FINDING
ENDURANCE

FINDING ENDURANCE

Shackleton, My Father and a World Without End

Darrel Bristow-Bovey

Jonathan Ball Publishers

JOHANNESBURG • CAPE TOWN

First published in the UK in 2024 by
Icon Books Ltd, Omnibus Business Centre,
39-41 North Road, London N7 9DP

South African edition published in 2024 by
JONATHAN BALL PUBLISHERS
A division of Media24 (Pty) Ltd
PO Box 33977
Jeppestown 2043

ISBN 978-1-77619-383-7

www.jonathanball.co.za
www.twitter.com/JonathanBallPub
www.instagram.com/JonathanBallPublishers

CONTENTS

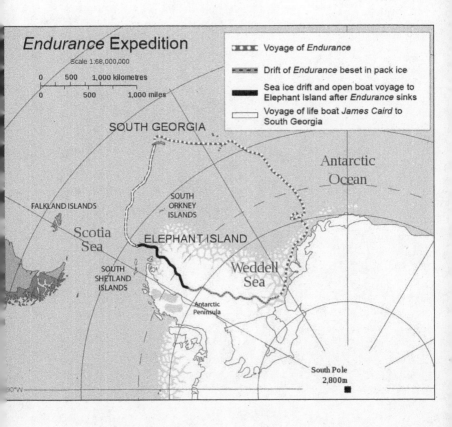

Endurance Expedition

Scale 1:68,000,000

| 0 | 500 | 1,000 kilometres |
| 0 | 500 | 1,000 miles |

Voyage of *Endurance*

Drift of *Endurance* beset in pack ice

Sea ice drift and open boat voyage to Elephant Island after *Endurance* sinks

Voyage of life boat *James Caird* to South Georgia

SOUTH GEORGIA

Antarctic Ocean

FALKLAND ISLANDS

SOUTH ORKNEY ISLANDS

Scotia Sea

ELEPHANT ISLAND

SOUTH SHETLAND ISLANDS

Weddell Sea

Antarctic Peninsula

South Pole
2,800m

90°W

ABOUT THE AUTHOR

Darrel Bristow-Bovey is a prize-winning screenwriter and travel writer and a newspaper and magazine columnist. He's the author of six books which have been translated into seven languages, including Spanish, Estonian and Portuguese. He was born in South Africa, studied under J.M. Coetzee and André Brink, and currently divides his time between Cape Town, the UK and a hillside on the Greek Peloponnese. His fascination with the *Endurance* expedition began as a small boy, when his father first told him that he had been south with Shackleton. He still believes him.

DEDICATION

Without Jeremy Boraine, and especially without Michele Magwood's conviction, passion and gift to encourage, this book wouldn't exist. It is at least half hers.

It is dedicated to Joanna Simon, who has read every word of it more often and more generously than I have, and whose love keeps me going like a fat gold watch.

PROLOGUE

Twenty-seven men stand on ice, squinting into the glare. The ice is very wide and very long, but no one mistakes it for land. A metre under their feet is the sea, and the sea moves, even when it's still. They know they're standing on the sea, and the sea is very deep.

They stare up at a figure on a wooden tower. He's not tall but he's solid. His shoulders bulk and hunch, like a bull with a scholarly stoop. He stands with legs braced, chin forward, peering through binoculars. Five minutes ago, trying not too obviously to rush, he climbed a three-runged wooden ladder to a square wooden platform, raised off the ice on low wooden stilts, and then a four-runged ladder to a smaller platform on top of a wooden column.

The tower isn't high but on ice any height gives advantage, and the man has a line of sight south-east over snow hummocks and white ridges and sastrugi. On a clear day, if the tower were tall enough, he might see all the way over ice shelves and mountain ridges and snow planes to the South Pole, but for perhaps the first time in his life he isn't looking to the horizon, he is looking just three kilometres to a black ship. The men on the ice watch the man on the platform as he watches.

The lines of the ship's stern are still clean but most of her is underwater. There's disorder on her decks – ropes, spars, tools, someone's thigh boot – and she's lost her masts. She lists to the left, as some of the men would say, or to port, as the others would. It's a little after 5pm and the southern summer sun bobs several fingers' width above the horizon so it's warm on the ice, perhaps as hot as 0°C. Some men have been working and as they stop to watch the watcher on the tower, sweat runs down their spines and chests, then freezes. There's a light breeze from the south, but the term 'wind chill' won't be invented for another 25 years.

The man is very still as he watches. It's a very still scene: still men watching a still man who watches a ship frozen in mid-roll. Then, on invisible wires, her stern rises. She holds like that, stern high and black above the ice, then the whiteness seems to part and the black ship slides into it, and disappears.

The men are silent and the man on the tower can feel the weight of their watching. He knows the next words he says will matter. He looks again through the binoculars, but already the ice has closed. It's his job now to offer the story of what this moment means, and so determine what will happen next. His own heart is pulling silently apart but there isn't time for that. This is one of the moments of life when what is solid suddenly cracks and splits and opens, and it matters very much which way he jumps.

He has been preparing. He spent last night in his cramped tent reading the poems of Robert Browning for inspiration, although just half an hour ago he was reading *Eothen* by Alexander Kinglake, that great breezy Victorian tale of exploration in the dusty Levant. Tennyson might be fit to the moment, or maybe his favourite Browning, but perhaps Kinglake – serious but not self-serious, optimistic and funny, more interested in a good story than fact – is closer to his character.

('A story may be false as a fact,' said Kinglake, 'but perfectly true as an illustration.')

The watching men know he has a habit of reciting dramatic lines at every opportunity, whether there's an opportunity or not. Usually it's annoying but now they're ready. They're as far away from the world as any human will be again until humans go into space. They *are* in space, adrift in space, alone and facing extinction in the cold, expanding, measureless reaches of a great and terrifying blankness, and there is no one to rescue them. They are human beings, alone in the universe, infinitely weak and immeasurably strong, and they need to be led.

Shackleton lowers the binoculars and makes himself meet the gaze of the upturned faces. He says: 'Well, boys, she's gone.'

And then: 'So now we'll go home.'

*

Freddie Ligthelm has the bridge of *SA Agulhas II*, as he does for six hours twice a day, every six hours while the other ice pilot tries to sleep. It's difficult to sleep in six-on, six-off shifts, which is what he and Knowledge Bengu have been doing since they entered the ice. Freddie Ligthelm and Knowledge Bengu: these are two very good names for your ice pilots.

Six hours off isn't long enough to sleep, not with the welfare of 100 people and a ship on your mind. Sometimes an ice pilot will lie in his bunk and see high-definition satellite photos taking shape on the ceiling, and wonder if that gale will keep coming in, or what the current will do with the pack ice. He'll think about the bergs that calved from the Larsen ice shelf last season and now circle clockwise on the vortex, clumsy and graceless as adolescents, and he'll squint up at that grey shadow in the north-west corner and wonder whether it's new ice or old.

But now Freddie Ligthelm has the bridge and he's fully engaged in his work but in a different shadow in the corner are his wife and daughters, who aren't really in the corner, they're back home in Cape Town. His kids are teenagers now. You always find strangers in your house when you come home from sea, and for a while you're a stranger yourself, but these are fast-growing strangers at a difficult age, who in their strangeness more than ever need their strange father around. Freddie and the ship have been down in the south longer than projected. They didn't find what they were looking for in the time they had, so they stayed a little longer. Freddie is thinking that maybe this time when he comes home from the sea he shouldn't leave so soon. After this trip he might never be on this bridge again.

The bridge of *SA Agulhas II* is one of the great rooms of the world. It looks the way you want the bridge of a spaceship to look, how a ten-year-old in 1981 would draw it: like the bridge of the starship *Enterprise*. The colour scheme is dirty-gull grey, but never mind that: it has 270 elevated degrees of view, and comfortable leather seats arranged on either side of the wheel. There are monitors and instrument panels and magnetic compasses and gyro compasses and things that flash and go beep. There are rolls of paper with needles ready to make marks, like old-fashioned seismographs. There are glowing buttons to launch photon torpedoes. There are radars and depth sounders and console lights on moveable goose-necks like the lantern antenna on deep-water angler fish. There's a coffee machine.

One of the screens should show the visual feed from the helicopter, but the helicopters have only flown once – onto the ship – and then they haven't flown again. (That's not actually true: they have taken test flights and noodled around but for the most part they've been grounded by cold and low visibility, and the other members of the expedition like to rib the helicopter gang about how the choppers will only fly twice, once onto the ship and once back off again. Simplifying the truth makes for a better joke.)

Since the helicopters aren't flying, that screen has been re-jigged to show the position of something three kilometres down. It's an autonomous underwater vehicle (AUV), sled-shaped and about the length and width of a 'fortwo' Smart Car, and it's moving in a small square right on the far edge of a search block that's nearly 200 kilometres square. Freddie is preoccupied and the AUV is none of his concern, but still: he notices the AUV has gone off on a tangent. Uh-oh.

In 2019, the last time the ship was in this location (the second time *any* ship was *ever* in this location), one of the AUVs went silent and awry under a floe and they broke their way through 114 football pitches of ice but still couldn't find it. (That is the standard unit of measurement for sea-ice: football pitches. For larger areas of ice, the unit becomes Luxembourgs, or sometimes Isles of Wight.) Then the weather came in and they had to leave it behind. People don't like to talk about how much the AUV cost, but an AUV costs a lot more than a Smart car. To lose one AUV in the Weddell Sea might be considered misfortune, but two AUVs … Freddie Ligthelm frowns over the screen. There's an emotional burst of French chatter over the comms. Freddie Ligthelm can read the water and the ice and the skies and the screens but he doesn't understand French.

Freddie calls Nico Vincent, who spends his days hunched over monitors in the cold of a shipping container on the poop deck. It's not just cold in the shipping container; it's very cold. The temperatures can drop to -35°C and Nico is in there four hours at a time, sometimes eight. Nico is in frequent danger of frostbite, but he is in charge of the subsea operations. 'Subsea operations' means the AUV. Nico is French. Nico tells Freddie that he can't say anything over the comms. He'll come up in person.

Nico walks into the bridge, with a camera crew in tow. In 1914 Ernest Shackleton pre-sold the publicity rights to the *Endurance* expedition to raise money for the trip, and went south with film cameras and an artist with sketch pencils and oil paints and a stills photographer lugging heavy glass photographic plates to make sure he had something to bring back and sell; in 108 years, some things haven't changed.

Nico takes Freddie aside and speaks in a low voice. The leaders of the expedition, John Shears and Mensun Bound, are on the ice, walking to a trapped iceberg nearly two kilometres to starboard, and haven't been informed yet, so Nico can't say anything officially. Freddie glances around. All eyes are watching him. The cameras are watching him. This is what it means to have command.

They do not say anything, but there is footage from the cameras of the expressions on the faces of the crew on the bridge as Nico Vincent and Freddie Ligthelm ceremonially shake hands.

*

It's March 2022 and I'm in an apartment in Greece. In January a cold front swept in snow from the east, turning the white Parthenon a whiter white and trapping Athenians in their homes. For two months they've been talking about it: 'Remember when it snowed and we couldn't go to work?! *Po po po*! Look, I have a picture of the snow on my car!' Now in March the snow has returned. Athenians have spent a lot of time trapped in their homes in recent times; we all have.

Snow in a place that's usually hot is like a magic trick: the world is transformed, it's made uncanny. I'm considering heroically trudging into the white silence in search of a breakfast bougatsa, leaving a note on the fridge saying 'I am just going out, and may be some time', when I start receiving messages from friends around the world. They all contain a photograph, and different exclamations: 'Have you seen this??!' 'Can you believe it?!!' 'I saw this and thought of you!!!'

I have two thoughts. One: it's gratifying to be remembered by friends. Two: my friends use too many exclamation marks. And then I look at the picture, and there she is, *Endurance*, the grain of her wood, her painted black boards, the bronze lettering proud and catching the light, the Polaris star bright and shining and pointing south, east, west and home. There she is, the way she was. She isn't gone, she's there, and also, she's here. She's on my phone, she's in the room with me, she's back in the world. I draw in air while gasping out loud, like an 'Oh!' in reverse. I want to show someone. My heart is racing. I want to use exclamation marks. There she is: the ice claimed her but it didn't keep her – it kept her safe. I feel joy, I feel envy that I am not there, a part of it. And I feel something bigger, something nameless. Suddenly, unexpectedly, I'm welling up. I haven't cried in years, but there she is: *Endurance*. So much has been taken from us and now, incredibly, like a gift, like a whispered half-remembered promise fulfilled and renewed, something has been given back. And I *am* part of it: we all are.

Then I receive another message. It's from an old school mate. We aren't close. I don't even know how he has my number. It says:

'Wasn't your father on the *Endurance*?'

*

I was astonished at the outpouring of delight around the world at the discovery of *Endurance*. I knew how much it meant to me, and to fellow polar nuts and Shackleheads and frosted weirdos, but in this world that – well, you don't need me to tell you what the world is like – how did this picture and this story manage to elbow anger and rancour off the timelines and front pages for as long as it did? How were so many ordinary people who don't know a nunatak from a barquentine so moved by the discovery of a small wooden ship once commanded by a half-forgotten Irishman?

When I first announced, aged ten in Miss Kincaid's English class, that my father had sailed with Shackleton, those kids hadn't been much impressed. Who was Shackleton? He never made it to the South Pole. He never crossed Antarctica. He didn't die tragically in his sleeping bag, pen in pale fingers and lashes frosted to his cheek while the snow piled up against his tent. He really didn't do anything except come back alive, and what's the big deal about that?

Kids don't understand death. No one does really, although we start getting an inkling around the time we turn 40. Kids understand being the best, or the first, or the last, but just surviving doesn't feel like much of an achievement. Shackleton wasn't the best or the first or even the last. He wasn't anything. He was, by most standards, a failure.

I suppose my father was too. He had once been many things: a nightclub bouncer, a travelling sales representative purveying lubricating motor oil, a policeman, a door-to-door encyclopedia salesman, a thirteen-year-old high-school drop-out, a middle-man for illicit booze, a diamond prospector, a professional wrestler, an elderly soldier, some sort of undefined handyman on a film set where he once met Roger Moore, a surf lifesaver, a railway worker, the prospective manager of a floating casino, a barman, the self-appointed leader of the St Margaret's Presbyterian church choir, a welder, a typewriter repairman, the manager and promoter of a rock band, a fraudulent night-school teacher, a con man, a hustler, a paid escort, a husband, a husband again, a husband a third time, quite possibly a husband a fourth time in between the second and third times although no one has yet produced any definitive proof, a bricklayer, a dad. And, once, a polar explorer.

But so what? He was a large man once but not any more; he was 30 or 40 years older than the other kids' dads; his wavy hair was grey. He sat all day in his comfortable faux-La-Z-Boy leatherette recliner (which looked, it strikes me now, a lot like the chairs on the bridge of the *SA Agulhas II*, except in the Durban humidity the leatherette would get sweaty and squelch if you sat in it without a shirt), reading cowboy books and telling me stories about his life. He was a failure – all he'd done was survive, and by the end of the year that I was ten, he hadn't even done that.

At some point since then it occurred to me that my father did not in fact sail on *Endurance*. At some point when I started reading about the expedition, thinking about it, literally at night dreaming about it, I must have registered that his name wasn't on the crew list and that even though he was unfathomably old, he wasn't *that* old. But still, it's possible for human beings to believe two opposite things at the same time; I think it's necessary. 'A great truth,' said Niels Bohr, 'is a truth whose opposite is also a great truth.' When the message came in from the old schoolmate, I very nearly replied: 'Yes he did!'

There are certainly questions to be answered: he knew a surprising amount about the ship and his shipmates who sailed with her – small details that I've subsequently read only in unpublished sources that weren't available in 1982, or certainly weren't available to *him*. Beyond that, my father was generously given to exaggeration and the embellished tale – he wasn't Irish, as Shackleton was, but had a distinctly Irish faith in the primacy of the true story over the accurate one – but why was he so persistent with Shackleton? Why did it mean so much to him?

He said to me once, 'Failure's not the end of the world. Shackleton was a failure. We should all be such failures.'

I don't know that my father thought himself a failure, but for a long time, I did. And I think that, marooned in a seaside town on the hot coast of South Africa, in sight of the sea, an aging man prematurely weak, an idle king by a quiet hearth, he thought about success and failure, and what makes a life and how best to live it, alone and together.

Endurance meant something to the world when she sank, and something else to my dad, and she means something new to us again. The meanings of things change because the stories we tell ourselves about them change. The Antarctic meant something once, and something else now. The ice summoned from nature's heart by humanity's hubris has changed its meaning too. 'Nature' means something different to what it meant in 1915; so does 'humanity'.

The story of *Endurance* and Shackleton is still one of the greatest stories in the world, and it has old things and new things to tell us, because in 2022 *Endurance* came back to us, but not the same as when she went down.

PART 1

LOSS

1. WHITE WARFARE

When they reached the whaling station on South Georgia Island the old Norwegian whalers warned them there was trouble down south. It was a bad year for sea ice: no one had ever seen so much of it so far north, so early in the season. The weather was being strange. Wait a year, they suggested. Next summer will be better.

It's not that Shackleton didn't listen. There's a long, exasperating tradition of English polar explorers ignoring good Norwegian expertise, and Shackleton was as prone to it as anyone, but this wasn't one of those times. Shackleton liked these grizzled old salts, these hard-bitten misfitting oddballs and outsiders making a community far from home, down here at the southern end of the world, and he respected them, so he waited a while in the blood-washed waters and the rot-stench and death-reek of the whaling station, hoping the ice would clear. He waited as long as he could, but he couldn't wait a year, and he couldn't turn back. From the moment *Endurance* left England, they were never going to turn back.

Shackleton had raised money for the expedition – and still owed it – based on a promise: that his Imperial Trans-Antarctic Expedition would be the first to cross the mainland continent of Antarctica. *Endurance* would sail from England to Buenos Aires, and from Buenos Aires to South Georgia Island, and from South Georgia south-east across the Antarctic Circle to land at an unsurveyed rocky indentation on the coast of Antarctica named – for the sake of naming things, since no one had ever actually set foot there before – Vahsel Bay.

At Vahsel Bay they would get their ice legs and maybe learn to ski, and then he would lead a group of six men and 70 dogs to the South Pole. They wouldn't be the first ones there – Roald Amundsen first reached the pole four years earlier, and then Robert Falcon Scott reached it one month after him – but they would be the first to reach it from the west, from the Weddell Sea, across geography unseen by another human being. Having reached it, instead of turning back, they would be the first to keep walking forward.

They would cross the continent from west to east, nearly 2,500 kilometres past the pole and across the high polar plateau until they reached the Beardmore Glacier that Shackleton himself had first discovered, six years before.

Then they would keep going beyond that, to the crystal minefield of the Great Ice Barrier, then down to McMurdo Sound and the frozen Ross Sea where a support ship would be waiting. They had budgeted enough food for 100 days, so as long as they covered nearly 25 kilometres every single day for three months and ten days, and didn't run into any of the Antarctic weather that had confined every other polar party to their tents for at least part of the time in every single expedition that had ever been launched, they would be fine. One thing was for sure: they were not turning back.

(It may be worth mentioning that after Shackleton's expedition, no one tried this particular journey again for 43 years, until the southern summer of 1957–58 when Dr Vivian Fuchs and his Commonwealth Trans-Antarctic Expedition, using mechanical vehicles equipped with heaters and radios, managed it in nearly four months.)

There had already been some close calls for the expedition. While *Endurance* was preparing to leave England, the world was preparing to go to war with itself. A month before departure, in June 1914, the Archduke Franz Ferdinand of Austria-Hungary was shot and killed in his famously tight-fitting tunic in front of Schiller's delicatessen in Sarajevo. A month later, on the day the *Endurance* left the East India Dock in London, where Canary Wharf is today, Austria-Hungary declared war on Serbia. *Endurance* was lying at anchor in the mouth of the Thames when Germany declared war on France. On the same day that King George V came aboard and his mother, Dowager Queen Alexandra, presented the ship with a hand-dedicated Bible, Britain declared war on Germany.

Suddenly everything changed. Shackleton had sold his expedition on demonstrating that the men of Edwardian England were still as strong in spine and will as their Victorian forefathers, and most especially stronger than their rising German rivals. 'War in the old days made men,' he said. 'We have not those same stirring times to live in, and must look for other outlets for our energy.'

The whiskered old men agreed that what young chaps needed was a damn good war, but failing that a polar triumph would do. But now they had their war. Did they still need Antarctica?

At the declaration of war some members of the party disembarked to go and fight. All remaining eyes turned to The Boss, watching which way he would jump.

Shackleton was not a navy man. Nearly 40, stocky, under-exercised, chain-smoking, nursing a nagging cough and hiding a time bomb of a heart condition, he wouldn't pass any military medicals. But still, he solemnly and – who knows? – perhaps sincerely wrote to the Admiralty, placing *Endurance* and her crew at the disposal of the war effort. If England wanted him to turn back, then never mind the loss of national prestige and his personal financial ruin: he would turn back.

'Financial ruin' is no exaggeration. Money was always a problem with Antarctic expeditions, especially the privately funded ones of the Heroic Age. Part of the problem was that there was no good reason to go to the Antarctic. There are no gems or gold to be found, no – so far as they had reason to believe – seams of coal or reservoirs of gas. There are no spices or timber or steppes of waving grain, or any of the other things that cause private capital to twitch its whiskers with interest. There was nothing to be found in the Antarctic but symbols; nothing to be extracted but stories. Stories are not nothing – the stories we tell ourselves shape who we are; a father's stories shape his son – but investors prefer them more as a means to an end than an end in themselves.

In the absence of wealth, polar expeditions usually promised science: they would bring back maps and measurements, knowledge and the prestige that knowledge confers. Some, like Scott, seemed more or less sincere about this. Others, like Shackleton, not at all. Either way, knowledge doesn't drum up nearly so much money as minerals.

Even after returning as a celebrity from his previous expedition, and being knighted by King Edward VII, Shackleton had financial problems. He had sailed off on that previous voyage leaving a cloud of unpaid bills, and returned to a consolidated debt of £25,000, nearly £3 million in today's money. It took years of slogging on the lecture circuit (travelling – he calculated airily – some 20,000 miles by train and sea) and flogging his book, *In the Heart of the Antarctic*, just to pay off the back salaries of his crew.

Shackleton was energetic and charismatic, but even his admirers didn't mistake him for a prudent financial investment. Charles Dornan, a wealthy solicitor, personally liked him but refused him permission to marry his daughter Emily until Ernest had proven himself as a provider. Dornan's death while Shackleton was away in the Antarctic cleared the way for Ernest and Emily to marry, but you couldn't accuse him of having misread his man.

Shackleton had promised Emily that he wouldn't go adventuring again, that he would use his fame to make money in other ways, but on land he was a better dreamer than a doer. He broke his heart on endless schemes: starting a fleet of taxicabs, manufacturing cigarettes, mining coal in Norway, logging the forests of Mexico, selling first-edition postage stamps from Antarctica, revitalising abandoned gold mines in Hungary, running for parliament, providing troop transport for Russian soldiers, getting in on the ground floor of a new truth-telling international news agency, searching for buried treasure.

His business reputation wasn't helped by his disreputable brother Frank, who was imprisoned for financial misdeeds and strongly suspected of stealing the Irish crown jewels from Dublin Castle, where his lover, Sir Arthur Vicars, was Ulster King of Arms. Shackleton at one point drew up plans to hunt for Captain Kidd's buried treasure in the Caribbean, but he might more profitably have started closer to home. The Irish crown jewels have never been recovered.

(The theft of the jewels was the inspiration for the Sherlock Holmes story, 'The Adventure of the Bruce-Partington Plans'. Conan Doyle was friendly with Arthur Vicars, and the villain of his story, Valentine Walters, has some delicate similarities to Frank Shackleton. Frank was never convicted of the crime – largely perhaps because an investigation threatened to expose the private lives of a number of fashionable gentlemen close to the crown – but Arthur Vicars himself was so sure that Frank did it, he included the allegation in his will.)

Ernest Shackleton did not thrive in civilisation. He finally accepted he had to return to the frozen wild. 'I have my own ideals,' he mused, 'and far away in my own White South, I open my arms to the romance of it all.'

Funding was even more difficult this time round. The race for the South Pole was over and England had lost, so Shackleton cooked up the idea of making the first trans-continental crossing as a way of scraping back some prestige. It would be much harder than simply going to the Pole and back: there would be much suffering involved, and English patriotic pride was best wooed by the promise of plenty of noble suffering. But still doors closed in his face; former backers stopped answering messages.

Shackleton wore out his shoe leather on the sidewalks and doorsteps of the City. He begged from rich contacts, borrowed from friends, accepted donations from well-wishers. One of these, assiduously courted, was the wealthy, elderly, unmarried Janet Stancomb-Wills, the adopted daughter of a tobacco tycoon. Tobacco was quietly taking away from Shackleton, but here at least he had the chance to get something back.

Ms Stancomb-Wills had led a very proper late-Victorian life, shaded from the rays of passion, before she met Shackleton in the golden Edwardian sunshine. It would be improper to suggest that her personal feelings may have outweighed her scientific zeal for polar knowledge, but here are the opening lines from a poem she wrote to him in violet ink with an ivory-handled fountain pen from her boudoir dressing table:

Into my life you flashed, like a meteor out of the dark
Flooding its peaceful dullness with a splendour of
glowing light.

Little by little, Shackleton raised the minimum needed to outfit the expedition. He bought a strong wooden ship, part steam-powered, part sail-, and painted her black and called her *Endurance*. He equipped her; he hired a team. But the longer he spent trudging the corridors of influence, the more he sagged as a person.

Shackleton was an emperor penguin, built to nobly withstand any degree of icy hardship, so long as it never sets foot on land. Someone who had met him before his first expedition and met him again now was shocked at the change. His skin was grey and his hair seemed thin.

He had a haunted look, a pale shadow peering from a dusty window. One of my favourite descriptions of Shackleton, one that always made me love him, was that he was unable to suppress laughter, especially in serious matters, but now he never laughed, and barely smiled unless he was talking, and then always with visible effort. Most strikingly of all: he seemed to have developed an aversion to shaking hands.

Much of the money Shackleton raised was contingent on completion: he pre-sold the rights to the book, to the photographs, to the motion picture. He was counting on the proceeds from the lecture tour, and the serialised rights already sold to the *Daily Chronicle*. Without the expedition, he had no way even of covering what he had spent. If he turned back now, he was finished.

But Shackleton sent the cable to the Admiralty. If England wanted him to turn back, he would.

He paced the deck, waiting for a reply.

Shackleton was a great pacer. In Frank Hurley's film footage from the ice he is often pacing or just post-pacing, staring at the camera, prow-faced and thoughtful. Often when he paced he recited poetry. The Russian poet Osip Mandelstam once wrote about Dante that his poetry – especially the *Inferno* and *Purgatory* – had the rhythm of pacing: linked to the breath, saturated with thought. Dante's inner ring of hell was frozen in ice; he climbed Mount Purgatory to try to get out. Shackleton paced his purgatory, trying to get in.

It's unclear whether the Admiralty knew about it, but there was a thrilling story in the making. In the previous months, an Austrian explorer named Felix König had announced he would launch his own Antarctic expedition, also using Vahsel Bay as his starting point. The two teams might land there at the same time. König and Shackleton had exchanged tetchy letters and there'd been a skirmish of words in the press, and that before the real war had been declared. It still stung the English that they had lost the last polar race to the Norwegians; could the King really afford to lose this race to the Kaiser? König's ship was named *Deutschland*.

Shackleton waited, and he paced.

At anchor in Trieste, Felix König kicked his heels fretfully on the *Deutschland* for word from *his* admiralty.

And then a cable arrived, quite possibly from the First Lord of the Admiralty himself, Winston Churchill. It said: 'Proceed'.

No less than Churchill, Shackleton knew the value of a phrase. Solemnly, he declared he would venture forth to wage 'white warfare in the south'.

(It's one of the great missed opportunities that there was no Churchill in the Austro-Hungarian war department. König was denied permission to go south. He was sent to war and *Deutschland* was conscripted into the navy. It was torpedoed and sank in the Adriatic. König fought in Galicia, was captured and imprisoned in Siberia and daringly escaped, but he never went to Antarctica.)

Endurance left Plymouth for the South Atlantic. The voyage took nearly two months. Shackleton stayed behind to wrangle some lingering finances and to patch up a last-minute quarrel with Emily. He caught up with them in Argentina, but then came the second close call.

In Buenos Aires, Shackleton was pale and unwell and spent long hours locked in his cabin. His second-in-command Frank Wild was startled by his appearance and covertly alerted Alexander Macklin, the ship's physician, who suspected a heart complaint.

Shackleton declined to be examined.

Two tales of death foretold cling to Shackleton. One: when he was a child, an Irish nanny with second sight told him he would not live to be an old man. Two: a fortune teller he encountered on a lecture tour said he would die before 50.

On Shackleton's first Antarctic expedition, with Scott on *Discovery*, Scott had selected him to trek southward toward the pole with him, along with Scott's friend Edward Wilson. Shackleton had been chosen for his strength and vigour, but on the march he collapsed and the others had to help him back hundreds of kilometres, occasionally pulling him on a sled. It was demanding on Scott and Wilson, humiliating for Shackleton.

He refused to be examined by the expedition doctor and was invalided home. For the rest of his life, he never submitted to a genuine medical examination. In particular, he never let anyone listen to his heart.

Now, in Buenos Aires, Doctor Macklin was concerned. If Shackleton had a heart complaint, he had to turn back. But Shackleton wouldn't be examined, and Shackleton was The Boss.

Once *Endurance* left Buenos Aires, he was a changed man. At sea he stood taller, and he laughed again. He looked men in the eye and joked with them, he slapped them on the shoulder. But still, Macklin was worried and Wild was watching fearfully.

A few days later came the first big test.

In Buenos Aires two sailors, William Bakewell and Perce Blackborow, had applied to be taken on as crew. Their previous ship had sunk in the mouth of the River Plate, leaving them without a berth. Bakewell was American but fearing prejudice from the English, shrewdly pretended to be Canadian. He was accepted. Blackborow was Welsh but he was eighteen years old. He was rejected for being too young.

Now, half-starved and seasick, Blackborow allowed himself to be discovered in the lower decks, a stowaway. They were too far from port to take him back. He was brought before Shackleton. A hush fell. Bakewell and another seaman named Walter How watched with particular interest, since they were the ones who smuggled Blackborow aboard, but in fact everyone was watching to see how Shackleton would react. So far he had been firm but easy-going, but character is only revealed by the unexpected, and when you're sailing towards the blank spaces of the map, you want to know who is leading you. No one watched Shackleton more closely than Frank Wild.

As the boy Blackborow slumped on deck, too weak to stand, Shackleton leant over him, bellowing what he thought of sneaks and stowaways, and itemising how he intended to punish him. He seemed incandescent with rage, trembling on the edge of violence.

Frank Wild was shocked. Wild had been with Shackleton in the Antarctic twice before, once on the Scott expedition, once on Shackleton's first voyage as leader. He had saved Shackleton's life and had been saved by him. He was the one who had first named him The Boss, but Frank Wild didn't recognise the man shouting at the stowaway. Shackleton had disapproved of Scott's temper and military style of discipline. Once Scott had ordered his cook tied to the mast for hours on an icy deck for refusing to cook seal meat, and Shackleton had trembled with fury. That was the Shackleton that Wild revered, but maybe The Boss really had changed in those last bad years on land. Maybe he was wearing out, a fraying knot. Maybe it was time for Frank to rethink his faith.

Shackleton was building to a crescendo: 'Furthermore,' he thundered at the hapless Blackborow, 'if we run out of food and anyone has to be eaten, you'll be first!'

The boy managed to lift his head and make a final appeal to logic. He eyed Shackleton's hefty frame. 'They'd get more food off you, sir,' he said.

Frank Wild watched as Shackleton turned away and paced to the railing and gripped it with both hands, knuckles white. He seemed to be trying to control his temper. But from where Frank Wild was standing he could see The Boss's face, so he could see that he wasn't trying to stop his rage, he was trying to hide his smile. And then Frank Wild remembered that Shackleton never lost self-control, not at sea. Everything he did was a performance, to establish character, to test its effect. This was the Shackleton he knew: the Shackleton unable to suppress his laughter. Shackleton liked his men with spirit. Next to optimism, the quality he most admired was humour.

Blackborow was set to work assisting Charlie Green, the cook, and *Endurance* sailed on, but Wild wasn't worried any more. Shackleton was back where he belonged.

When they arrived at South Georgia, the whalers told him not to go this year, and he listened, but on a misty day in December, with the clouds covering the cliffs and the grey mist on the sea's face, *Endurance* sailed south. They were never turning back home.

2. SMALL HANDS

Do people still shake hands? I do. I spent a lot of time as a teenager practising my handshake on my left hand, or on imaginary other hands. A boy who wants to be a man must learn to shake hands like a man, and then like the particular man he wants to be. Not too firm, not too weak, dry of palm, wrist cocked at a convenient angle for the other shaker. Don't hold too long, don't drop too soon. Subtle adjustments for men and women, for young and old, for friends and strangers. It's a lot to teach yourself, and what if there's something you haven't thought of, and how do you know you're getting it right? It's difficult for a boy to figure out how to be a man.

In the passage dealing with the land-bound and greatly reduced Shackleton, I wrote that he developed an aversion to shaking hands. That detail comes from Roland Huntford's biography of Shackleton, and as best I can establish, Huntford found it by reading an interview with a certain Miss Ireland, a clerk in the office of a German businessman from whom Shackleton was trying to cajole funding. In the same passage, Huntford records her observation that Shackleton's hands were incongruously small.

It's an odd detail to include at that moment, in a passage describing how reduced he was on land. His tribulations, presumably, hadn't caused his hands to grow smaller. It's also an odd thing to notice. Without shaking hands, how could she tell? I have studied photographs, and Frank Hurley's film footage aboard *Endurance* and on the ice: Shackleton's hands aren't often visible – they're usually bunched in the pockets of his overcoat – but when they are, they're not noticeably smaller than you'd expect.

My father also once told me about Shackleton's hands. He said that when The Boss spoke to you he seemed to give you his full attention, like pausing the swinging beam of a lighthouse. He had a way of putting his hand on your arm to make a point, or to hit the punchline of a joke. He gripped you firmly, and even through your jersey or your coat you felt a jolt of electricity, similar to the charismatic charge some politicians have. It's the gift of making connection in a crowded room, the electrifying wordless intimation that of all the people in the world who could be here, at this moment, thank God it's *you*.

And my dad also said that Shackleton had small hands.

He didn't say it to diminish him but as a loving detail, an expression of joy at the wonders of the world: that so forceful, so electric a man as Ernest Shackleton should have such unexpectedly small and precise hands.

I didn't think about Shackleton's hands again until I read about them in Huntford's biography, on a beach in Mauritius in 1999. The biography was first published some years after my father died. How could my father have known?

Details matter when you're telling a convincing story, or trying to tell a story convincingly, but it's a wonderfully strange detail to have made up, especially when your only audience is your small son who has never considered any gradations of hand-size other than 'child' and 'adult', and who in any case will believe whatever you say, just because you say it. It's also a wonderfully strange thing to have guessed, and been right about.

Shackleton's small hands felt like a clue. No, not a clue. A clue – a 'clew', a ball of yarn, Ariadne's length of string that let Theseus find his way through the Minotaur's labyrinth – leads you to a fixed destination, a set goal. A detective follows a clue to find the truth, the identity of the murderer. The clew my father gave me was a different kind of yarn.

The detail of Shackleton's small hands was more like a spark thrown up by a wood fire, that darts and drifts against the black sky on invisible breaths of heat. It still dances when I think of it: a fugitive electron, a scintilla of some larger heat or long-ago blaze, escaping from the unreachable cold past and the unknowable privacy of a personality, some light-catching mote that I want to chase and understand.

My father couldn't have read about Shackleton's small hands, and he couldn't have seen them or felt their grip, because when *Endurance* set out from Plymouth in 1914, my father wasn't quite yet born.

His father, George Bovey, had been a porcelain-clay digger in the village of Bovey Tracey, on the banks of the Bovey River, eight miles south-east of North Bovey in Devon. This, to George Bovey, was a surfeit of Boveys, and in 1914 he sailed to South Africa for a new life. His timing was good. The Great War would claim many Boveys, but not George.

Even without going to war the Bovey men die young, and I never met George Bovey, but from all accounts he was a drinking man, with a temper and hard fists, and I didn't miss much. He settled in Pretoria and married and had a son, Gerald, and then my father, Richard, and then a daughter, Mary. Gerald was called Gerry, and Richard was called Dick, and Mary was called Molly. I don't know how George Bovey made a living. I can find no official records and if my father told me, I've forgotten.

My father was born in 1922, almost 100 years to the day before the rediscovery of *Endurance*. He grew up poor in the Great Depression and English in the capital of Afrikanerdom, so from an early age he learnt to fight. He shoplifted tins of bully beef and stole fruit from neighbours' trees to bring home for his mother. She was furious and ashamed that he stole, but the human heart has space for opposite things, and she was also grateful.

(I have just remembered that when I was very young we had an avocado tree in the bottom of our garden, and my dad used to keep watch in early summer and yell and chase the neighbour's kids who came to steal from it. When their father came round to apologise, my dad took him aside and said in a low voice that they were welcome to all the avocados they could steal: he was just playing the game because it's more fun to steal fruit when someone's trying to stop you.)

My dad left school at thirteen. He and his brother Gerry worked odd jobs and learnt trades and cooked up various schemes. For a time, he lived on the street.

My father was a great survivor but seldom a thriver. He was charming and capable and always found a way out of scrapes but nothing ever paid off as fulsomely as he dreamed. He was, it strikes me now, out of his element. Being out of your element is a common predicament; it's only really sad if you never find it.

My father moved away from Pretoria and around the country, finding jobs, losing them, giving them away. He was happiest when he was moving. He found himself in a boarding house in Durban. He thought he might go down to the harbour and find a ship and try his luck in Mozambique or up in East Africa. He thought there might be good things in Dar es Salaam or Zanzibar or Mombasa.

In the boarding house he met a young schoolteacher from Cape Town with auburn hair. She was shy and twenty years younger than him. They married in the City Hall one day in early summer and she won't like me being this precise with numbers, but eight months later I was born. My dad never found a ship.

It was the 1970s, and soon enough, like most white men in South Africa who might elsewhere have faced more limited prospects, my dad was doing all right. He was now a travelling sales representative, supplying needs in lubricating motor oil and related products up and down the coast. He was a big man, six foot four and strong. His hair was smoothed back in steely corrugations with La Pebra's hair tonic, and he had a neat moustache. In photographs he looks like Ernest Hemingway in his Paris years, before Hemingway grew a beard. He smoked a pipe loaded with a mix of Old Fox and Rum and Maple tobacco. We had a car, almost new. We lived on the Bluff, a big working-class suburb that sticks out into the Indian Ocean on the other side of Durban harbour, where the tankers come in and out. The Bluff has train tracks and factories and a former whaling station and an oil refinery but we lived on the sea-facing side, quite far from the oil refinery. Above all, we had a house. It was the first house my dad had ever owned.

When I was seven we flew to Cape Town, where my mother's mother lived. My mother's mother had refused her permission to marry my dad, for reasons similar to those of Emily Dorman's father when he refused Ernest Shackleton. When my mom disobeyed – perhaps for the first time in her life – her mother cut her dead. This was to be our first visit. I wore my Sunday best.

When we arrived at my grandmother's house in Constantia, where rich people lived, my grandmother gave us tea on a table spread with an embroidered white cotton cloth under the oak tree in her very pretty garden, but she refused to allow any of us into the house.

When we left her garden we drove to Sea Point. On the long promenade beside the cold Atlantic there was a little playground with swings and a seesaw and a jungle gym and an odd recreational contraption I haven't seen elsewhere: a metal oil drum, weighted for maximum turn, mounted horizontally on a metal pole across a pit at ground level. It was free to spin around the metal pole. The entertainment value of this drum consisted in standing on it and taking little steps to make it turn while you stay in the same place and keep your balance. If you've ever seen a Canadian lumberjack log rolling, you have the idea.

I put a foot on the drum but as I leaned my weight it moved under me. It didn't seem possible to keep your footing on such a thing. My father had never seen this apparatus before either, and he hadn't been intending to stand on it, but he didn't like to see me give up. He told me to watch and he would show me how to do it. I watched closely. There's nothing in the world I can't do, so long as I've seen my dad do it first.

I remember looking up at my father as he stood on the drum. He was tall. He was so tall he blocked out the sun; it formed a kind of corona around him, an incandescent white fogbow, a parhelion halo.

I once saw a photograph of an elephant hanging from a tree. The elephant's name was Mary and the photograph was taken in Tennessee in 1916. While Shackleton was in the Weddell Sea, Mary was being hanged. The Sparks World-Famous Traveling Circus came to Erwin, Tennessee, and the townsfolk lined Main Street to watch Mary lead the parade, but when she stopped to eat a watermelon rind a man poked her behind the ear with a stick, and she threw him to the ground and stepped on his head. In vengeance the townsfolk hanged her from a crane. An elephant is not supposed to be hanged. An elephant's feet are not supposed to leave the ground, not all of them at once. Looking at that photograph felt like an unclean act, the inversion of some natural law, something terribly, unspeakably *wrong*. That's also how it felt when my father fell.

Big men are not supposed to fall, especially when they're your father. Nowadays playgrounds have rubberised surfaces but this was the late 1970s and his head hit on tarmac. I remember the sound. It was heavy and wet. I remember how he lay there.

3. ANGLES OF LIGHT

*I try in vain to be persuaded that the pole is the
seat of frost and desolation; it ever presents itself
to my imagination as the region of beauty and delight.*
MARY SHELLEY

The *Endurance* left South Georgia in November and
sailed south towards the Weddell Sea. Although
the ocean was clear they saw ice blink on the southern
horizon – a daytime brightness in the sky, made by the
sun reflecting off sea ice.

In its remoteness and distance from the warm world
of people, Antarctica is often compared to the moon;
then the Weddell Sea was the dark side of the moon. It
was unknown, almost untouched; every previous expedition on the continent had started in the Ross Sea, on the
eastern side of Antarctica, closest to New Zealand.

The Weddell Sea is on the west, near South America,
one and a half million square kilometres of ice and waves

and wind. The ice changes by the day, by the minute. There had been three attempted expeditions to the Weddell Sea before *Endurance:* one fled, one was trapped then fled, one was crushed.

But *Endurance* went south and all aboard had their reasons for going: the crew for their salaries, the scientists for their science, young men like Captain Frank Worsley to test if they had what it took. And Shackleton? Shackleton was looking for something too.

In early December, near Candlemass volcano in the South Sandwich Islands, they encountered the first ice. The sea changed from salt-streaked green to indigo. They were still a thousand miles from Vahsel Bay, but sea ice isn't necessarily a problem. *Endurance* was built for ice, her prow and hull clad in greenheart oak, a wood so dense and heavy it weighs more than iron. Besides, Shackleton had a plan.

If you look at Antarctica from above, it's blobbily circular: Sara Wheeler calls it an irregular splodge of white pancake batter, or a cross-section of a brain with one creepy protrusion pointing towards South America. This protrusion is the Antarctic Peninsula, and just east of it is a vast indentation in the continent, with a coastal fringe of permanent ice. This indentation is the Weddell Sea, and Vahsel Bay is on the eastern side, the far left if you're facing south, of that indentation.

Shackleton knew about the circular sea current in the Weddell Sea, a clockwise gyre that drives the ice westwards – to the right – where it bunches and piles up against the peninsula, leaving a clear space on the opposite side, where he wanted to go. His idea was to sneak across through the thinner sea ice then slip south down the open edge of the ice-pack to reach Vahsel Bay.

The plan was a good one, and like many good plans, at first it worked.

In the unending summer days, the ice was pure delight. Shackleton described the pack as a great white jigsaw puzzle whose pieces hadn't yet been joined. The sea was purple and blue between the floes, like the seams of gold that bind the broken porcelain in Japanese *kintsugi*. The scientists gathered on deck to marvel and coo.

Shackleton was reborn. He had written to Janet Stancomb-Wills that he was feeling old, but 'hopefully the Antarctic will make me young again'. Now he was out of reach of home and family, beyond the 'no' of governments and banks. He sparred with the crew and teased the scientists and sang on the bridge. Like a stern father he mock-tormented Perce Blackborow to do his schoolwork. A condition of not being eaten, he reminded him, was that he learn to read.

When Shackleton or Frank Wild had the bridge, *Endurance* picked and weaved thoughtfully through the ice, like Theseus tiptoeing in the labyrinth. When Worsley was alone at the helm he would work up a head of steam and leap straight at the thinner floes. When keel encountered ice there was a judder and a pause and an ominous grating, then a most satisfying surge and release as the ice gave way and the *Endurance* broke through with a sound almost loud enough to conceal Worsley's whoops of joy.

Each day the world was giddyingly new and beautiful. The Antarctic summer air is dry and cold and when it meets the warm blood of your lungs it fizzes like pure oxygen. The air cures depression and malaise, astigmatism and tuberculosis. Your skin, your heart, your cells burn with health. In four voyages to the Antarctic, Wild could only ever recall one occasion when anyone caught a cold: on the *Nimrod* expedition, when they opened a packing case containing clothing. There must have been some germs in the case, they decided, because everyone present caught a cold which lasted a day, except the cook who went on sniffling until Shackleton sent him out for a long curative walk on the ice.

George Marston, the expedition's official artist, set up his canvas on the deck but his oil paints froze so he turned to chalks. The photographer Frank Hurley climbed the masts to rig up cameras, wrestling with how to frame whiteness and how, without perspective, to give it shape.

Edward Wilson, who died with Scott, said in his diaries that there are no similes in the natural world to account for the pale brilliance of the lights of the ice. He preferred to evoke the radiance of incandescent metals like strontium and potassium. Herman Melville, who had seen the ice but never reached the frozen seas, imagined in *Moby-Dick* that the Antarctic is a seascape as white as a shroud, but it's not quite like that in the light.

Under the circling sun the ice does things to light to which we are not accustomed. Colours emerge and dance in the crystal depths. At the waterline of icebergs, where the lapping sea carves out grottoes and caves, the refracting sunlight makes rainbows in the ice that mirror in the water below then reflect back up onto the ice in overlapping rings and polychrome hoops. In the ledges and faces of the bergs are unexpected hues: not just blues and purples but golds and ochres, sage green, herb green, all the greens of the forest. On clear bright days the world opens, immense: you can see the flaws and cracks in distant bergs, a flying petrel on the horizon, a penguin on the moon, but although your eyesight is newly keen, you cannot trust your eyes: they have evolved to predict and make sense of an altogether different world.

In the Antarctic summer light everything is mirror or mask, prism or scrim; the sky reflects in the ice and the ice in the sky; the sky upon the sky and ice upon ice. Shackleton climbed the mast and saw icebergs hanging upside down, the land in the sky like layers of silver and golden cloud, clouds that become islands, bergs that bulk like clouds.

The men saw rainbows of pure, glittering white, formed by the droplets within fog. On windless days crystals in the air caught the light and made parhelic circles: four satellite suns around a real sun, north and south and east and west. Sometimes perpendicular lines of light would connect the four new suns, intersecting to form Constantine's cross in the sky with our sun at its centre. Reality depended on the angle of the light, and your angle of looking.

Admiral Richard E. Byrd, who decades later spent more time alone on Antarctica than anyone else, wrote about visual beauties so sensual they almost became spiritual: a rainbow round the moon, pale pink ice in front of a horizon redder and brighter than blood, 'a straw-yellow ocean whose shores were the boundless blue of night.'

He was a man of science, but he concluded that such unsettling beauty was reserved for distant, dangerous places, surely as compensation for the life the viewer is in danger of losing. He said: 'This is the way the world will look to the last man when he dies.'

*

They made their way south through the ice, but in December the ice began to tighten.

They spent Christmas feasting around the long wooden table. They sang carols at the piano and wore paper hats and drank toasts to the King and to their wives and to each other, and wondered if the war was over yet. The walls of *Endurance* were made from Norwegian mountain fir – Christmas trees. I like to think of these 28 Englishmen and Irishmen and Australians and New Zealanders and Welshmen and Canadians having Christmas in the ice, singing inside a Christmas tree.

On Boxing Day the ice ahead seemed to thin and by the New Year there was clear water and they were steaming again. The sea was flat and the evening sun turned the water crimson-gold. It was a good omen for 1915.

On New Year's Day Thomas Orde-Lees pondered what resolution he could make. He had already given up swearing and there was nothing else at sea to tempt him. He thought about giving up sugar but decided to save that for Lent. He settled on washing the back of his neck more regularly.

They steamed south but the water grew thick with icy brash and slowed them down. A gale blew up from the south, pushing the ice to meet them.

They were passing between two large ice floes, a kind of pillared passageway, when a larger floe drifted across the narrow channel ahead of them. They pressed against it but even with their 350 horsepower engines at full speed, it didn't budge. They were burning too much coal and getting nowhere, so they tied up behind a large berg and waited for the ice to open again.

The gale blew for a week and when it stopped the slushy sea started to freeze. They needed a wind from the north to clear the path ahead, but for days the north-easter kept blowing.

Finally the wind dropped and *Endurance* was moving again, past vast bergs standing twice as tall as her masts, glowing white-blue in the purpling depths like capsized castles. Two years earlier an iceberg one tenth their size had sunk *Titanic*, but *Endurance* was stronger in the ice than *Titanic*, and ahead on the horizon there was a water sky: the dark matte reflection of open water in the air, the opposite of an ice blink.

In open water they made good time, running south at ten knots, almost full speed, parallel to the unnamed eastern shore of the Weddell Sea. A man named James Caird had donated money to the expedition, so Shackleton named it the Caird Coast.

Spirits were high. When they were at a standstill, wrote Orde-Lees in his journal, 'everyone feels despondent and some are actually snappy.' But when they were steaming south everyone was good-tempered and contented. 'Sir Ernest alone is always cheery and optimistic, be the weather what it may.'

They were closing in on Vahsel Bay: by 15 January they were just 320 kilometres away, perhaps twenty hours under steam. Then, around 2pm, there was an unsettling sight.

There are many collective nouns for seals – a rookery, a crash, a colony, a pod, a harem, a bob, a plump, a spring, a herd – but this was more like an evacuation, an exodus of seals. No one had ever seen so many crabeater seals before, a great dark floe of them, single-minded, the sea shiny and black with their glittering arching backs, all heading north, all of one mind to get the hell out of there.

The men uneasily eyed the direction from which the seals were fleeing, the way humans on the savannah might look past a herd of fleeing impala to wonder what is chasing them. Crabeater seals run north in the polar winter: they can't survive the frozen months. But this was the middle of January, only three weeks past the summer solstice. The deep freeze, surely, was months away.

Later that day, around 5pm, they encountered the ice pack again. A number of large bergs had grounded on a rocky shoal, making a barrier that trapped the floes and loose ice, forming a kind of perpendicular wall in their way. They turned west along the wall, looking for a way in.

A gale blew up and they tethered to another berg and waited. After two days the gale died. It had opened up cracks through the barrier. Worsley lifted the propeller to protect it and they went in under sail, between what Edgar Allan Poe had perfectly imagined 85 years before as 'stupendous ramparts of ice, towering away into the desolate sky, looking like the walls of the universe.'

They emerged into open water, and gave a cheer, and then they came to another ice pack.

Later, after many bad things had happened, the men agreed that bad things very often happened at 5pm. At 5pm on 18 January 1915, they entered the new pack.

The new pack was made of thick old ice – ice that had been around for years, the snow falling on it in winter and freezing, growing thicker and more compacted each year, accumulating layers as a tree gathers rings.

Freddie Ligthelm, the ice pilot on *SA Agulhas II*, told me that even today, with nuclear-powered icebreakers, captains are afraid of old ice, but this was even worse: the old ice had been covered in snow from the gale, and soft, padded ice is doubly hard to break. In the gaps between the floes the sea was a congealing slush of ground ice, broken ice, grease ice, water not quite liquid, not quite hard. Again, it closed around them. Again, they stopped.

Shackleton wasn't troubled. Only a fool expects constant forward motion, either in the Antarctic or in life. Stopping is part of the journey. You only had to wait for the ice to grind and part, a crack to appear. Being motionless in winter would be a problem, but not in summer. In summer it was just a matter of patience.

A week later, the crack opened ahead, about five metres wide. It kept opening through the morning and Shackleton ordered the engines stoked. Worsley edged forward and positioned the bow in the crack, like a wedge. *Endurance* was built to push through cracks and floes. They gathered up to full steam. They leant in.

And didn't move.

4. SMALL HANDS II

My father lay on the tarmac next to the barrel and then he gathered himself up on one knee with his hands on the tarmac on either side of him. He gathered himself up some more and then he pushed with his hands and managed to stand and then he went to the public toilets to comb his hair and splash his face with water. When I am in Sea Point, walking the promenade, I go into those same public toilets and look in the mirror. His face was once in that mirror. He looked in that mirror at the mask of his face, and he couldn't see what was happening behind it. It confounds me that he and I could be standing there in the same place, separated only by time.

He said he was all right, and he seemed to be all right, but he had a headache and he didn't say much else. We flew back to Durban. The next morning, Sunday morning, my mother tried to wake him for church. My dad woke but he didn't seem to want to get up. My mom pushed him and he still didn't get up. She pushed him harder and he fell out of bed and lay on the floor, and he still didn't get up. I came to the doorway and saw him lying on the floor, and when my mother saw me in the doorway she told me to get dressed for Sunday School, and she would call Aunty Joan to pick me up.

When I came back from Sunday School, my father wasn't on the floor any more. He had been taken to hospital. He'd had something called a stroke. It might have happened anyway, but the doctors thought it was probably brought on by his head hitting the tarmac.

Afterwards my dad said he was lucky. His movements were affected, but not too much. His speech and his thinking were affected, but not too much. He became more irritable and less tolerant of noise and of movement in his peripheral vision. He couldn't work any more. He couldn't leave the house. We needed money so my mother sold the house, the first house my father had owned, the first house she had owned too, and we moved into a rented house.

Each year after that, we moved to a new rented house, always on the Bluff, always a little closer to the oil refinery. We moved but we weren't fully migratory. We were like gorillas or chimpanzees, caught between migration and domesticity, sleeping each night in a new nest, made from a new tree, but always within the same small range.

My father spent his days at home but I never thought he was doing nothing. He read all day and that seemed proper for a grown-up to do. He read large-print hardback novels from the library. He read Louis L'Amour and Ian Fleming and Alistair MacLean and books set during the Second World War. He read Hemingway, especially the war novels, but he thought Hemingway tried too hard to be tough. My father had been a nightclub bouncer and a boxer and a dock worker; he knew what tough was. I remember him apologising to me for being like this. It upset him that my memories would be of him reduced, smaller. He wished he could be restored, made whole again, just for a little while, so that I could see.

My little sister slept in the bed with my mother and my dad moved into her room. On Sunday nights, when the good shows were on the radio, I lay in the single bed beside him, my head on his chest, and we listened to Springbok Radio. He would put his arms around me if it was a scary show like *Squad Cars* or *There's a Twist in the Tale*. I was scared easily, and afraid of the dark, but in those days I could afford to be afraid, because my dad was there.

Once we listened to a radio play set in the Antarctic. It may have been set in Scott's last tent, with actors playing Scott and Oates and Wilson and Bowers. Their voices were thin and brave as the blizzard howled and the canvas flapped and cracked and the ice crunched under their bodies as they moved. It scared me. They were tiny pockets of heat clinging together to defy a cold far vaster and more pitiless than I could imagine on my own. Their voices in the dark – their dark and my dark – whispered that there is more cold in the universe than there is heat or life, and their small human voices were all they had to hold it at bay. When you're a child you ask yourself: how would I have behaved in that tent? Not well. I would have been a coward. I would have cried for home. The Antarctic for me was conceived in fright.

My dad saw I was afraid and tried to comfort me. He said they were just actors reading off scripts and after they recorded it they went home and had supper with their families. He told me how they made the sound effects in the studio. His guess was that the snow being crunched was really cornflakes.

He turned off the radio and put his hand on my head, lightly on the side of my face, and started telling me a story about his life. His hand smelt of soap, and underneath the soap, of pipe tobacco and skin. I don't remember which story he told me, but that may have been the start of all of them. Every night after that, not just Sundays, I came and lay in his bed and he told me stories.

He told me about his childhood and about loves he'd loved and fights he'd fought and the times he'd let people down. He told me things he'd learnt, and things that made him laugh, books he'd read and old movies. There was no end to the stories, and he told some of them more than once, never the same way twice. They drifted into side currents or became other stories. Sometimes there were fresh details, new characters, small bits that had nothing to do with the story but that struck him as interesting. Sometimes he would start at the end or the middle, and work his way backwards and forwards. You can't think about one thing without somehow thinking about everything; everything opens into something wider; everything is connected.

I can't remember everything he told me; it's unpredictable what lodges in the mind. This is a silly thing, but once, when I was older, I stared at a dictionary thinking that all the words he spoke to me are in there, just dispersed. All I would need to do is gather them up and put them together in the right order, like the *Shahnameh*, the Persian Book of Kings, which the poet Ferdowsi claimed had been scattered in fragments and lost in antiquity until it was pieced together by wise men. If I could gather them up, like Ferdowsi, or like a Kabbalist gathering the sacred shards of light, I could make the world whole again.

Most of the stories my dad told me were true, some were not. He told me how during the war he'd trained for an SOE mission that involved parachuting into occupied France disguised as a Frenchman with a wooden leg. He had a trick with a matchstick and its matchbox that would imitate the creak of the leg. It worked best if you made it creak while stiffly swinging your leg in an exaggerated limp. (He used to do this at cocktail parties.) (So do I.) He warned me against cliché: 'Don't wear a beret. Only a Frenchman can wear a beret without looking like someone trying to look French.' He also told me that he went to Antarctica on *Endurance*, and that Shackleton had small hands.

Where was my mother all those nights? She was in the lounge, marking schoolbooks, or making our school lunches, or worrying over the accounts. She was studying for a further qualification so that she could qualify for a higher salary. She was looking in the newspaper for somewhere to rent that would be cheaper. She must have heard the low rumble of my dad's voice from his bedroom. Maybe sometimes she came to the half-open door and listened to what we were saying. She must have felt a thousand miles away, eavesdropping on the pulse of a telegraph signal passing faintly through the atmosphere. In the daytime I went to my mother for help and comfort, but at night, in that bed with my father, was when I was whole. In that bed I was home, and my mother was as distant and strange as the moon. My mother kept us alive, she saved our lives, but my father was my hero. It isn't fair, how things work.

When I think of Antarctica, and Shackleton, and time, and home, and loss, I think about lying in that bed, forty-some years ago, two pockets of warmth surrounded by cold. Heat flows in one direction only, and as my father spoke in the darkness, the greater concentration of warmth transferred its heat to the lesser one.

My father loved the world and loved being in it, and he sang it into being as something vast and wonderful that would never be finished, neither the world nor the song: to even dream of finishing would be to make the world insultingly smaller than it is. The world, my father told me, in words that didn't need saying, is infinite in its wonders and its gifts, and it pours endlessly into our small hands, and as small as our hands may be, they are never filled.

His hands were very strong, and they were scarred from the fighting he had done in his life. But when he laid them on me, they were very tender.

5. ANGLES OF LIGHT II

The ice should have groaned and cracked and eased apart, but nothing happened.

They backed off and gathered steam and tried again. They rammed it and it didn't open. This time as they leant and pushed, the ice closed around them. Captain Knowledge Bengu, the master of *SA Agulhas II*, explained to me that ice from behind is the ice you cannot fight. Modern icebreakers can create backdraft in the water to drive ice clear of the stern even while they're motionless. *Endurance* could not. They couldn't back up and they couldn't go forward. They were frozen in place.

But Shackleton didn't worry. The wind had packed the ice around them, but wind is like luck: soon enough it turns around. When the wind turned it would open the pack again and allow them to go.

Time passed. It's bad in a wooden ship when the wind blows. The wood creaks and groans and howls, and so does the ice. If it blows long enough it can affect your mind. Sailors hear voices in the wind, someone calling their name, someone shouting a warning.

The wind died and it was a relief, but it didn't turn around. There were breezes and airs, skiffles and cats-paws, but they needed something closer to a gale.

The men were on edge so Shackleton sent them down with saws and chisels to cut away the ice around the hull. The exposed water froze over again straight away.

For something else to do, they tried the ship's radio. Radio had been recently invented – in 1909 Guglielmo Marconi shared a Nobel Prize in Physics for his work on wireless telegraphy – and they had it in order to receive time checks to synch their chronometers, and in the hope of picking up news bulletins sent once a month in Morse code from the Falkland Islands. The Falklands were 2,700 kilometres away. No one was entirely sure how the radio worked. Even if it worked, it couldn't send messages, only receive. Even if it could send messages, what could anyone do about them? To no one's surprise, it didn't work.

Shackleton still wasn't worried. They were immobile in the ice but the ice wasn't immobile. It was drifting with the current southwards and westwards, towards Vahsel Bay, taking them with it. And it was still summer, the sun was still up all day, there would be a thaw. Any moment now they would be released and then they would land, and build a winter base and then in spring, on schedule, they would set out on the grand Imperial Trans-Continental Expedition, to glory.

But for Shackleton and Wild and Worsley, keeping watch from the bridge, the world and their senses conspired to taunt them. Wavy dark lines appeared in the sky ahead, like illustrations in black ink, like the lines Hergé draws to show Captain Haddock's confusion. They were distant leads of dark open sea, escape routes through the ice, reflected unreachably in the sky.

After the long nightless summer, the sun started lowering again. Soon it would skim the horizon.

Shackleton kept an eye on the coordinates from Worsley's daily readings. The ice had taken them in the right direction, but it was a clockwise current, and they were just 96 kilometres north of Vahsel Bay when the gyre started moving them westwards, away from land. They had travelled 20,000 kilometres, and they had stopped 96 kilometres short.

For now they could still see the Caird Coast to port across the ice, but every day would take them further away. One option was to take the men off the ship and lead them across the frozen ocean to land. But what a decision that would be. It would mean abandoning a ship in perfectly good order – their home – and marooning themselves on an unknown shore on the dark side of the moon. And in any case a frozen sea isn't flat. There are pressure ridges formed by colliding ice floes, hills and walls of ice, stretches of open water between one floe and another. Could they drag all the supplies needed to survive a winter? And if they did, would they ever get away from the shore again?

No, they would stay with the ship, even as it veered helplessly away. The thaw would still come.

Shackleton recorded in his journal an effect of the sun on the vapours rising from the ice, suffusing them so that they shimmered gold like a stage curtain, about to raise 'to reveal a stage-set of heaven'. The beauty of nature was like the effect of art, and it was all appearance. What was truly there was yet to be seen.

They kept the steam high in the ship's boilers, ready to seize on any release in the ice, but they had used too much coal coming through the pack: their 176 tons were down to 75: perhaps another 33 days' worth of steaming. On 24 January Shackleton called an end to ship's routine, ending the sea watches and allowing the men to sleep through the night, but he ordered the stokers to keep up the steam. As long as the fires burned, there was hope.

On Valentine's Day the lookout in the crow's nest spotted a line of open water snaking through the ice ahead but not quite reaching the ship. The men went down and worked all day to carve a V-shaped canal between the bow and the open water. Hurley filmed them sweating in the cold, two men to a saw, Shackleton watching, hands in pockets. The canal needed to be 140 metres long. The ship burnt shovel-loads, bin-loads of coal, three tons in a single day, trying to smash through the ice that kept forming as they cut it away. They were metres short when the open water closed up again.

The next day was Shackleton's birthday. He turned 41.

In March, for the first time in months, the sun dipped below the horizon. The night lasted only a few minutes, just a pearly twilight, but that was the end of the endless days. From now on the nights would grow longer by minutes at a time. Winter was coming.

Four days later they started drifting north as well as west, deeper into the Weddell Sea. Out of sight of the coast, the frozen sea seemed wilder: there were great troughs and sculpted crests, like waves frozen in the act of breaking. A bad thought was occurring to the men.

Now that there were sunsets and sunrises again, the low angles of sun offered a kind of cold enchantment, shining through the rims of ice hills like polished silver, cycling shadows through blue palettes from azure to a modernist periwinkle to a decadent mauve. In the twilight a fine violet gauze descended over the world. But the bad thought was getting stronger.

Shackleton banned all discussion of it, and no one raised it in front of him, but it was there: what if there isn't a thaw? What if summer is already over? What if we must winter here?

Secretly, the thought excited Frank Worsley. Worsley was a New Zealander, sandy-haired and good-looking, and he was 42 but had the heart of a happy schoolboy. He always claimed to have been led there by a dream: one night he had dreamt that certain streets of London were filled with ice. The next morning he walked down through the streets of his dream, and in Burlington Square he came across the office where Shackleton was interviewing candidates for his expedition. He walked in and explained his dream and 30 seconds later Shackleton made him his captain.

Worsley had come south to test his mettle, and this was a mettle-tester from a Victorian boy's adventure book. He struggled to hide his enthusiasm. Walking on the ice with Wild and Shackleton one afternoon, he spotted a flat plain of ice and cheerily declared, 'Oh boys! What a jolly fine football ground that will make!'

Able seaman Walter How didn't mind too much either. He was 24 and had been at sea since he was eleven. He was one of the few married men aboard, and his daughter was six weeks old when *Endurance* sailed. He missed her and he missed his wife, but – he wrote in his last letter home, from Buenos Aires – if he was back home, he would just be sent to war. 'It's always the poor who suffer.' Anyway, he was earning £4 a month, and by the terms of his contract, if they should be gone longer than a year, that would rise to £7.

But the others weren't as sanguine. They were a disparate company: Oxford dons and illiterate trawlermen, scientists and merchant officers, artists and Australians. Few of them would have associated with each other in normal life.

Thomas Orde-Lees, the motor expert and storekeeper, was an eccentric former public schoolboy. He worried about spending so long with people so thoroughly unlike him. He objected to Walter How's table manners, and he privately deplored Chippy McNish's habit of sniffing, and of eating his peas with his spoon. He didn't much like Shackleton's policy that all men should share chores, regardless of rank. 'I hate scrubbing floors,' he wrote. 'Scrubbing floors is not fair work for people who have been brought up in refinement.'

They were on the crumbling edge of a crevasse, this shipful of strangers. They had boarded the ship as Edwardians with an idea of themselves in a stable and knowable universe – whether it be a universe of God or of science – and they had gone out to test themselves against it. They couldn't know that while they waited in the ice, their world was ending, torn apart in the trenches of Europe and on the hillsides of Gallipoli, crushed in a new age of combustion and machine. And they couldn't know that it would be followed by a new one, less obviously ordered, accelerating in the direction of chaos.

While they fought for their lives, perns in a gyre, back home the old hierarchies were already starting to devolve into a new and more entropic system. A faster and less human age was starting – the age in which we still find ourselves. The men on *Endurance* had not seen the First World War, far less the Second, so they couldn't yet conceive a universe in which we could destroy the world. They were struggling for their lives against an idea of nature still too big ever to be hurt by them.

At night the light glinted on the floes in the unending dusk and kept them awake. Then even the dusk drained away.

They tried the radio again. Anything – a pulse, a dot, a dash, anything to persuade them they weren't alone.

Only static.

Orde-Lees thinks 16 March was the day Shackleton realised that the game was up.

Roland Huntford identifies 16 March as the day Shackleton started rising to greatness.

On 16 March, Shackleton extinguished the boilers. They would need to save their coal.

They would have to winter in the ice.

6. SMALL HANDS III

I had a year with my father that way, nearly two years, but then he had another stroke, and another, and another, and each stroke made him smaller and took him further away, and then he had another stroke and was taken to hospital. I didn't visit him in hospital, and he didn't want me to. Then one night at three in the morning when I was ten years old, my mother received a phone call, and he had died.

My father once said that all he had to leave me was his self-winding gold watch, but while he lay in his hospital bed, his body cooling to the temperature of the world, someone stole the watch off his wrist, so really all he left me were his stories. But stories are not nothing.

I lay in my bed that night, listening to my mother on the phone, and when she came to my doorway I pretended to be asleep because I didn't know what to say.

I lay in bed and thought about one of his stories, about when he was in the army and represented one of his buddies in a disciplinary hearing, even though he wasn't a lawyer, and the secret system they had designed for communicating during cross-examination – a scratch of the nose if he should answer 'yes', a tug on the ear for 'no' – and I panicked as I realised that I had missed a detail. I went back and remembered it again, but I knew one day I wouldn't.

Marconi's wireless telegraphy was one of the great inventions of the Edwardian age. In 1910 it was used to catch the murderer Dr Crippen as he made his escape from England to Canada with his lover, Miss Ethel Le Neve, who was disguised as a boy and pretending to be his son. In 1912, as *Titanic* sank, RMS *Carpathia* picked up her transmissions of SOS (actually CQD, the Marconi distress signal) and came racing to save the lives of more than 700 people. Days later, a crowd gathered at the New York Electrical Society to cheer Marconi – who had himself been booked on *Titanic*, before changing his mind – as a saviour, and a hero.

Titanic made Marconi a celebrity. Years later, when he was old and declining, lurching through a cascade of ever more serious heart events, he became obsessed with the idea that every transmission ever transmitted, every sound ever made, every word ever spoken still exists, travelling through space and therefore through time, in frequencies and radio waves that decay and grow ever fainter and move further away, yet still survive. If we could only devise a receiver sufficiently strong, thought Marconi, we could reach out through space and hear anything, everything that has ever been said.

We could hear, clear or crackling, the Wright Brothers whoop when their first plane flew and we could hear Bach giving music lessons to his son. We could hear Jesus talking in his sleep. We could hear our child's first laugh again, and the laugh of every baby that has ever laughed. We could hear our fathers first meeting our mothers. We could hear their last words to us, and all the words we've forgotten. We could hear our mothers kiss us goodnight, night after night. We could hear, over and over, the ones we love tell us they love us. We could hear them say our names. Nothing would be lost, nothing would ever be lost, if only we had the right radio to hear it.

7. PLAYING THE GAME

Roland Huntford says 16 March 1915 was the beginning of Shackleton's rise to greatness, because it was the moment his dreams were devastated yet he carried on with the same smile as before. Doctor Macklin noted in his diary on that day that Shackleton's outward face didn't change, not that day and not the next.

To understand the context in which this is called greatness, and the debate between pessimism and optimism in which it is framed, we must think about Robert Falcon Scott.

The Antarctic has a way of manufacturing rivalries. It started from the very beginning: it's commonly accepted that the Antarctic continent was first sighted by a human being in January 1820, but it's not agreed which of two people, on opposite sides of the world, happened to see it first.

27 January 1820: On the east coast of Antarctica, Captain Fabian Gottlieb Thaddeus von Bellingshausen, aboard the Russian sloop *Vostok*, at just about the right coordinates, records seeing a wall of ice.

By sheerest coincidence, three days later in the west, an Irish officer in the Royal Navy named Edward Bransfield comes upon the northernmost tip of the Antarctic Peninsula and reports two high mountains, covered with snow.

Those three days make all the difference. Although he never actually recorded seeing land, Von Bellingshausen is credited with the discovery of the Antarctic. He becomes an admiral and a military governor and has a sea named after him. Bransfield fades into the sea mists of history and is buried in an unmarked, crumbling grave in Brighton. No account of his voyage is ever written. In 2000 the Royal Mail issues a commemorative postage stamp in Bransfield's honour, but no likeness of him has ever been made, so the stamp shows a drawing of his ship.

(Later that same year, entirely unaware of the other two, an American seal hunter named Nathaniel Palmer *also* comes upon the Antarctic Peninsula. For the next 150 or so years, the Americans call the Antarctic Peninsula the Palmer Peninsula, in much the same spirit that they call their baseball tournament the World Series.)

Competition, even unwilling and unwitting competition, appears to be bred into the DNA of the human history of Antarctica. I don't like comparing Scott and Shackleton, and I don't like taking sides (although I do), but it's almost impossible to avoid, especially when considering the qualities that might best help us live.

Their destinies were intertwined from the beginning.

Scott's expedition to the Antarctic in 1901 aboard the *Discovery* was the first of what has become known as the Heroic Age of Antarctic exploration. Shackleton was third officer. He was popular, but also an outsider: it was a Royal Navy expedition but he was from the merchant marine; it was an English ship and he was a little too Irish. Even the men below him were confused: they adored him, but he spoke with them too informally and it wasn't clear whether he belonged above deck or below deck, in the wardroom with the officers or the fo'c'sle with the sailors.

But when it came time for Scott to trek south, he selected two men to accompany him: his friend and confidant Edward Wilson, and Shackleton. Scott wrote to his wife Kathleen about Shackleton's vitality and strength, his good humour, his enthusiasm.

There had been some friction between them – Scott was a navy disciplinarian, and Shackleton was temperamentally more comfortable giving instruction than receiving. But on the southward trek things turned more seriously sour.

Simmering differences and silences finally erupted in words. Wilson says Scott called Shackleton a 'bloody fool', and Shackleton replied 'You're the worst bloody fool of the lot.' It's not edifying badinage, but we've all been there. Wilson kept the peace, but they made slow going and didn't come within 400 miles of the pole. Then, on their return journey, Shackleton fell ill with his mysterious malady.

Shackleton was sent home, while *Discovery* stayed another year in the Ross Sea. Back in England, he made the best of things by writing articles about the expedition, giving talks and interviews, inevitably raising his own profile. There was a feeling among the rest of the expedition, when they heard, that 'Shackleton isn't quite playing the game'.

'Playing the game' is one of those English ideas. There are rules to the game but you can't be told them – you only belong to the game if you already know them. You might think you are playing the game, only to find that you are playing a very different game. Shackleton also wasn't playing the game when he decided to lead an Antarctic expedition of his own, to be first to the South Pole.

Scott was annoyed: Antarctica was *his* terrain, and *he* intended to claim the South Pole. He couldn't stop Shackleton going, and he couldn't raise his own second expedition in time to beat him, but somehow, by somewhat schoolyard rights of precedence, he extracted a promise that Shackleton would not use the landing point in McMurdo Sound that the *Discovery* expedition had used.

It was 1908, and Shackleton was sailing south in command for the first time. King Edward VII came aboard *Nimrod* to wish them well. Scott was the favoured explorer of the Royal Geographical Society and the establishment in general, but Edward was a life-loving and swashbuckling king, and in some ways he and Shackleton were temperamentally better suited. His last words to Shackleton were: 'Play the game.'

But when *Nimrod* reached the Ross Sea and couldn't find safe harbour anywhere else, Shackleton broke his promise to Scott and landed at McMurdo Sound.

Some members aboard worried that he wasn't playing the game.

The Royal Geographical Society and its former president Sir Clements Markham grumbled that Shackleton wasn't playing the game.

Scott definitely didn't think Shackleton was playing the game.

The broken promise confirmed Shackleton's status as an outsider, a chancer, an arriviste. Scott wrote of 'the terrible vulgarising which Shackleton had introduced into the Southern field of enterprise, hitherto so clean and wholesome.'

One way to shake off accusations of not playing the game is to win the game. Shackleton set out with three companions, including a short, durable Yorkshireman named Frank Wild, to reach the Pole. They went with ponies as pack horses but the ponies died in the snow, or broke through the surface and tumbled down bottomless crevasses. When the ponies collapsed with exhaustion, it was Wild's job to shoot them and butcher them for meat.

After a month of hauling their food and equipment up black-rocked mountains they discovered a great glacier, which Shackleton called the Beardmore, after one of his donors. It stretched away south, a shining highway that would lead them all the way onto the polar plateau and the South Pole.

After another month of trudging and hauling and freezing, they were running out of food. They were further south than any human beings had ever been. They carried on walking.

After 73 days, Shackleton stood looking south. Somewhere beyond the mists was success. They were 156 kilometres from the Pole, nearer than 100 miles, and this is the moment, long before *Endurance*, that for me is key to understanding Shackleton and what he has to tell us.

He was then a young man, in his early 30s, burning with ambition, aching to be someone. As a young man he had dreamed of being a poet, and submitted poems to magazines under the pseudonym 'Nemo'. Nemo was the mysterious captain in the Jules Verne novels, who avoids dry land except for deserted islands and the empty edges of Antarctica, and whose name in Latin means 'Nobody'. Shackleton discovered that he was not a good poet, but he decided that exploring was like writing. He had told Emily that he was Nemo, but one day he would be somebody. One day he would make her proud.

And here he was, so close to the South Pole he could walk there. But not close enough that they could make it back alive. So Shackleton turned them around.

They only just made it back. They had 50 days to reach the coast before the ship would leave. Shackleton went snow blind and Wild had to position him on the edge of crevasses and tell him how far to jump. They couldn't find a food depot and were only saved when they found a scarlet stain marking where they'd shot a pony, and made a soup from the ice. Wild became ill with dysentery. A blizzard struck. Everyone was roped together, and when a snow bridge gave way and the lead walker fell into a crevasse, he would dangle there above the infinite, waiting for the others to haul him up. Wild remembered being so exhausted that he prayed his rope would break and he could have a proper rest.

They were starving. One day Wild stumbled and was too weak to get up. Shackleton offered Wild his morning's ration: a Huntley & Palmers biscuit, specially fortified with milk protein. Wild refused, but Shackleton threatened to throw the biscuit in the snow if he didn't take it. In his memoirs, Wild wrote: 'All the money that was ever minted would not have bought that biscuit, and the remembrance of that sacrifice will never leave me.'

(As it happens, that biscuit – or one very like it – was left behind in the hut on Ross Island when they departed. It was sold at auction in 2011, not for all the money ever minted, but for a disappointing £1,250.

The historical biscuit market is capricious. In 2015 a Spillers & Bakers 'Pilot' biscuit from a *Titanic* lifeboat – saved by James Fenwick, a passenger on the *Carpathia* – sold at auction for £15,000. I have inspected the lifeboat biscuit, and it resembles a hybrid between a Salted Cracker and a Tennis Biscuit.)

Wild and Shackleton shared a tent. Wild wrote in his journal that in the unlikely event of making it out alive, nothing would ever induce him to return to that terrible place ever again. The next day, hollow-eyed and starving, still twenty days from safety, Shackleton said he thought that next time he could make it to the Pole. Would Wild come back with him? Without hesitating, Wild said yes.

Shackleton brought his men back. They had scurvy and frostbite but they recovered. Shackleton never cursed his rotten luck, never complained about the ponies that let him down or the blizzards that held them up or plans that hadn't worked.

When Scott realised that Shackleton had failed, he heaved a sigh of relief and organised his second expedition.

He sails south on the *Terra Nova* with an enormous scientific party. He has ponies and mechanical tractors. He has the backing of the Royal Geographical Society and the Royal Navy. The Pole is his to claim. At the base in McMurdo Sound, he takes his time. This will be a stately triumphal procession. He will do enormous amounts of science, and return with the Pole to present to the King. Shackleton had first shot, but Scott will not miss.

It is a shock when Scott receives news that Roald Amundsen has unexpectedly come south, landing at the Bay of Whales, a little way round the coast. What business has Amundsen there? And a discomfiting thought sinks in: Amundsen is Norwegian, and he can ski and handle dogs. He will be faster than Scott.

Scott pretends it doesn't matter, but it does matter, very much. He sinks into a scowling black depression, becomes remote, complains bitterly. It is agreed that Amundsen isn't playing the game. It is agreed that skiing and using dogs is cheating. Man-hauling – using your own feet, dragging your own equipment – is the English way. Man-hauling is playing the game.

Scott sets out for the Pole, fearing that Amundsen might beat him, but in his journals Shackleton most occupies his mind. He compares the weather to the weather Shackleton had, he decides Shackleton had exaggerated the difficulties, had taken incorrect readings, had lied about the inefficiencies of ponies. He has one eye constantly out for Shackleton.

Scott is intent on playing the game, but he is also locked into winning a different kind of game, and when his party arrives at the South Pole, sick with scurvy and frostbite, the soles of their feet cracking open in their frozen boots, one of them days away from death, and they see Amundsen's Norwegian flag flying, Scott is defeated. He sits down and writes in his journal: 'Great God! This is an awful place, and terrible enough for us to have laboured to it without the reward of priority.'

Scott is defeated in that moment in a way that Shackleton is never defeated.

When people compare Scott and Shackleton, they sometimes quibble over who was the better explorer. It's pointless, not least because neither of them was any good at all, measured against the contemporary metric provided by Roald Amundsen. They were both bad planners, bad preparers, slow to take advice, slow to adapt their thinking, suspicious of foreign ways, foolishly brave, too infatuated with willpower and proud of their capacity to suffer.

The real point of comparison is temperament. Wild, who went south under each of them, unhesitatingly called Shackleton an optimist, and therefore a survivor, and Scott a pessimist, and that is why he died. The question of optimism and pessimism as strategies of survival is an important one – more important to us now than ever – and perhaps it's not quite as straightforward as it seems.

It's true that Scott broods constantly in his journals about bad luck, the obscure intentions of Providence, the lingering conviction that success will be snatched from him at the last. He is a moody leader, prone to tempers or sulks, nursing grudges. Of course, he can also be cheerful and inspiring and no one can doubt his willing or his courage. Like Shackleton, he has the gift of inspiring loyalty. But it is a fair consensus that he is a pessimist, while Shackleton is the man with the fierce conviction that everything will be all right.

And yet – *and yet* – it is Shackleton the optimist who turns back from the Pole, and it is Scott who goes on.

And the South Pole *is* an awful place, of course. The South Pole is the great secret nothingness at the heart of human vanity – a howling, featureless plain atop a high, flat, white dome, without views, without beauties, without tenderness, without illusions for human succour. And critically for Scott, it is without even 'the reward of priority', because for Scott it is the awful place where he *lost*. And his conception of what it means to win or to lose the game is fundamentally different to Shackleton's.

Scott and his men tried to make it back home. Taff Evans died on the polar plateau and they left him covered in snow. On the Beardmore Glacier, seventeen kilometres from their last food depot, bogged down in a blizzard, Titus Oates took his long walk in the snow and Scott and Wilson and Birdy Bowers lay in their tent, waiting for the end. There have been long debates about what killed them. Bad planning, bad luck, bad weather. Scurvy, starvation, snow. It is distasteful to point out that other men – including one of those men in that tent – survived conditions worse than those that killed Scott's party. It is distasteful to sit at a warm desk and pass lofty thoughts about how other men failed, but I want to at least consider this: that the profound difference between Scott and Shackleton is ultimately a matter of philosophy. It may have been that Scott was playing the wrong kind of game.

8. POLAR NIGHT

....

*Civilisation is like a thin layer of ice upon a
deep ocean of chaos and darkness.*
WERNER HERZOG

....

Shackleton readied for winter. He cleared the main
hold and instructed Chippy McNish to construct
sleep cubicles for the men. The hold was in the centre
of the ship, insulated by wooden decking on all sides.
Shackleton personally laid linoleum on the floor.

He moved the dogs and pigs onto the ice and built
them 'pigloos' and 'dogloos' from ice blocks. He turned
his cabin into the ship's library. There was a range of
books available: Browning and Tennyson and Shelley,
Encyclopedia Britannica, *The Brothers Karamazov*, *Anna
Karenina*, Carlyle's *The French Revolution*, some Walter
Scott, manuals of grammar – but the book most in demand
was *Through the Antarctic Night* by an American doctor
named Frederick Cook. Shackleton barked and scowled at

anyone he caught reading it, regarding it as seditious, but they couldn't stop. It was passed around like contraband.

Outside, a lumen at a time, the light slowly left the world. The colours went first, then the edges of objects, then depth and distance. There were no shadows any more; ice and sky became the same. The beauty vanished, to reveal what Herman Melville considered to be the face beneath.

In *Moby-Dick*, as he paints the terror of whiteness, Melville writes that all we see and love in everyday life are visual illusions, stage paint, set designs: 'All visible objects, man, are but as pasteboard masks.' Whiteness, he says, is the world stripped of decoration, revealing – like a nightclub when the lights come up – that it is 'painted like the harlot, whose allurements cover nothing but the charnel-house within.'

The men of *Endurance* didn't have to go as far as that to feel a creeping dread. They knew that one day soon the sun would set and stay set. There would be no sound out there but the wind, no animal pulse, just a crystal, mineral, unliving stillness. The sun would set and break the primordial promise of life: that it will rise again tomorrow. And if the sun doesn't come up tomorrow, how can we be sure that it will ever come up again?

As the light goes, temperature follows. The only heat in all that frozen ocean will be the heat they bring there, and can sustain. It's a mythical story: you are the bearer of the beleaguered spark of life and must keep it kindled against the darkness until life returns to the world. It's a spiritual story: you must look inside for the heat that animates the universe. It's a science story: you have a sample of what ordinarily we only sense, appalled, on a deep-time scale of extinction: the eventual heat death of the universe.

Shackleton forbade any foolish talk like this, but the men couldn't help turning their eyes to the lowering sun, and their minds to what was to come. They were about to be examined and their innermost selves revealed, and each quietly feared he wouldn't pass the test. That's why they read Frederick Cook.

Cook had been the ship's doctor on the exploration ship *Belgica* in the Bellingshausen Sea, not far to the east. The expedition leader was a young Belgian named Adrien de Gerlache and the crew included a young Norwegian officer on his first polar voyage named Roald Amundsen.

De Gerlache had promised his backers a patriotic triumph – glory for the new country of Belgium – but they had been slow reaching the Antarctic. Summer was ending and the crew were agitating for home and there was still no triumph, no glory. De Gerlache deliberately froze the ship into the ice, claiming it was an accident. They would be the first ship ever to overwinter while frozen into the southern ocean: there would be *some* triumph, if only the reward of priority. It went horribly wrong.

'The curtain of blackness which has fallen over the outer world of icy desolation has also descended upon the inner world of our souls,' Cook wrote. 'The night soaks hourly a little more colour from our blood.'

A strange condition began to afflict them. Cook had never seen it before: he called it 'polar anaemia'. Individuals became restless, irritable, physically weak. They refused to move. Their legs swelled. Their heart rates surged to 150 beats per minute, and dropped to 46.

Some of their symptoms are familiar from the effects of Covid isolation: they were unable to focus on conversations, they lost their appetite, were unable to read, unable to work. They sank into melancholy as a boot sinks into snow. The melancholy became anxiety, then depression, and then something worse.

The Eskimos of Alaska have a word for it: *perlerorneq*, 'the burden'. The writer Barry Lopez characterises it as feeling with sudden intensity something that is always there but waits for the long dark before showing itself. When it arrives, it lays upon you the full weight of life: the past is no consolation, the future seems empty and bleak, you 'retreat to the present feeling defeated, weary before starting, a core of anger, a miserable sadness.'

The Inuhuit of northern Greenland don't experience *perlerorneq*, but rather winter attacks of *pibloktoq*: episodes of manic, delusional, occasionally violent behaviour. Individuals turn on their companions. They bite and claw. They strip naked and run into the snow. Afterwards they have no words to account for it.

The Gothic and Romantic literature of the 19th century imagined the Poles as places of madness, beyond the pale lamplight of what language can describe. In Coleridge's *Rime of the Ancient Mariner* the old salt is driven near insanity by Job-like tribulations; Mary Shelley begins and ends her narrative with Victor Frankenstein's unhinged pursuit of his monster of ego, even to the frozen Pole; Edgar Allan Poe's short stories describe polar journeys as irrational pursuits of a terrible incommunicable knowledge with which no one can return; H.P. Lovecraft would set *At The Mountains of Madness* in the sub-Polar city of the Old Ones, haunted by mad, dark visions of what he thought Poe had glimpsed there.

But the Eskimos of Alaska and the Inuhuit of Greenland have ways of mutual support and community diffusion that share and so alleviate their winter afflictions. On *Belgica* there was no community. The company was divided, wary of each other. The officers and crew ate apart and seldom interacted. De Gerlache holed up in his cabin for days and weeks on end, weak with scurvy and melancholy. The men, bottled together, were profoundly alone.

They lay awake through night-dark and day-dark, dwelling on their aloneness. They thought about the light-washed world to the north, and their families and friends and enemies walking around under the sun. They felt the great weight of the Earth piled up and spinning above their heads. They contemplated the brief ember-glow of their lives and trembled at the waves of darkness mounting to engulf them. And they grew afraid.

The deckhand Jan van Mirlo became hysterically mute and deaf. He became convinced the chief engineer hated him. He recovered his faculties, but not his mind. When he could speak again, he swore he would kill the chief before the chief could kill him.

For Frank Wild on *Endurance*, reading Cook's account, this was uncomfortably familiar. He remembered how on Scott's *Discovery* expedition one man became convinced he had a mortal enemy among the crew. He ran out into the snow and crouched in the darkness with a crowbar, waiting. He knew a search party would come looking, each man holding the hand of the man behind him, a human chain of care reaching into the night, and he hoped his enemy would be the one to find him: then he would split his skull.

On *Belgica* the Norwegian bosun Adam Tollefsen was next to become paranoid. He lost all memory of how he had come to be on the ship, like a man waking from a dream into a more terrifying dream. His shipmates were murderers conspiring to kill him, so he hid from them in nooks and dark corners, whimpering at sudden noises, the crack of ice, the groan of timbers. He wrote heart-breaking letters to his wife and posted them in the snow. At night he disappeared into the bowels of the ship with a knife. His shipmates heard him creaking through storage holds and stairs, and lay awake afraid of what he would do.

The official Belgian report said that Tollefsen 'was smitten with terror and went mad at the spectacle of the weird-sublime and in dread of pursuing fate.' He never fully recovered, and afterwards his shipmates burnt his diary, appalled by the darkness they found there. He spent the rest of his life in isolation in an asylum in Norway on the outskirts of Oslo.

(Not all cases of Antarctic violence and paranoia are irrational: in 1959 one Russian scientist on the Vostok Station in the interior of the continent, where the temperature has been measured at -89°C, making it officially the coldest part of the coldest place on Earth, attacked and may have killed another scientist with an ice axe over a game of chess. The KGB investigated and made the obvious KGB decision to ban chess at their polar research stations.

Again with the Russians: in 2018, in the cafeteria of Russia's Bellingshausen Station, an engineer named Sergei Savitsky stabbed a welder named Oleg Beloguzov in the chest. It was later revealed that Beloguzov kept checking books out of the library before him, waiting till he was halfway through them, then telling him the endings. If this is true, I think we can agree that Beloguzov was asking for it.)

In 1934 Admiral Richard E. Byrd spent five months alone in a cabin buried under the snow of the Antarctic continent. He was there to take scientific measurements but also, Poe-like, to conduct an experiment upon his own soul. He noticed a kind of edgy restlessness stealing over him, making him 'strangely irritable'. He started feeling uncharacteristically anxious about the outside world and became increasingly depressed. He worked through check-lists and positive self-talk, willing himself whole, but still he felt like 'a clock wound up to strike in an empty house'.

He longed for things: not specific things, but frag-ments and scintillas, pointillist dots of memory and sen-sation that swirled to form a symbolic impression of the world, 'fragments of something vast and not wholly rec-ognisable, that I had lost forever.'

He felt himself splitting and separating along unguessed-at geological seams. His will was still strong, but he was discovering how profoundly mind and body are connected. Eventually he realised that 'my body is waiting, as if with bated breath, for the intrusion of familiar stimuli from the outside world, and could not comprehend why they are denied.'

He says that a man can distract himself, or force his mind to forget, but a body is not so easily side-tracked: it remembers its natural element, and its natural element is social. 'I don't think that a man can do without sounds and smells and voices and touch, any more than he can do without phosphorus and calcium.'

On *Belgica*, Cook tried various ways of combatting polar anaemia. He marched them on the ice in a narrow circuit round the ship: 'the madman's promenade'. They shuffled like inpatients in the pale glow of hanging lan-terns, at arm's length from the hull lest they wander into the dark and be lost. It didn't seem to help.

He sat with the afflicted, asking about their state of mind, the condition of their emotions, even the content of their dreams. He was the first to propose treating an affective disorder with exposure to light. He had the suffering men strip naked and sit for hours before an open fire piled high with wood. Then he questioned them again. How were the symptoms? How were they feeling? The men said they were feeling better.

Of course, a wood fire can't generate enough light, nor the right kind of light, to treat Seasonal Affective Disorder. So what accounts for the improvement in their condition? In his excellent account of the long night of the *Belgica*, Julian Sancton notes something vital: Cook sat with the men, enquiring with genuine and intense interest into their well-being. He gave them the full glow of his attention: he looked at them, and seemed to care about what he saw.

We know this, but we seem to keep forgetting it: humans are not whole, in and of ourselves. We need certain conditions in order to be most fully, healthily human. Those conditions are not climatic but social. We need touch, yes, and light, yes, but also warmth, and not just the warmth of the sun or other bodies: we need the warmth of other people's attention. We need the sensation of being seen and acknowledged as a part of something larger than only us. We need a shared experience of being alive, our existence to be a collaboration. Without that, we are out of the element in which we flourish. We are like those jungle cats or primates in zoos, those killer whales in Sea World who languish in depression or lash out in violence. It's a truth so old it feels trite: we exist in and through each other.

9. A DIGRESSION ABOUT BEARS

He speaks to the sun and it does not shine;
He seals off the light of the stars.
He alone stretches out the heavens
And treads on the waves of the sea.
He is the maker of the Bear ...
and the constellations of the south.

JOB 9:7

It's a primal scene: the men huddled on *Belgica*, fearful of the circling dark. But is the fear of the dark a metonym of the fear of something *in* the dark? In the Antarctic there is nothing in the dark, and it's precisely that nothingness that terrifies, but in the Antarctic the distance between the elements of a metaphor becomes very narrow indeed.

The Antarctic is the opposite of the Arctic, and the Arctic means 'the place of the bear'. 'Arktos' is the Greek for bear, and the Arctic has polar bears. The 'Arktos' in Arctic, though, is not a real bear, it's the bear as a metaphor: it's the constellation Ursa Major, or perhaps Ursa Minor – the Great Bear or the Little Bear. (The North Star, Polaris, is in the Little Bear.) In other words, the Arctic is the place where you can see not only bears, but also the Bear.

Medieval geographers theorised that the Earth is a place of balance, so if there is an Arctic, there must be a continent, as yet undiscovered, on the other side of the world. On the map he drew up in 150 AD, Ptolemy draws an imagined continent and calls it *Terra Australis Incognita* – the unknown southern land. It would be the equal but opposite of the Arctic, a counter-Arctic: the Antarctic.

It makes good linguistic and celestial sense that the Antarctic is the place without the Bear – in the south the Ursas can't be seen in the night sky – but there's no good reason for it also to be the place without the bears, and yet, in one of those irresistibly sinuous and sensuous entwinings of stories and metaphors, the Antarctic when it was discovered turned out indeed to have no bears. And yet the bear is also there.

The word 'bear' itself doesn't mean 'bear'. Bear is derived from the word *bera* in Old English, from the Proto-Germanic, and means 'the brown one'. It's generally agreed the northern tribes of Europe used the word 'bear' to avoid saying its real name, perhaps for fear of summoning it.

Avoiding the name of our greatest fear is a common human need, hence the many nicknames for the Devil ('the Old One', 'the Dark One', 'Old Nick'). (Hence also, possibly, the word 'nickname' itself.) Hence also Voldemort – He Who Must Not Be Named – and the various sobriquets Russian citizens used for Stalin, or Cubans for Castro, and how the woodcutters of the Knysna forest in the Western Cape said 'Big Foot' instead of 'elephant', and the way the characters in Neil Simon's *Brighton Beach Memoirs* lower their voices to say the names of diseases. Hence why we're sorry your father passed away, or passed over, or left us, instead of being sorry he died.

Mary Shelley never named Frankenstein's monster. For the first theatrical production of *Frankenstein*, in London in 1823, the monster was listed on the programme as '---'. Mary Shelley commented: 'This nameless mode of naming the unnameable is rather good.'

(In the 1931 movie, he is called 'The Monster' in the credits, but Boris Karloff is named only as '?')

The bear was a northern monster, prowling the edge of human settlements, seeking what it may devour. The word 'berserk' comes from the Old Norse, used by the Odin-worshipping tribes who wore bear skins in battle to appropriate the totemic force of the bear and encourage their own ferocity. Berserk literally means 'bear shirt'. Until near the end of the 13th century bears were regarded as supernatural devils of the forest: they changed shape, they came back as ghosts, they abducted women and impregnated them with monstrous children.

But humans, faced with the terrible-sublime, are driven to measure ourselves against it. In the pages of polar history there are plenty of arguments about the motivations for this expedition or that, or for the enterprise in general. The usual candidates are science or nationalism or imperialism or commercial exploitation, but I think this is really what makes humans go out to the extremes of the Earth: because written into our genetic blueprint is the impulse to test the limits of our humanness, first by contact with that which is bigger than us, then by enduring, then, through endurance, by overcoming.

This is true of the Antarctic, and before that it was true of bears. For better or worse, when we encounter the vast and frightening non-human, we are driven to make ourselves big enough to match it. Perhaps that's a bug of being human, perhaps a feature. But if it's a feature, it comes with a bug: in the course of making ourselves bigger, we can't seem to stop ourselves making the non-human smaller.

Bear-baiting was a popular entertainment in Europe and especially England in the 16th and 17th centuries. Bear gardens offered shows the way theatres did, and competed for the same market. Clowns and acrobats dressed in bear suits and capered for laughs. Shakespeare wrote a famous contemporary bear – Sackerson – into the dialogue of *The Merry Wives of Windsor*. To torment a bear was to make small an ancestral fear: the bear comes from the darkness at the edge of town but then is declawed, made pitiable, paraded at the end of a leash and prodded by a stick, the way Mary the elephant would later be marched through Erwin, Tennessee.

Having been humbled, they were domesticated: by the 20th century the bear was the most beloved and unthreatening of nursery characters: Winnie, Paddington, Rupert. Care Bears, Gummi Bears, Berenstein Bears. In the darkness of childhood night, seeking comfort, we tightly hugged our Teddy Bears.

Today polar bears are the furry child-friendly public faces of climate change. We show them forlorn on tiny ice floes, or picking dolefully through trash heaps on the outskirts of town. 'Make sure you throw that plastic in the recycling bin,' we tell our children. 'We have to save the polar bears.'

But Bruce Chatwin suggested that even the bear was a memory of an earlier, more intimate beast. In *The Songlines* he floats a theory adopted from the South African palaeontologist Bob Brain, who excavated the Swartkrans caves at Sterkfontein.

Wherever early hominid fossils have been uncovered, from South Africa to Ethiopia, we have also found the fossils of a now extinct predator: Dinofelis, the false sabre-toothed cat. Chatwin suggested Dinofelis may have evolved alongside us to hunt, specifically, us. It wasn't just a monster, it was *our* monster, our original Beast. Chatwin wondered if our human fear of the dark isn't a genetic memory of this cat in the night, its yellow eyes gleaming only for us. Since then, sighed Chatwin, 'has not the whole of history been a search for false monsters ... a nostalgia for the Beast we have lost?'

He pictured our early ancestors sitting tightly together around our campfires, feeling the weight of its eyes on our backs. We can't think so much about something without becoming fascinated by it, a little infatuated. We look around nervously, draw closer to the light, tell stories about the Beast. Perhaps here, around this fire, a huddle of small mammals, shoulder to shoulder and feeling the same fear in a hostile night, is where stories were born. The stories connect us; they overcome the dark. The Beast created our capacity to create.

What I most love about Chatwin's story is that it's a hopeful one. We're pessimistic about the future these days. We are, we're convinced, a *bad* species: aggressive, despoilers, the planet's super-predators. In our hands, the world has no choice but to end. But in Chatwin's story we are not the predators: we developed from vulnerability. In the shadow of the Beast, we evolved to cooperate and so to survive.

To bear, of course, is also another way of saying to endure.

(Is it worth mentioning that Chatwin's story doesn't stand up to strict study? There's no evidence that Dinofelis was a specialised predator upon humans, but the beauty and truth of stories is that the strict truth doesn't matter. Dinofelis is like the bear, or Antarctica – if he didn't exist, we'd have to invent him.)

On *Belgica*, the men had no community to bind them against the fear. They weren't sitting shoulder to shoulder against the darkness, they were small, scared individuals, and the dark was in between them. 'We have told all the tales, real and imaginative, to which we are equal,' wrote Cook in his diary. 'Time weighs heavily upon us as the darkness slowly advances.'

Fifteen years later, on *Endurance*, Shackleton's men looked ahead with trepidation. By now they all knew what had happened on *Belgica*, and how some men had gone into the darkness and hadn't come back. Now they were going too. What would happen to them?

But they didn't yet fully realise the difference. *Belgica* had fallen to the fear, and was taken by the bear. But *Belgica* didn't have Shackleton.

10. POLAR NIGHT II

*We seem to be a wonderfully happy family, but I think Sir
Ernest is the real secret of our unanimity.*
THOMAS ORDE-LEES

Ernest Shackleton was not by modern standards a model father. His children were three, eight and nine when he left on *Endurance*, and he'd been away for many of the years before that. When he was home he was loving but not entirely there, but on the ice Shackleton was a very good father. One shrinks at modern jargon, but on the ice he was very present.

Each man felt Shackleton took special interest in his well-being. He asked questions, remembered details, let him know – a quiet word, a joke, a glance – that he saw him. If they needed discipline, he provided it. A universally loathed crewman named John Vincent had been made bosun, but there were accusations of bullying, so Shackleton took him aside and demoted him.

Shackleton set a routine. He scrapped unnecessary duties but made it compulsory to gather for breakfast at 9am, and again after dinner to talk or play cards or sing. They rationed the wind-up gramophone because Wild had ordered 5,000 spare needles without specifying 'gramophone'. The unofficial song of the expedition was 'The Wearing of the Green', an Irish street ballad. It was perhaps an unexpected choice for a predominantly English ship:

> Then since the colour we must wear is England's
> cruel red
> Sure Ireland's sons will ne'er forget the blood that
> they have shed
> You may take the shamrock from your hat and cast
> it on the sod
> But 'twill take root and flourish there though under-
> foot 'tis trod.

Shackleton banned the educational lectures that bored him on Scott's expeditions, but Frank Hurley delivered monthly 'lantern-chats': slide-shows of places he had photographed. The most popular was called 'Peeps in Java', its popularity due perhaps to the lush tropical scenery in the background, perhaps to the topless Javanese women in the foreground.

Shackleton insisted they exercise. Some walked on the ice. Hurley went skiing. Worsley took naked snow-baths each morning. Orde-Lees became the first man to ride a bicycle in Antarctica: his beloved old Rudge-Whitworth, which he'd owned for sixteen years.

Perhaps it's time to introduce Orde-Lees more fully. One wants to be impartial in the treatment of a large cast of characters, but even the most scrupulous dad has his secret favourites, and Thomas Hans Orde-Lees is one of mine.

None of the expedition diaries gives more pleasure than his. He is the very best of company: gossipy, interested, candid, cheery and apparently completely unaware of how thoroughly unpopular he is. In their diaries, the other men complain about his snoring, his greediness, his laziness, his stinginess when rationing out food, his pernickitiness, his clumsiness, his propensity for wandering off and getting lost, the argumentativeness that apparently only he understood to be collegial and good-natured. When we are young we think we'd be the hero of the story, but with age we have fewer illusions: I have finally accepted that in the story of *Endurance* I wouldn't be Shackleton, or Frank Wild or Worsley. I would probably be Thomas Orde-Lees.

When the wind died down they rigged up lights and played football and hockey on the ice. Dr Macklin and the scientist Robert Clark were the stars, although Wild played a crafty game in midfield. When the sky was clear the full moon was bright enough to play without lights.

They practised dog sledding and held the Antarctic Derby, with one driver and one passenger per sled. Wild had Shackleton as his passenger – a distinct weight handicap – but still won, only to be disqualified when it was revealed that Shackleton had fallen off on the sharp turn for home. The stars were bright and clear. They marvelled at the low-hanging Southern Cross. One night Hurley returned from sledding and described the exhilaration of 'driving into the face of the moon'.

They played parlour games. Orde-Lees was especially fond of 'Twenty Questions', although the number wasn't capped at twenty. Players had an infinite number of yes/no questions in order to guess an assigned and increasingly abstruse historical identity. 'Sir Ernest had to guess the left eye of the snake who tempted Eve,' Orde-Lees recorded with enthusiasm, 'and I was the dorsal fin of the second fish in the miracle of the five loaves and three small fishes.'

They staged Edwardian entertainments. One night Worsley was put on mock trial for stealing a button from a Presbyterian church. Wild was the judge. Orde-Lees the defending attorney was crestfallen when his client was found guilty.

They played pranks on each other. Someone sneaked handfuls of cooked spaghetti into the scientists' dredging buckets and Clark's jars of formaldehyde. Exercised by Orde-Lees' snoring, Hurley and Hussey dropped sardines in his open mouth. When he swallowed them whole in his sleep without breaking snore, seeming almost to open his mouth wider, like a hungry baby bird, they poured in a cup of dried lentils.

Each Saturday night they were issued a ceremonial tot of grog and proposed the traditional toast: 'To our wives and sweethearts!' And the traditional reply: 'May they never meet!'

Doctor McIlroy considered himself a great man of the world, and instructed them on how to make cocktails, including a guaranteed aphrodisiac he called 'The Bosom Caresser'. I'm sorry to say the recipe is lost to history.

One Saturday Chippy McNish sneaked some extra grog and had to be subdued before he could wake Shackleton. Orde-Lees disapproved of McNish. Scotchmen are a nuisance around alcohol, he mused, 'and never have singing voices worth speaking of.'

In late May they took turns shaving each other's heads and posed newly shorn for Hurley's camera.

The earliest accounts of *Endurance* don't make as much as they might of the class and social distinctions. Shackleton's biggest challenge was to 'keep the fo'c'sle': to maintain the morale and loyalty of the crew. They worried Shackleton, because he understood them. They were jobbing sailors on salary, with no particular interest in the Antarctic, no sense of mission or larger purpose. Orde-Lees called them 'sea lawyers': acutely aware of their rights, leery of responsibilities. He was especially wary of McNish. Scott's crews had been seconded from the navy, so he could always count on obedience through weight of authority, just as Field Marshal Haig could at the Somme and Arras and Ypres, but the *Endurance* crew were civilians and Shackleton couldn't command their agreement, he had to win it. On *Belgica*, De Gerlache faced mutiny from crew members before they'd even crossed the Antarctic circle.

But Shackleton bonded them all, the upper decks and lower, the wardroom and the fo'c'sle. They weren't frightened individuals, huddled against the dark; they became a community. They mocked Frederick Cook's account of *Belgica*. Surely he must have been exaggerating. No one was going mad. If anything, morale was improving. They felt safe in their home, safe under Shackleton's eye. They would ride out the winter and thaw and sail free in the spring and return with stories to tell. Worsley confessed to his journal that he was enjoying himself.

Late in May, temperatures plunged. The wood held in the heat from the stoves but the metal bolts exchanged heat: outside the ship was covered in a permanent sheet of ice except for the bolt heads, warmed from within, which stood out sharp and clear of ice. Indoors the bolt heads formed icicles which melted and soaked bunks and blankets. Gusts of cold air from open doors formed billows of fog that condensed to make everything permanently wet.

Frank Hurley rigged twenty flashes on the floe and took a photograph of the *Endurance* by night, rimed with ice, shining against a velvet sky like a spirit ship. The flash blinded him and he staggered into an ice hummock, cracking his shins and tumbling into a snow drift.

Meanwhile, Orde-Lees was fretfully monitoring the food supplies. There was just about enough to last the winter, but he was worried about fresh meat. Fresh meat was their best defence against scurvy, but in the frozen winter the seals and penguins had long disappeared.

On *Belgica* De Gerlache was so afraid of scurvy that he forbade Frederick Cook even saying the word, even while he was being diagnosed with it. For sailors, scurvy was more frightening than fire, more frightening than the deep. It killed an estimated two million sailors between the 16th and 18th centuries, but even by 1915 scientists still weren't sure what caused it or cured it. It's a terrible disease: physical weakness, bleeding gums, loose teeth, subcutaneous bruising, new wounds not healing. Perhaps worst of all when you have scurvy is watching scar tissue dissolve and old wounds opening up. What can be more cruel than a disease that bends time's arrow and makes old pain new again?

That there was no scurvy aboard *Endurance* is largely to the credit of Orde-Lees. In March, Charlie Green the cook had taken to his bunk with a case of 'housewife's knee'. Green was a curious character, somewhat scattered and disorganised, with a comically high voice. The men called him 'Doughballs', apparently because he only had one testicle, and Orde-Lees suspected him of malingering, but was press-ganged to temporarily replace him in the kitchen.

Until then, the officers had been eating freshly-killed seals and penguins, an excellent source of vitamin C, but the crew had refused. Their contracts did not say they had to eat penguin and seal, so they insisted on their cans of jugged hare and bully beef. Tom McLeod thought penguins contained the souls of drowned sailors.

Orde-Lees chafed at their prejudice. Seal meat is dark and slightly gamey, rich in iron and Omega-3 oils, with a texture like veal. It needs to be prepared well and patiently – slow, on low heat, to prevent it becoming too chewy and to minimise the loss of vitamin C – but as long as you remove every trace of the blubber, it doesn't taste fishy.

With Perce Blackborow as his assistant, Orde-Lees worked up a plan. He prepared savoury slow-roasted seal with onions, letting the aroma waft through the ship. When members of the crew sidled by to see what was cooking, Orde-Lees shooed them away, saying it was for officers only. Orde-Lees knew his audience. If they can have it, demanded the crew, why can't we? Watching them enjoy his seal, wrote Orde-Lees in his journal, was his finest achievement in the south.

By the time Green was well enough to return, Orde-Lees had conceived a range of seal dishes, including a seal curry made with chopped ham, sugar and desiccated coconut, and his personal favourite, 'kidney wallop': shredded seal kidneys simmered with seasoned stock and thickened with penguin hash, breadcrumbs and onions. Ten kidneys were enough to feed all 28 men.

The seals and penguins had kept the crew healthy so far, but now their stocks were finished, and who knew when the animals would return? Orde-Lees worried, but Shackleton scowled and called him a pessimist.

By June *Endurance* had been frozen in for four and a half months. She had drifted more than 1,000 kilometres. The average temperature was -27°C.

On 22 June, Midwinter Day, there was a concert involving singing, dress-up, Spanish dance, and recitation of verse. The hitherto reserved physicist Reginald James appeared as Herr Professor Schopenbaum, offering a learned disquisition on the Calorie. They had reached the worst of winter and the ship rang with laughter. In the moonlight the ice looked spectrally lovely, washed with silver milk.

But as spring approached, blizzards confined them to the ship. In mid-July the wind was 120 km/hour and Worsley said the rigging shrieked like a man in fear of being murdered. The temperature dropped to -36°C. It snowed. Antarctic snow is coarse, dry powder, infinitely fine, and it finds its way through the edges of hatches and hinges and porthole frames, through the threads of screws. Snowbanks built up on the windward side of the ship, and the ice floe subsided under the weight.

The air was colder than ever but Antarctic ice is melted not by air but by the warmer water beneath it. They felt movement in the ice, a sign it was beginning to open, but it wasn't a good feeling. Shockwaves came rumbling through their wooden walls. The ice plains broke and pushed together again, and as they collided, they pushed up at the edges, the way tectonic plates make mountains. Pressure ridges rose as high as two-storey buildings in a couple of hours. The ridges were like sails, catching the wind, driving the floes faster.

The men began to feel uneasy.

Shackleton met each day with Wild and Worsley in his cabin, where they wouldn't be overheard. Shackleton paced in the narrow space, and said to Worsley: 'What the ice gets, the ice keeps.'

At noon on July 26 the sun appeared in the sky for a minute. It wasn't really there – it was only refraction from just below the horizon – but it was the first time in 79 days they had seen it. Corridors of water opened and froze over again, and delicate fields of ice flowers bloomed on the new ice, lit red by the morning sun, like poppies.

As long as they were frozen in, they were safe, but they didn't want their floe to break up and set them free without open water, because then the ice could smash closed again, crushing them in between.

On 1 August there was a great scrape and grinding, and *Endurance* rose and listed to port and dropped and landed with a splash and rolled from side to side. She was free of the ice, in a little dark pool of ocean water. But there was no way out of the pool, and the ice was all around. There was a lull and the men half-cheered but then a floe lunged from the front, pushing her bow up in the air. *Endurance* toppled to port again ... and stopped.

The men held on but she didn't move again. The ice held.

Three weeks passed and the sun stayed longer in the sky each day. Shackleton worried and paced, but the men felt encouraged. The ice had attacked but they had survived. She was a good ship, a strong ship, possibly the strongest ice ship ever. She had Shackleton as her

Boss. Hurley said the ice frosted the ship's rigging like Christmas tinsel.

Summer was approaching. Clark's measurements showed plankton increasing in the water. The temperature rose. The sun was in the sky ten hours a day.

On 20 August a beautiful Fata Morgana mirage appeared. Shackleton describes great white and gold cities from the Arabian Nights floating in the blue sky, set about with lakes and lanes of water. Wavering cream and violet lines dissolved, reassembled, trembled, dissipated, came together. The southern icebergs were golden in the sun, the northern bergs were purple and distorted in the refracting light, becoming 'balloons, mushrooms, mosques, cathedrals'. Orde-Lees described the sun dropping against a pale yellow-green sky streaked with purple clouds, underlined with brilliant gold. The moon was apple green shining through a pink mist.

On 2 September there was a loud crack and the hull shuddered as though rammed by a whale. The ship leapt in the air. Hurley described it as popping upwards like a pip squeezed between three pursed fingertips.

The next pressure attack came at the end of September. Each attack seemed worse, as though the ice was gaining confidence. They were in the tightening vise of the world, a million-ton ice floe on each side and another in front, all pushing inwards on this tiny wooden ship to see what would break first. One of the floes broke first, and the pressure eased again.

With each attack, Shackleton seemed calmer. He stopped pacing. The men took comfort.

October came. In October in Antarctica the seals pup on ice floes, leaving smears of blood against the white. There were no seals. Seals live beside open sea. Open sea, for the ship, would mean safety, and going home. *Endurance* was hundreds of miles from open sea.

A killer whale appeared in the narrow pool and circled them. She rolled on her side and eyed them, and the men stared down at her lines and markings. Tom Crean, who had been on Scott's last expedition, remembered the horses that fell through the ice in the Ross Sea and were eaten by killer whales.

Clouds of sea smoke rose from open water in every direction. They were like a stagecoach with a broken axle, surrounded by war parties of Plains Indians. The sun from behind lit the smoke scarlet and crimson.

On 18 October there was another attack. They rolled to port again and everything slid. Chairs tumbled, crockery smashed. They heeled 20 degrees to port, then 30 degrees. The floe on the starboard side wedged under the bulge of her hull and drove under, flipping her. They ate on deck, feet propped against the fo'c'sle, plates balanced on their knees. Chippy McNish nailed strips of wood on the tilted deck to give the dogs a foothold. Reg James said the growling ice made a sound like London traffic when you're sitting quietly in a park.

There was a 24-hour watch for a lead – a channel of open water that forms when the ice parts. The men were ready to go. Shackleton started the boilers.

Four days later the barometer dropped and the temperature dropped, and the wind turned around to blow from the north-east. The men were in the wardroom, listening to 'The Wearing of the Green' on the gramophone.

The wearin' of the green
The wearin' of the green
They're hanging men and women for the wearin' of
the green

There was a sudden crash and the ship lurched. The men finished listening to the song, then went to look. A floe had smashed into the stern and torn away the sternpost. A great tide of dark water poured into the hold. The crisis had begun.

Chippy McNish built a cofferdam to contain the water and others helped caulk it with clothing and sail-cloth. They set the steam pumps to emptying the water but the pipes kept freezing over. They stood side by side and shoulder to shoulder in the icy water, work-ing hand pumps, crew and officers, scientists and art-ists, fifteen minutes until their hands were frozen, fifteen minutes off, fifteen on again, hours on end. All day and night, they worked. They fell asleep and kept pumping while they slept. No one complained. They worked till they dropped, and stood up and carried on working.

Men went over the sides to crack the floes and ease the pressure, but they were like men with shovels trying to break an island in half.

Just as the final squeeze began, eight emperor penguins emerged from the white. They were the first pen-guins seen in half a year. They stood staring at the ship, then slowly, together, began to bray a low, mournful dirge.

The scientists pretended to be unaffected. The sailor McLeod, the one who thought penguins contained the souls of sailors, turned to Dr Macklin and said: 'Hear that? That means we'll none of us get back home again.'

PART 2

HOPE

11. THREE CONVERSATIONS ABOUT NATURE

I mentioned to three different friends that I was writing about Shackleton and *Endurance* and the Antarctic ice.

1.

'Oh god,' said a friend. 'I hope it's not about climate change.'

'Well, not really, but ...'

'We get it. The ice is melting. We should recycle, or change the economic system. Got it. I'm not paying good money for you to tell me again.'

'No, I see that ...'

'Can someone just tell me an old-fashioned story for a change?'

2.

'Oh god,' said a different friend. 'You're telling me you're going to write about *Antarctica* – about being literally *threatened by the ice* – about surviving a catastrophe brought on by human hubris *in the ice fields of Antarctica*, and you're *not* going to write about the climate?'

'I thought maybe I would just tell an old-fashioned story.'

'Are you an Edwardian?'

'No.'

'Are you writing for an Edwardian audience?'

'No, but ...'

'Are you still a child?'

'I don't know. Maybe.'

'Okay, whatever. Good luck with pretending it's the 20th century.'

3.

'I hope,' said a third friend, 'that you aren't giving some kind of meaning to ice.'

I didn't think so, but I wondered what that meant.

'I mean,' she said, 'Nature isn't there to teach you some kind of lesson.'

No, no, I could see that, I said.

'There's no meaning to nature,' she said. 'It just is.'

Well, I said. There's no meaning to anything until we give it one.

Exactly, she said.

But, I wondered, you can't really think about things without giving them meaning and isn't it good to think about things? Are you saying we shouldn't think about the world?

She looked at me with some disdain.

'Clearly,' she said, 'you are part of the problem.'

From these conversations I have come to the conclusion that it's not a good idea to talk to people when you're writing a book.

12. THE MARTINGALE

This was the *Endurance*'s maiden expedition and her first time south. She was originally Norwegian, the last of the great wooden expedition steamships, hand-crafted in the famous Framnaes shipyard in Sandefjord under the supervision of master shipbuilder Christian Jacobsen, who only hired shipbuilders who'd had experience sailing on whaling or sealing ships. Mensun Bound, who in 2022 would be the man to find her again, calls her the second-strongest non-naval wooden ship ever built. The strongest was the *Fram*, which took Roald Amundsen to the South Pole.

Endurance was commissioned by a Norwegian whaling tycoon named Lars Christensen, who had been talked into a scheme to charter her to rich people to hunt polar bears in the Arctic. Everything is connected, especially in the Antarctic, so it's no surprise that Lars Christensen's partner in the scheme was someone we've met before: Adrien de Gerlache from *Belgica*, most wretched of explorers. She was originally named *Polaris* – the North

Star, the brightest in Ursa Minor – and her name was written in an elegant arc across her stern, above a bright copper five-pointed star.

De Gerlache, in time-honoured polar tradition, couldn't meet his financial obligations, so the scheme fell apart. The Arctic safari industry's loss was Shackleton's gain. Using De Gerlache as his agent, he bought *Polaris* for £11,600 – a steal – and renamed her *Endurance*, after his family motto: *Fortitudine Vincimus*.

Through endurance, we overcome.

He painted *Endurance* black to absorb the heat of the sun. He replaced *Polaris'* name on the stern but he kept the star.

She was 44 metres long, 7 metres across the beam and designed for ice. Each timber in the bow was worked from a single oak tree, laid together to make a bow more than a metre thick. The shipbuilders put a copper krone under each of her three masts as good luck, to ensure she wouldn't break.

On the morning of 27 October 1915, as ten million tons of ice pushed in, her beams bent like bamboo canes and her timbers in the fo'c'sle broke. Her back hunched and she rode up and down as the pressure eased and surged. The metal plates of the boiler room floor buckled and sprang their bolts and lifted and slammed down again with a sound like rifle fire.

The ship was held between two floes – one jammed against the starboard bow, the other on the same side at the stern. A third drove in at midships from port. She was like a stick being broken over a knee.

As the floe in front pushed in, the ice mounted and climbed over the bow, towering half the height of the mast till it broke off and crashed to the foredeck, its weight pushing the bow further under, angling her for a nose dive.

When a wooden ship is being squeezed to death she makes a sound like an animal that knows it's dying. She bucked, she wailed, she howled, she threw back her head and shrieked. But it was worse when her sides constricted and strained to open, rasping for air. On the other side of the world, in the field hospitals of northern Europe, boys who didn't yet know they were dying called in their delirium for their mothers. The ship was like a mother answering them, groaning for the children she would leave behind.

She was flooding with the water pouring in at the stern, and she was being held up only by two great spears of ice piercing her sides. The three dark crosses of her masts still stood on their sloping wooden Calvary, but not for much longer. At any moment the ice might draw back, and then she would sink.

On the bridge, Shackleton turned to Frank Wild. Wild's thin hair was neatly combed, and he pulled calmly on a pipe that had been given him by Rudyard Kipling. They often didn't need to speak to exchange words. Wild's soft eyes met Shackleton's and he nodded and went below.

He started at the bow, where Walter How was trying to sleep. In the opposite bunk, William Bakewell turned restlessly, kicking his boot against the bulkhead. They'd been working the pump for three days in iced water to their waists. For at least the last day, they'd known it was no good.

Frank Wild didn't apologise for waking them. He said: 'I think it's time to go.'

Wild left to complete the rounds of the ship and in his wake men gathered up their possessions. There was no panic. She was going, but she was going both fast and slow, with that fearful two-pacedness of a dream, the way we age, or the world ends: the way an unstoppable thing is happening both in the future and also right now.

On deck the scientists slumped against the bulwarks, broken from the pumps. The lifeboats were already lowered and lay uselessly on the ice, awkward and out of their element. From the floe, his cine camera rigged on a tripod, Hurley filmed the crew sliding dogs down escape chutes made from sailcloth.

For months the dogs had been rowdy, howling and snapping at each other, but at the moment of crisis they conducted themselves with the quiet gravity of gentlemen. The men did too, carrying goods and crates down one by one, back and forth onto a thick floe to port. Shackleton leaned on the railing and supervised, smoking a cigarette, apparently unconcerned, reminding each person as they passed about this or that personal item. He reminded Orde-Lees to bring his diary.

Chippy McNish carefully carried down his cat, Mrs Chippy. She was the worst ship's cat in expedition history. She habitually walked across the top of the dog kennels, driving them into a frenzy. No one had ever seen her catch a rat. On the voyage out she had jumped overboard through a porthole, and the navigator Huberht Hudson, whose parents didn't know how to spell Hubert, had the ship heeled round so she could be fished from the sea. She wasn't even a female cat, she was male. She didn't much like people but she loved Chippy McNish, and Chippy McNish, who didn't much like people either, loved her back.

It took two hours to get everyone down to the ice, and they stood, piled around with gear and dogs and canned goods, a little stunned. 'Let's eat, drink and be merry,' said Macklin. 'For tomorrow we diet.'

'What time do we die at?' asked Orde-Lees.

Then the ice under their feet cracked and opened. They scrambled to gather their things, and leapt across the splitting floe to regroup behind a pressure ridge on the starboard side of the ship, a little further away and hopefully more stable. It was the long crystalline twilight of the early October summer, and a light breeze blew from the south. The skies were clear. It was a balmy 8° below zero.

Shackleton sent some men – including Dr Macklin, perhaps as punishment for his pun – back to the ship to salvage a stock of timber: if they were going to make their home on the ice, they would need walkway planking, a cooking shack, a lookout tower. The timber was stored in the forepeak, the awkward narrow lightless storage space in the hold, below the waterline, between the narrowing bows of the ship. The forepeak was almost flooded.

Macklin and Frank Wild lowered themselves into the hold. They heard the ice scraping at the buckling wooden walls like a bear trying to get in. Alexander Macklin was 25 years old and wore glasses. He was on his first voyage. He was good-humoured and brave but he was a doctor, not a spelunker or a polar explorer. He froze with fear.

If Frank Wild was ever afraid, no one had ever seen it. Frank was a small man, a little over five foot four. He had been at sea much of his life and to the Antarctic three times before, once with Scott, once with Shackleton, once with Douglas Mawson, but he was also, in his way, a gentle man. He shared with Shackleton the principle of never asking someone to do something he wouldn't first do himself. He eased Macklin aside and climbed into the flooded darkness of the forepeak, into the dark frigid slurry, fumbling with numbed fingers and arms for the wood, passing it back through the narrow hatch.

For the rest of his life Macklin remembered the terror of crouching in that low tortured space with the walls warping around him, knowing that the ship might any moment tilt and lurch and sink three kilometres down. He willed Frank Wild to come back out so they could flee to the safety of a sheet of ice floating hundreds of miles from land. He looked up at the hatch that led to the light. He was afraid he was going to run.

It's only under pressure that a person's shell cracks to reveal what's there. It can be a terrible thing to discover. Sensible men and women avoid situations like this for fear of what they might find.

Several times, Macklin thought his nerve would break but Wild's faith kept him there. Afterwards he glowed with the pride of knowing that under examination, he hadn't flunked.

An hour after they were clear the ice pushed in again and drove the bow further underwater. Ice smashed through the fo'c'sle from starboard and only the ice spurs held it from sinking. Their home was no longer whole; it clung to the world purely by grace of the same force that had destroyed it.

On a white field beside the dark rubble of their ship, these 28 men gathered. They had been iced in for 281 days and had drifted 1,200 kilometres. They were nearly 2,000 kilometres from the South Pole, and nearly 2,000 kilometres in the other direction from the nearest human being. They made tea.

Shackleton overheard the men talking. One man asked for strong tea. The other asked for weak. He turned and informed them with asperity that the tea would be the same for everyone, and that in two months they would be lucky to have any tea at all, but secretly he was fascinated by the mystery of human beings, their home crushed, adrift on the frozen ocean with little hope of survival, taking a passionate interest in the strength of their tea. Humans are surpassingly odd and annoying and varied creatures. That may be why we survive.

They made camp in a line of pale green expedition tents. Some slept on sailcloth, some on boards of salvaged timber, others, not so lucky, on the ice itself. There were 28 men and 28 sleeping bags, but there had been no expectation that the ship's crew would ever have to sleep outside, so only eighteen of the bags were reindeer fur. The other ten were woollen Jaeger bags, not nearly as warm, so they drew lots. The lottery was rigged.

Walter How remarked that it was the only time they were aware of uneven treatment on the ice. The rigging was blatant: it was the officers who conducted the lottery, and it was the officers who, without exception, including The Boss, drew the lesser bags.

At 2.30am the ice broke in half under the line of tents and they had to scramble to safety again. Somehow, after that, they slept well, except Shackleton.

Even up until the moment he nodded to Frank Wild on the bridge, Shackleton must still have cherished some half-extinct ember of hope that the expedition could yet be saved, that with luck they might still make it to the continent, still carry out the expedition, still save the future, still succeed. With the ship, there was hope, but now, he wrote in his journal, 'It is hard to write what I feel.'

And then he wrote, in seemingly casual words that mark him apart from someone like Scott: 'A man must shape himself to a new mark the moment the old one goes to ground.'

When Scott lost the South Pole, he lost everything. When Shackleton lost the ship, he looked for a different game to play. 'I pray God,' he wrote, 'I can get the whole party back to civilisation.'

He stayed awake all that night, pacing the perimeter, watching over his men as they slept on the sea, watching for cracks in the ice, watching the ship. A chain attached to the martingale boom stretched onto the ice, and as the boom swung in the breeze the chain dragged and grated like the chains on a ghost in a Victorian horror story.

(The accounts all say the chain was attached to the martingale boom. There's no reason we should know what a martingale boom is. The scientists and civilians on the ice didn't know what a martingale boom is. I have found out what a martingale boom is, and it is a small vertical spar between the bowsprit and the martingale, redirecting the tension in the forward end of the martingale slightly more vertically. The martingale is a stay running from the end of the jib-boom to the dolphin striker, which holds the jib-boom down against the pull of the fore topgallant mast stay. All of this is to say: I still do not know what a martingale boom is.)

But every good story, if indeed it is good, offers sinuous, sometimes hidden entwinements of meaning. A martingale is also the name of a gambling strategy. The simplest form of it holds that when betting on a 50-50 call, every time you lose you must double your bet for the next round. Playing the martingale, you are guaranteed at last to profit, unless you run out of money first. If you play the martingale, you cannot lose, so long as you can keep playing.)

In the morning the men were woken by Wild and Shackleton and Worsley. Shackleton had made them hot tea, and Wild and Worsley delivered mugs to their tents, like a trio of Victorian wives tending husbands who have worked a long shift. Some of the men omitted to say thank you, and Wild was enraged. If anyone would like their boots cleaned, he snarled, they should leave them outside the tent and The Boss would attend to them by and by.

Shackleton calculated where they were. Where they were, no one had ever been before. The closest any human had ever been was Nordenskjöld on the *Antarctic* when the ice crushed and sank it, and that was a full degree north. It would be at least another four months before anyone even started to wonder where *Endurance* might be, and months more, maybe years, before anyone looked for them, and when they did look for them, they would not be looking there.

The nearest land where they could find food and shelter was Paulet Island, 557 km to the north-west. It was a speck of soot in the frozen sea, a dull black chip of stone set in a vast brooch of silver, only 2.5 kilometres wide. It was uninhabited, of course, but a cache of stores had been left by the ship that rescued the crew of the *Antarctic*, in case anyone was ever again so unwise as to venture so far into the Weddell Sea and be marooned. Shackleton knew about these stores, because he was the one who had been commissioned to buy them.

To reach Paulet they would need to walk there, dragging their stores and their belongings in the boats behind them, but it would be like dragging several deadweight tons across a volcanic landscape after – and during – a series of eruptions. There was no real chance they could do it, but they couldn't stay where they were: the ice-pack was drifting north, and in time they would be dropped into the sea. Doing something seemed impossible, or at least useless. Doing something might well make matters worse. But not for the last time in human history, *not* doing something was even worse than that.

Shackleton addressed the men matter-of-factly. He gave no stirring speeches, he simply explained what they would do: they would play the martingale. They would walk to land.

They would drag two boats, leaving one behind. There was no space for luxuries and personal items. Each man could bring:

the clothes on his back
one pair of fur mittens
six pairs of socks
one spare pair of boots or finneskos (soft reindeer-
    skin slippers)
a sleeping bag
half a kilogram of tobacco or cocoa
one kilogram of personal effects (soap, brush,
    toothbrush, etc.)

It seemed shockingly little, but he believed it was better to move fast and decisively than to be prepared for anything. The doctors were allowed to bring medical equipment for emergencies. Hurley could keep a fraction of his photographic plates. Men with diaries could add them to their allotted weight. In a special dispensation, Leonard Hussey was allowed to bring his banjo, even though it weighed nearly 6 kilograms, and even though he only knew six songs. 'Music,' said Shackleton, 'is vital mental medicine.'

To demonstrate his seriousness, he dropped his solid gold cigarette case on the ice at his feet. He threw down 50 gold sovereigns beside it. It was the last money he had in the world.

Then he took the Bible that Queen Alexandra had given them before departure. It was the Revised Version of the King James, printed by Cambridge University Press 'for the universities of Oxford and Cambridge'. He tore out the flyleaf on which the Queen had written:

'May the Lord help you to do your duty & guide
you through all the dangers by land and sea.
May you see the Works of the Lord & all His Wonders in the deep.'

He turned to the 23rd Psalm – 'The Lord is my shepherd', the one with the green pastures – and ripped out the page. He turned to the Book of Job and tore out the page with the verse:

Out of whose womb came the ice?
And the hoary frost of Heaven, who hath gendered it?
The waters are hid as with a stone.
And the face of the deep is frozen.

He folded the pages and put them in the pocket of his calico Burberry jacket. Then he dropped the Bible on the ice beside the gold and walked away.

Silently, the men made a pile of their personal effects. Cufflinks and belt buckles and best Sunday clothes. Tie pins and pen sets and fine photo frames. The second mate, the massive Irishman Tom Crean, was assigned to kill the animals too small or weak to be taken along.

He had to shoot four puppies. He had to shoot Mrs Chippy, the cat. Chippy McNish kept only the most rudimentary of diaries so we don't have his real feelings, but some men believed that when Shackleton told Crean to kill Mrs Chippy, something broke deep inside Chippy McNish.

Macklin took the responsibility of killing Sirius, his favourite puppy. He had bonded with Sirius, and it wasn't right to make Crean do it. Sirius was friendly and excited when Macklin took him behind a pressure ridge, carrying the rifle. He thought they were going for a walk, and was confused when they stopped. He stared up at the man behind the barrel, wagging his tail. Macklin's hands trembled so much he only wounded Sirius. He had to shoot him a second time to close his eyes.

On 30 October it was snowing but warm, and the snow turned to sludge. The boats were fully laden. They tied ropes to the boats, and took hold of the ropes. Each boat weighed a ton. It was 3pm. They started to walk.

13. AUNTY MOLLY

One day a friend sent me a news report from the local Afrikaans newspaper. I was writing a weekly column for an English newspaper then, and always on the lookout for stories. It was a small item about a man in Maitland in the northern suburbs of Cape Town who died at his local grocery store after a wall of spaghetti and meatballs collapsed on him.

I pondered whether I could use it. It's possible, if the conditions are right, to be entertaining about a man perishing beneath a wall of tinned spaghetti. You would need to use words like 'perish' instead of 'die', but other details matter too. Tragedy plus time equals comedy, but time's not enough, you also need things like juxtaposition and resonance and some luck.

The playwright Aeschylus died a long time ago but that's not entertaining. It helps that he died because an eagle dropped a tortoise on his head, but it *really* starts to work with the detail that Aeschylus was only under the flight path of an eagle because he'd been troubled by a dream of something falling on his head, so started sleeping in the open air where it's safe. It's also a nice touch that his friends agreed the eagle thought Aeschylus was a rock because he was so bald.

Graham Greene wrote a very funny story about a boy whose father died when a pig fell on him from a balcony in Naples, but he had the advantage of making it up. When dealing lightly with a real-life death you need just the right victim. It's never funny when a woman dies, or a child, or someone frail. Regrettably, the man who succumbed to the leaning tower of Heinz tins was in his 90s.

I was putting the report aside when my eye snagged on the man's name. Neville Carter. That's funny. My Aunty Molly, my father's younger sister, was married to a Neville Carter. They lived in Kensington, in the east of Johannesburg. Once when I was very young I went with my dad to visit them. We went up on the train and I slept on the top bunk and he slept below me. Aunty Molly and Uncle Neville lived around the corner from a movie theatre, and he took me to see Dino de Laurentiis' remake of *King Kong*. There was an age restriction but my dad persuaded the cashier I was ten. My dad could do anything.

Aunty Molly must be long dead by now. She and my dad fell out even before he became sick, and we hadn't seen her since. (This is not unusual on either side of my family. We are like a constellation of stars in the night sky: related only by a trick of perspective that makes us seem conjoined when seen from a certain angle that collapses distance, but really we are light years apart and almost oblivious to each other's existence.)

I read the second paragraph. Neville leaves behind a wife, Molly.

I had never been to Maitland before. It's an area of Cape Town similar to the Bluff in Durban where I grew up, similar to Kensington in Johannesburg. I drove there from Sea Point and found a quiet street named after a flower. There was a vibracrete wall around the front of the property with a pattern of half wagon wheels. At some point someone had tried to raise the height of the wall, but the effort had been abandoned. There was a glazed ceramic letterbox moulded to look like it was made from miniature logs. On the wall beside the front door was a ceramic cactus, and a ceramic man dozing in the shade of the cactus, wearing a ceramic poncho and a ceramic sombrero pulled low over his eyes. There was a dog's plastic water bowl on the veranda, but no sign of a dog.

There was a dog next door that barked the whole time, but it wasn't an aggressive bark; it was chasing its own tail round and round. That dog needed a longer tail.

I rang the bell and the door was opened by a man named Roy. He was Neville and Molly's grandson. My cousin, I suppose, or second cousin, something like that. I had last seen him when he was five or six and I was three or four years older than that. Roy didn't have a moustache, but he gave the impression of one. He wore jeans slightly too big for him, and a t-shirt that was clean but had a small hole along the shoulder seam. There was a silhouette on the front of a cowboy on a horse.

We greeted each other and shook hands. We stood in a narrow entry hall. Molly and Neville had been living with him for the last twelve years, he said. Roy lived there alone, and sometimes with his wife. Roy's marital status was a little unclear, but he had moved down from Johannesburg, and then his wife had found him and moved down too, and then a few years after that Neville and Molly had also moved down and moved in with them.

'Johannesburg is no place to get old,' I said sympathetically.

Roy had moved down in the expectation of work, but someone had let him down. He was waiting to hear about Neville's life insurance. There were questions about whether Neville was covered for death by supermarket. There were also questions about the status of the policies. Insurance companies can be very tricky, I agreed. Roy looked hopeful. Was I maybe in insurance? No, I said regretfully. Did I know anyone in insurance? Again, regretfully no. That's a pity, said Roy. It helps to have contacts. He didn't say that bitterly or knowingly, just as a statement of fact. It does, I agreed.

He took me down the corridor to his grandmother's room. The corridor was dark, and there were pictures on the wall but I couldn't make them out. The corridor was wooden parquet.

Aunty Molly was 94 years old. She was mostly blind and spent her days in bed. It was a double bed and took up most of the small room and she lay on one side of it, her feet under the bedclothes pointing towards the door. The other side must have been Neville's. The burglar bars on the window behind her threw grey shadows on the bedspread, which was white with a waffled pattern of raised square ridges, like pressure ridges in a frozen sea, although far more regular. There was a photograph frame on the bedside table, without a photograph in it. Hanging on the wall was a bronze relief of a pair of hands clasped in prayer. The hands were well-rendered male hands with knotted veins. The fingers were long and sensitive, with slender tarsals but pronounced knuckles. If the bronze had been clean, it would have gleamed in the sunlight.

There was a wardrobe to the right of the door as you came in. There was a mirror on the door of the wardrobe and if she wasn't blind, she would have been able to see herself in it. I sat on a white wicker chair beside the bed, on Aunty Molly's side. I hadn't seen her in 40 years. The back of the chair was against the wall and I had to sit sideways on the chair to have space for my legs. Aunty Molly wasn't always clear about who I was. I didn't ask her how she was; it was obvious how she was. She had the look of someone who had once been much larger.

I told her that I was sorry about Uncle Neville, but that made her cry. She was stronger on things that had happened a long time ago than things that had happened more recently and I think that she had forgotten that Uncle Neville was dead, so I avoided reminding her again. I didn't know what else to talk about, so I asked her about the only thing that interested me. I asked her about my dad when he was young.

She told me that their father was often a very angry man, especially when he drank. He never hit her, or not often, but he often hit my father, and he used to hit Gerry even more. Gerry was the oldest and he was the naughtiest but he was also the weakest. She spoke as though it was last year. My father tried to protect Gerry from their father, she remembered that. Gerry and my dad both left home young.

'To make money,' I said. My dad had told me that.

She thought about it. No, she thought. Or maybe. But mainly to get away from their dad. She stayed at home much longer, because her father never hit her. Or not often.

I asked her if she could tell me anything else about my dad. What he was like as a boy? She thought about it. Once, she said, he put a frog in her bed. To that day, she still didn't like frogs.

When I left, Roy walked me to my car. He knew about cars, and he said he could service my car the next time it needed a service. It would be cheaper than the garages. Garages rip you off. He knew that because he used to work in a garage. I told him I would remember him, the next time my car needed a service.

At home, I sat and stared into space. I remembered that once when I was young I found a frog and put it in my sister's bed.

'When are you going back?' my wife asked. That startled me. I hadn't thought about going back.

She reminded me how often I'd said that I'd lost my father entirely, that there was no one alive who knew him when he was young, that he was a memory as far away and fading as a signal beamed into space. But here was a gift. There had been nothing, and now something was given back.

I agreed, but I was troubled. In a way, total loss is comforting: there's nothing you can do about it. Now I could do something, I *should* do something, but I didn't quite know what.

You have to go back, my wife said. You can't wait for her to die, and then complain about that loss too. (I realise now, remembering those words, that it can't always be fun, living with me.)

I took some groceries when I went back. The dog next door was still barking and chasing its tail. I didn't want to insult Roy so I didn't say anything about the groceries, I just carried them in and left them in the kitchen and neither he nor I ever mentioned them. I went back a number of times. Sometimes Aunty Molly seemed to have slipped a little further away, but then the next time she would be closer again, then next time further. She was like a shortwave radio signal fading in and out, and there was always a lot of static. Each time I came I tried to ask for stories about my dad.

She told me some things I didn't know. She told me that his favourite movie was *Bad Day at Black Rock*, so I went home and watched it. It was directed by John Sturges in 1955, and it has Spencer Tracy coming to a small town with a secret. Spencer Tracy was a big man, and aging, with wavy steely hair. He is strong but he's vulnerable, because he lost an arm in the war. I didn't get much else from watching it, except the moment when Robert Ryan, the villain, says to Spencer Tracy, 'A man's only as big as the thing he's looking for.' I think that's probably a good line.

Sometimes she told me stories that I couldn't follow. Sometimes she became confused between Gerry and my dad. Sometimes she told a long story that by the time it ended turned out to be about Neville. The most detailed and uninteresting stories were always about Neville. Sometimes when she spoke about her life with Neville she wandered away into how her old Kensington neighbourhood had changed when black people moved in. She didn't use the words 'black people', she used other words. There were times when I wondered what I was doing there, sitting in that room in Maitland, listening to the racist ramblings of a blind old woman. Of course, my father would have been racist too. He grew up working class and white in Pretoria in the 1920s and 1930s and there are some people who did that and weren't racist but not a great many, and I have no reason to think my dad was one of them. I don't think it's disloyal to say that.

As she lay in bed with her head on a pillow that had been doubled over and placed on top of another pillow, I studied Aunty Molly's face for traces of my father, but I realised I don't really remember my father's face. I feel that I would recognise him on the street, if he still looks the way he looked in 1982, but I would be recognising the whole face, the pattern of it. I can't, in my mind's eye, parse out the details. I studied her face for traces of my own face, but after a while I realised that I don't really know my own face either.

One day, in a long silence during which my mind had wandered, I asked, 'Was my dad always interested in polar exploration?'

She swam back through galaxies and came into focus. 'He met that explorer once.'

I sat up straight.

'What?'

'The explorer. He met him. They were friends.'

'Shackleton?'

'Oh, ah, I can't remember.'

I stared at her.

'My dad met Shackleton?' I said again.

I knew he couldn't have, but already the story was forming in my head.

'They were going to go mining together,' she said. 'They were going to mine for ... not diamonds, the green ones ...'

'Emeralds?'

'Him and the explorer. The one who went to the South Pole.'

14. A BRIEF DIGRESSION ABOUT HEAT

Digression is a strategy for putting off the ending, a multiplying of time within the work, a perpetual evasion or flight. Flight from what? From death, of course.

ITALO CALVINO

It turns out it's heat that's to blame.

Anyone who has deeply mourned knows how impossible it feels that we can yearn and long so powerfully, applying our will with such intensity, more wholehearted and undiluted than anything we have ever done, and yet still not find some way of bringing what is gone back into what is here. It feels like some unfathomable misunderstanding.

A friend once told me that theoretical physics would clear it all up for me. It's all about heat, he said. The reason time is irretrievable, the reason it goes one way only, the reason what's lost is lost for ever and what is no longer whole will never be whole again is all explained by heat. When I asked him what he meant, he became a little uncomfortable and told me to read Carlo Rovelli.

Carlo Rovelli is the Italian physicist who wrote *Seven Brief Lessons on Physics* and also *The Order of Time*. He's a humanist and loves life and the world and literature, which is appealing, and he writes very elegantly and poetically.

Rovelli helpfully explains that from a physicist's point of view, and from a microscopic point of view, there's no such thing as time. In the microscopic view of the world, 'past' and 'future' are meaningless. Time, in fact, doesn't belong to the universe – before and after, cause and effect belong only to our limited, human perception. This is apparently a matter of some solace to theoretical physicists, which makes me wonder about theoretical physicists.

Under pressure of questioning from dummies like me, Rovelli offers this: another way of thinking about time is as the movement of heat. In every scenario in which linear time is present and meaningful – in other words, any sequence of events that would be absurd if reversed – heat is involved.

He gives this example: film footage of a football merely rolling on the flat surface of an ice floe could be shown backwards and it would still make perfect sense. If we merely see the ball rolling, we don't know if the film is being shown forwards or backwards. A ball could roll in this direction, or it could roll in that direction. But if the ball rolls along the level floe and then stops, we know that piece of film is running forwards, and cannot be running backwards, because a motionless ball on a flat ice floe cannot by itself start rolling.

Everything that can only go in one direction in time involves heat. The ball slows then stops because of friction, which involves the production of heat. It cannot start rolling without some external application of energy. In the same way, a hot cup of strong tea, or a nice bowl of seal hoosh, will cool to the temperature of the room, not lower, and cannot spontaneously heat up again. Heat can only move down a gradient, from a warmer body to a cooler one. The arrow of time exists where there is heat, and only where there is heat. Life requires heat. Thinking creates heat in our heads. So does remembering.

There's a paradox that feels very keen to us today: the Antarctic is taking heat, and eventually will melt. Heat, thought of in these terms, doesn't feel like life to us, it feels like death. It's not really a paradox – it's only a paradox because we are looking at it through the narrow perspective of the human scale of time and distance.

But of course, we *are* humans, irreducibly we are humans, tragically and triumphantly we are humans, and even if our perceptions tell us a misleading story, as they do all the time, for us that story is what's real. I cannot enter the microscopic state of things and abolish time and go back to lying in that bed beside my dad. The men in Scott's tent on the Beardmore Glacier, once they had lost their heat to the cold universe, could not get it back again.

If we could get far enough away from here and look back through an instrument powerful enough, maybe the moments of time would all co-exist, past and present and future, all observable right now, whatever 'now' means, but we can't get far enough away, because those distances are not available on the human scale.

Perhaps on a microscopic level there is no before and after, no cause and effect, but we are humans, and for us, the arrow of time never turns around. We have to figure out how to ride the arrow, away from wholeness but also away from the aching conviction of loss, and try to steer it somewhere better.

15. OCEAN CAMP

*What saves a man is to take a step. Then another step. It is
always the same step, but you have to take it.*
ANTOINE DE SAINT-EXUPÉRY

The boats sank into the snow. When you're pulling the equivalent of a small car without wheels, you want no snow, or you want lots of very cold, dense snow, but the temperature soared to 4°C and the snow was like mashed potato. The men heaved and pushed with their bodies almost parallel with the ground.

Shackleton went ahead with Wordie, Hussey and Hudson, hacking passes through pressure ridges with axes and saws. At higher ridges they built ramps of snow before cutting the pass. At even higher ridges they led the long caravan zagging and weaving in search of an easier way through.

Norwegian polar explorers had always been amazed by the English love of man-hauling. The Norwegians preferred to minimise exertion – Amundsen swished south and back on skis and dog sleds – but Scott and his men trudged all the way there and not quite back, dragging laden sledges. But this – dragging one-ton lifeboats from the middle of the sea to the land – this was the Pythonesque *ne plus ultra* of the era of man-hauling.

The plan was to cover ten kilometres a day. After three hours they dropped their ropes and stretched their backs and wiped away the sweat. They turned and looked back at the ship, one straight kilometre behind them. As soon as they stopped, the sweat in their clothes froze.

That first night they made a temporary camp and didn't sleep well. They had to carefully pry open their frozen sleeping bags without breaking them in two or splitting them down the middle. Then they had to wriggle in between cold solid boards and wait for their bodies to defrost the ice. Then it was like lying in a damp ditch, until the temperature dropped in the night and the damp-ness froze around them again.

The ice they slept on was very thin. With their bags on the bare floe and their heads on jackets rolled for pillows, they heard the clicks and grunts of killer whales and felt their movement below their cheeks. They were like the Nantucket sailors in *Moby-Dick*, who like land-less gulls at sunset fold their wings 'and lay them to their rest, while under their very pillow rush herds of walruses and whales.'

Shackleton must have suspected, even before start-ing, that they couldn't haul the boats all the way across the ice. Adrien de Gerlache's escape plan on *Belgica* was almost identical: drag lifeboats to the edge of the pack, then sail to the South Shetland Islands. But De Gerlache made his plan in the grip of depression. He wrote in his journal, and said to the men around him: 'I estimate our chances of success at 100:1 against.'

Shackleton wasn't interested in calculating those kinds of odds. On that first night he wrote that 'the issue is beyond my power either to predict or control', but he wanted his men to recognise – to feel it with their skin, to *believe* – that 'human effort is not futile'.

When faced with looming catastrophe, said Shackleton, thinking of a different looming Antarctic catastrophe to ours, there are three choices: give up, wait for someone else to save you, or do the best thing you can think of doing until you think of something better. He wasn't wedded to the outcome of this action: it was just something to try.

For two days they marched. The second day they covered much the same distance as the first. It's easy to dehydrate in the Antarctic: when the snow covers the ice there is only snow to melt for water, and snow reduces to only a few tablespoons at a time. They sweated and dehydrated. They slept on the ice.

On the third morning Shackleton woke before the others and saw that pressure had come in the night, throwing up even higher ridges and breaking up the ice between them. He went for a closer look and sank to his hips in snow.

He called the men together. By his calculations the ice was drifting towards land faster than they were walking. He would keep marching if they wanted to keep marching, but otherwise they could set up camp right there and take a free ride. The men, exhausted and sore, liked the idea of the free ride. They came away from the meeting with the impression that somehow they had voted on it.

They called it Ocean Camp. Despite all their labours, they were still so close to *Endurance* that Shackleton sent back men to fetch more stores. Setbacks are disheartening but sometimes they are the best way forward; much of what they retrieved would save their lives.

The men who went back to the wreck found a distressing sight. All was disorder, litter and mess. The pile of their personal effects was still there, jumbled and snowed under, a sprawl of vanity, a litter-heap of uselessness, the things and works of man lying unravelled and abandoned and cold. Some objects had melted through the upper layers of snow and then frozen into the ice below. The ice was stained with coal dust and soot, blubber and blood.

But there was life to be had from the wreck. The lower ship was flooded but they cut away the thick planking of the upper deck to access the wardroom, where goods had been moved when the holds flooded and Chippy McNish built his coffer dam. Using boathooks, their arms submerged, they pulled out 100 crates, four tons of food, three months' full rations. Frank Hurley stripped to the waist and swam down to retrieve his photographic plates.

They carried the wheelhouse back to Ocean Camp and used it as the galley. Hurley constructed a stove to burn seal blubber as fuel, billowing great filthy clouds of black oily smoke that clung to skin and beards and wouldn't wash away. They built a lookout tower from salvaged wood and used it to scout for seals and to gaze thoughtfully over the hummocks and ridges at the black wreck of their ship.

In the camp their priorities narrowed by the day. Food was the great obsession: not for the stomach, for the stomach soon adapts, but for the warmth. On Scott's expedition, Edward Wilson had called hot food 'a hot water bottle applied directly to the heart'. For breakfast the cook made bannocks – muffin-like concoctions of fried flour, mixed with dog-food pemmican or lentils to add flavour.

To their relief, the seals came back. The seals, like the penguins, let the men walk right up to them. They would stun the seal with an oar, then cut its throat. Sometimes they brought back the blood for the dogs.

Sometimes they killed the seals with a pickaxe, but the doctors worried about damaging the brains, making them inedible. Weddell seals live further south than other seals, because they can create holes in the pack ice and maintain them with their teeth, but on the whole the men preferred crabeater seals to Weddell seals. The Weddells were tubby and lazy, and the slender figures of the lively crabeaters made their meat seem cleaner and lighter on the palate.

Usually they went out hunting, but on happy days seals wandered into camp, mistaking it for land. One orphan pup came in all alone, mewling for comfort. They figured its mother had been taken by an orca. They saw the rake of the orca's teeth on the pup's flanks. It must have been very lucky, or very ingenious. It was a survivor. Orde-Lees kept the pup entertained while Kerr went to fetch the oar.

They added incremental amounts of the blubber to their seal stew to get used to the taste. At first it tasted like cod liver oil. Four months later Shackleton would be writing in his journal that it had the delicious savour of bacon. The human palate, he wrote, can get used to anything.

November brought their first blizzard, which pinned them inside their tents. An Antarctic blizzard is like a desert sandstorm: it whips up the loose dry snow from the floe so that there might be no visibility at eye-level while the skies are perfectly clear overhead. The wind was so strong you could wake suffocating in your tent with the canvas blown tight over your face. Frank Wild said that a man facing steadily into a 160 km/hour wind could drown as surely as though he were underwater – he wouldn't be able to expel the air from his lungs. He had seen anemometers registering wind speeds of 240 km/hour before they broke. Once, the wind picked him up off his feet and threw him 25 metres through the air. Modern anemometers have measured Antarctic winds of 200 mph (322 km/hour).

At least the gale was blowing them in the right direction: after 48 hours, it had driven them nearly 26 km north-west: a month's worth of suffering if they were still walking. When the wind dropped their drift slowed, and they wished it would start blowing again.

When the sun came out and the sky was clear, it became unpleasantly warm. The men on *Belgica* had decided that the most comfortable temperature in the Antarctic is -15°C, when all the moisture is frozen from the air. Above that, humidity seeps into cloth and fabric. You're always cycling between damp and frozen, far colder than you were before. When the wind dropped on the ice it became unbearably hot in the tents, as high as 0°. Good and bad in life is just a matter of what you're used to, Orde-Lees wrote in his diary.

Away from the men, Shackleton, Wild and Worsley pondered the prospects. There were broadly three futures: if the ice took them far enough north-west before winter, they could make it to land. But if the Weddell gyre kept them where they were, they would face a second polar winter, this time on the ice, with no food, no fire, no wooden ship around them. If the ice took them east or north-east, into the great empty nothingness of the south Atlantic on the wrong side of the winds, it was certain death.

In fact they were just about precisely on the split of two oceanic streams, one running north-west, the other north-east. Their floe was jagging erratically, tugged between the currents, a tiny prize fought over by two impersonal destinies. One way or the other, they would know soon, if their floe didn't break up first.

Shackleton had them fetch the boat they'd left behind, and prepared the fleet of three by giving them names. The largest, the whaler, he called the *James Caird*, after his most generous donor. He named the second the *Dudley Docker*, after a former first-class Derbyshire cricketer, now banker, who had contributed £10,000. The large-hearted Janet Stancomb-Wills, who was back home writing poems in violet ink and supporting Shackleton's wife Emily with a monthly stipend, was immortalised in the third lifeboat, the *Stancomb Wills*. (In naming the boat, they left off the hyphen. Such is the unending lot of the hyphenated name.)

Shackleton put Chippy McNish to work heightening the sides of the *James Caird* to make her seaworthy. McNish had very few tools, and used nails he'd personally pulled from the superstructure of *Endurance*. There was no oakum or pitch for caulking, so he filled the seams with cotton lampwick and George Marston's oil paints.

Oddly, there was a danger of complacency. Perhaps it was denial, perhaps too much confidence in Shackleton – human reactions are always difficult to predict, especially in the face of crisis. Worsley was stung by the abandonment of *Endurance* but confessed to his diary that he felt deeply and almost mysteriously content. Doctor Macklin was gratified to be far from civilisation, from trains, timetables, collars and ties. Orde-Lees fretted about future food security, but still, this was what he had been searching for all his life. He had a sense, at last, of being present at the real thing, the real event. All three used the word 'happy'.

I often think of what Sara Wheeler wrote after her time alone in a tent near McMurdo Sound: that the Antarctic in its vastness, its un-ownedness, represents everything beyond man's little world: it stands for everything, all of experience, all that we intuit about a life not yet rendered man-sized and small. It aroused in her a deep sense of well-being, a release from what she calls 'the crippling fear of the human condition'. It made her happy.

Shackleton didn't mind the officers being complacent. He was more concerned about the crew. Maybe that's why he turned on Orde-Lees.

Orde-Lees took his responsibilities as store-keeper very seriously. He kept counting and re-counting the food, doing sums, worrying there wouldn't be enough laid by should they have to overwinter again. He wanted to reduce rations, and stockpile seals and penguins. But Shackleton worried about putting the wind up the fo'c'sle. The official line was that they would be out by the end of summer: if the crew saw rations being reduced, and thought they might spend another winter, the effect would be unpredictable. Lassitude would be dangerous; depression might be fatal. And there were worse possibilities still.

Shackleton was always balancing what Caroline Alexander calls 'a gamble of morale against practical necessity'. He never hedged his gambles – he played the full martingale. It didn't matter that Orde-Lees was obviously, by any reasonable measure, correct. Officially everything was in hand, and Orde-Lees couldn't be allowed to unsettle that.

It's not that he bullied Orde-Lees, but he was a shrewd judge of character. Shackleton knew Orde-Lees could withstand a little scapegoating, and that scapegoating would diminish his influence, so he was scapegoated. In small, subtle ways, Orde-Lees became the butt of jokes, a figure of fun. Shackleton referred to him as the Old Lady. His old nemesis Chippy McNish called him The Belly Burglar, for his assumed habit of hoarding unguarded morsels of food. Most damagingly, Shackleton let it be known that Orde-Lees was a Pessimist.

Orde-Lees never took anything personally. He was ejected from his tent for snoring and had to move his sleeping bag to the storehouse beside the galley. It was much colder there than sharing the body heat of the tent, and he missed the sun filtering through the green tent fabric, but he was grateful they still let him eat his meals with them, and sit on their sleeping bags instead of on the ice. Orde-Lees was quite possibly very annoying in real life, but in his journal he is terribly sweet.

Time wore on. Tensions ebbed and flowed, flared and died. People inside tents were always forgetting that the canvas was very thin, as thin as skin, and had ears on both sides. Every gripe and every gossip was overheard; grudges easily grew. But on the whole, they agreed, it was remarkable how peaceably they lived together.

The books brought back from the previous camp provided fresh conversation. The volumes of *Encyclopedia Britannica* were especially good for starting and settling debates, until they were finally used as pipe lighters. Poetry had a brief vogue: they read Browning, and had long discussions about Coleridge's *The Rime of the Ancient Mariner*.

Those who couldn't read had the woes of the Mariner read to them, and they sympathised with him, he who on his wooden ship was driven down to the cold places of the south by fearsome weather, and there among the corridors of ice killed an albatross with his crossbow, incurring Job-like plagues of bad luck. The winds died, the sun blazed from a hot and copper sky, the ship suffered thirst while slimy things crawled from the deep upon the sea. Even as they drifted north the Mariner's shipmates became convinced that some dreadful dark force had followed them from the south, so to punish his sin they strung the corpse of the albatross around his neck.

The Mariner finally came to appreciate, nay, to *love* the things of nature all around him, even the wretched sea-snakes:

A spring of love gush'd from my heart,
And I bless'd them unaware

With that, some partial grace descended and the albatross fell from his neck into the sea, but still he was doomed to wander the Earth, warning people what he had learnt, and where salvation lies: the truth that all the world is connected – nature, beast and us.

> He prayeth best, who loveth best
> All things both great and small.

The picture of the men on the ice, talking about *The Rime of the Ancient Mariner*, is the most wonderful entwining of life and art. Coleridge drew heavily on the Antarctic descriptions of Captain Cook (Coleridge's tutor had been the astronomer on Cook's flagship). It was Cook, on his second voyage, who first discovered Antarctica, setting in motion the long chain of events that brought these very men right to this very place. What did they make of it, the sailors and scientists, suffering in the icy south as the Mariner himself had suffered?

The Ancient Mariner, these modern mariners agreed, seemed to be having a rum time of it, and none for the life of them could see what he'd done to deserve it. But what they really debated was what he did with the albatross.

*

Twenty-five days after they had abandoned her, on 21 November, a little after 5pm on a Sunday, as Shackleton watched from the lookout tower, the ice pulled back from *Endurance*'s sides and she raised her stern in the air and sank.

She fell and fell, stern-first, through the clearest sea water in the world. Down three kilometres she fell, gradually righting as she dropped so that she landed and settled on her keel, almost upright, a gentle list to port.

She came to earth again on the abyssal plain of the Weddell Sea, a vast flat seabed like a salt-pan, studded here and there with glacial boulders dropped from melting bergs in summers long past. She was the largest geographic feature for hundreds of kilometres. Below 260 metres she had been in perfect blackness. From the moment she vanished, the men knew as a fact – the way things are facts before things change – that no one would ever see her again. She was lost to the world.

Above the ice, it took ten minutes. From his lookout, quietly, Shackleton said: 'She's gone, boys.'

Endurance had gone already, but it was a shock when she sank, the way it's a shock when your parents or your former spouse sell the home where you once lived. Now some part of yourself is gone from the world, and a new stage must begin.

Depression loomed. Orde-Lees, to raise spirits, produced a treat at supper: one and a half tinned pork sausages per man, magicked up from his specially hoarded stock. But Shackleton made a fuss, waving the sausages about indignantly. You call this a supper fit for the grown men of a polar expedition? he bellowed at the Belly Burglar. Sausages are any self-respecting man's birthright, and they should all have two instead of one and a half, because they were such little ones.

All the men laughed and cheered The Boss, and were doubly cheered by the boost in rations and the unexpected variety, and by bedtime the camp was happy again. It wasn't fair on Orde-Lees, but Shackleton was a shrewd man.

But still there were danger signs. When the ship went down, the fo'c'sle lost more than the wardroom did. Many of the officers and scientists had been planning to camp on the ice anyway, as members of the expedition party. They had signed up for an adventure, more or less, but the sailors had not. They were part of the ship, and when the ship sank, an existential dusk descended. Why were they there? What was a sailor without a ship? If they had been sailors before, what were they now?

As they ran out of chores, time began to drag.

The north-west drift of the ice slowed.

Shackleton was laid low in his tent with sciatica.

They were approaching the midpoint of summer again, and soon the days would start shortening towards winter.

Day after day, day after day they were stuck, without breath, without motion, as idle as a painted ship upon a painted ocean.

In December, Worsley took his daily readings, and checked them, and checked them again. There was no doubt – the ice was starting to take them east, away from land.

Shackleton knew they had gone too long without doing anything, but the only thing to do was what they had already done. Gradually he allowed the news to spread: they would resume the walk. They were 320 kilometres from land.

Already, the difference in attitude was noticeable. They were divided about the walk. Some wanted to go, others to wait. Of those who wanted to wait, some were being prudent – to march they would have to leave behind food and equipment and one of the boats. But for others it just seemed like too much effort.

But there were no votes on the ice: Shackleton said they would leave on 23 December. They would travel at night when the temperature was lower and the snow firmer underfoot. They would leave poor old *Stancomb Wills* behind again, on the shelf. Since they would have to leave so much food behind, and since they would be walking on Christmas Day, they held an early Christmas feast before they left.

Orde-Lees privately fretted that this seemed a terrible waste but he had to concede, you can't take it with you. With the passion of a last meal, they gorged themselves on sausages and ham, jugged hare, anchovies in oil, Heinz baked beans, tinned peaches, Viking condensed milk, unlimited jam and nuts.

It was hard going from the start. The weather was mild and the snow was wet and loose. They broke through thin ice and sank to the thigh. Their knee-length Burberry-Durox boots filled with water, adding 3 kilograms to each leg. The eighteen men hauling the first boat could only take 200 or so metres of this at a time, then they would walk back to the other boat, using the walking time as recovery, and pull that to where they had left the first, then take up the ropes of the first one again. In this way, they covered 800 metres in five hours. They rested an hour. Then they went again. For supper they had cold seal steak and tea.

On Christmas Day they trudged and pulled and pushed and it was quiet at meal times because they were thinking about home, what their loved ones were eating, what they were doing. It was a silent day and a silent night.

Boxing Day was harder still. The ice was smashed up and littered with pressure ridges. Progress slowed. It was punishing, it was pointless. And at last what Shackleton feared came about.

On the fourth day of the march, there was a mutiny.

16. A VERY BRIEF DIGRESSION ABOUT ALBATROSSES

The Wandering Albatross is one of the great sights and symbols of the south. It has the widest wings of any bird and the whitest feathers of any albatross, spending the first six years of its life without touching land, able to circumnavigate the Earth in 46 days and fly 120,000 km in a single year. For days and weeks it can shadow a ship, hanging in the sky like the inverse of a shadow, like a tutelary spirit or a conscience. Did harming an albatross bring bad luck? No one ever claimed so before Coleridge, nor really after him. The crew of *Belgica* had fished for albatrosses by throwing baited hooks in the air. The birds snapped at them before they hit the sea, and were pulled onto deck. Their hollow wing bones made good tobacco pipes, and the sailors puffed on them while they froze in the ice and slowly went mad.

Herman Melville read *The Rime of the Ancient Mariner*, of course: he says so in *Moby-Dick*, and Ishmael saw his first albatross in Antarctic waters, singing in religious terms of 'a regal feathery thing of unspotted whiteness and with a hooked, Roman bill sublime. At intervals it arched forth its vast archangel wings, as if to embrace some holy ark ... Through its inexpressible, strange eyes, methought I peeped to secrets which took hold of God.'

In Beryl Bainbridge's novel about Scott's last expedition, *The Birthday Boys*, for which she drew largely from journals and first-hand accounts, Edward Wilson sees a vision in the light spangling off the sea. It's as though he has seen the same albatross as Melville: 'And in that heavenly dazzle I clearly saw a creature, half man, half bird, soaring above the waves ... I gazed down into those lidless eyes fixed on mine, observed where its powerful shoulders jutted into wings, followed the silver spray kicked up by its cruel talons as it skimmed the bright water. There was no doubt in my mind that the apparition was a harbinger of death, and yet, in the blaze of that terrible second a sensation akin to joy, something pitched between sexual arousal and fear bubbled up inside me.'

Wilson relays his vision to Henry 'Birdie' Bowers, a famously cheerful man, who would soon die in the tent alongside Wilson and Scott. Bowers tries to persuade him that he has seen something of God, but Wilson knows better. He knows he has seen the Devil.

I like thinking of the men of *Endurance* on the ice, smoking in their tents after supper, discussing albatrosses, God and the Devil, and their own endeavours in the frozen world. But I also like to remember something the author Zoe Gilbert wrote, and the perils of nature writing too enamoured of its own rapture: 'There is nothing like a struggle to get warm and dry, or find your way to safety, to do away with the hunt for meaning.'

Discussing the albatross over their umpteenth supper of seal hoosh, the men thought it was careless of the Ancient Mariner to let it slip into the sea. They all agreed they wanted it right there at that moment. They would like to eat it.

17. THE OPTIMIST

My father was never involved with the mines, or with emeralds, but my Uncle Gerry was. Emeralds are unlucky stones, but my Uncle Gerry was a great optimist.

Gerald Bovey was only Gerald Bovey for a short time. Some time in the 1930s he changed his surname, for one reason or more likely another, and kept changing it so many times that it's pointless to think of him in any way other than my Uncle Gerry. I never met him, because he died just before I was born – or maybe soon after, reports vary – and there are no photographs, but I know he had a twinkle in his eye and a rakish gap between his front teeth that was irresistible to a certain unlucky strain of mid-century woman.

In my mind's eye my Uncle Gerry is played by Terry-Thomas, the English character actor who made a respectable living playing cads and charming bounders, whose career largely overlapped with my Uncle Gerry's. (Like my Uncle Gerry, Terry-Thomas also changed his name. It was originally Thomas Terry, but he switched it round and, in a cavalier reversal of the usual fortune, added a hyphen, allegedly to represent the gap between his teeth.)

Uncle Gerry was a travelling man. He would disappear for months at a time, even years, then reappear on my dad's doorstep with a new wife and a new scheme. 'This one will work, Bonzo!' he would say, about both. 'This one can't possibly fail!'

He was married four times that we knew about, and after his funeral another two candidates came forward with marriage certificates, wondering if there was anything to be had from the estate. There wasn't.

Whenever Uncle Gerry reappeared, he and my dad would sit up late, drinking brandies with ginger ale until the ginger ale ran out, then just brandies, discussing what to do with all the money they would make from the latest scheme. My Uncle Gerry was an ideas man. Some optimists think having the idea is half the work, and those optimists are often disappointed, but I suspect that for my Uncle Gerry, having the idea was *all* the work.

Uncle Gerry had phases of imaginative interest. There was a racehorse phase, and a scrap metal phase, there was a plan to buy a fishing boat and turn it into a floating casino running between Richards Bay and Lourenço Marques. At one point he somehow acquired a de Havilland DH.82 Tiger Moth biplane and spent several years finding increasingly inventive ways to make no money from it.

He wasn't criminal, depending on how you define criminal. Perhaps from time to time he was crime-adjacent, and occasionally he found it prudent not to be somewhere too long with the same name, but really, I don't think there was harm in him, except to himself. There are different kinds of optimists. There was something missing from Uncle Gerry, something unnameable and impossible that might have taken him home and made him whole, and I think his optimism was the unending hope he would find it somewhere.

He also had a mining phase. Aunty Molly remembers him arriving one night after a lengthy absence, jingling something in a leather pouch. 'Hello, Bonzo!' he said. 'I've got something for us!'

He leaned over the dining room table and emptied out a handful of bright stones that jumped and danced like casino dice. Some of them fell on the floor, and Aunty Molly hastened to pick them up. 'Leave 'em!' said Uncle Gerry expansively. 'There's plenty more where they came from!'

Aunty Molly can't remember if he was trying to involve my dad in buying a mine, or transporting gems, or what. She remembers that he came back a few times with different gem-related schemes. Each time his sales pitch became more elaborate and impressive with the names of other people involved: successful people, famous people, people connected to the world where things happen. Maybe it was around that time that he mentioned Frank Wild.

When Frank Wild returned from Shackleton's last expedition he moved to South Africa. With the help of a personal loan from the prime minister, Jan Smuts, who was puzzled that the English government wasn't assisting such a distinguished man, he bought a farm in Zululand, at the foot of the Ubombo Hills. First came floods, then came drought, and that was the end of Frank Wild's farm in Africa.

Frank Wild stayed on in Africa. He became the manager of the Gollel hotel in Zululand. The wall of the bar was decorated with the crossed skins of two gigantic pythons he'd shot. There are stories of him swimming the crocodile-thick Pongola River in a dinner jacket on a bet after a few drinks. He went prospecting in Rhodesia. He had no luck, but it took him into the world of gems.

Everyone loves buried treasure, but for some people the glimmer of riches behind the dreary face of the world is an enchantment impossible to shake. Wild became the manager of G Stone Quarry, on a diamond mine in the village of Ottosdal, on a dreary plain west of Johannesburg. It was boring there. It was hot and empty and everyone spoke Afrikaans. He spent days on his own, sifting through piles of slag and gravel, looking for something glittering. Then the economy crashed and the mine closed. He was 57.

He drank. Perhaps he was alcoholic, although it's not certain. He gave public talks, and his pencil-written notes are still preserved in the Scott Polar Institute in Cambridge. In his talks he compared Shackleton's optimism to Scott's pessimism. He described the long, starving walk back along the Beardmore Glacier and his delirious conviction that devils were waiting at the bottom of crevasses. He spoke about his horror of loneliness and how he never felt lonely on the ice.

He lived in Klerksdorp, not far from the Swartkrans Caves where Bob Brain excavated the fossils of Dinofelis and Chatwin held them in his hand. He worked mines and lent his energies to the schemes of men who thought his name would get those schemes off the ground. He had some schemes of his own. Frank Wild knew what he was and was proud of it: he was a second dog who would follow his lead dog to the bottom end of the world and then back again. He only needed the right leader to follow, and he found him once and absorbed his lessons: he stayed optimistic, he did the work, he endured and kept walking forward.

My Uncle Gerry spent a lot of time in Klerksdorp – one of his wives was from there – and I imagine them meeting around this time, two haunted men hiding their fears, fumbling in the cold of the Depression for the ember of an idea that would change their lives one more time.

It would be good if I'd found some sort of provable connection between my Uncle Gerry and Frank Wild, so that I could put it forward as a hypothesis: my dad and my Uncle Gerry sitting around the dining table late into the night, talking and talking, Gerry's eyes glittering, arms waving: 'This time, Bonzo, this one's the charm! Frank Wild! He went south with Scott! Ever heard of the *Endurance*?! Shackleton's right-hand man! A name to conjure with! Put him up front, and the investors will flock in!'

'What's he like, Frank Wild?'

'Impressive man, Bonzo. Told me stories. Told me what it's like to eat your dog. Fell into a crevasse once, dangled from a rope. Did you know, Bonzo, Shackleton had very small hands?'

I can see Frank Wild and my Uncle Gerry together. I see Frank Wild warming to Uncle Gerry's energy, his optimism. I see him nodding thoughtfully at Gerry's ideas as they drink together, smoke, plan to hunt treasure together. I see Frank Wild measuring Uncle Gerry for the role of leader. But I don't see Uncle Gerry measuring up.

In many ways my father had the same blood as Uncle Gerry, the same instincts, like a wild goose locked in a cage that batters its beak bloody against the bars when it's time to migrate. Some are built to stay and some are built to move. Shackleton was built to move, and so was Roald Amundsen and Uncle Gerry and my dad. But just like there are different optimists, there are different reasons for moving.

When Uncle Gerry brought the gems to my dad, my dad said no. He must have wanted it, those gems must have glimmered and called like snow blink on the south horizon, but my dad wasn't available any more. 'You can't win the game if you're not in the game,' is something my Uncle Gerry said, but my dad had a family now, children to raise. He had a home. He was playing a different game.

Frank Wild's life was not unhappy; it was not tragic. He loved his wife Trix and she loved him. No one remembers him bitter or complaining. He was never defeated. Right to the end, Frank Wild was making plans. He owned land in Nyasaland that he bought after the war. A man and his wife could live cheaply in Nyasaland. With hard work, with endurance, they could make the farm work, they could live a good life. Frank was making plans for a last holiday with Trix, meeting up with old friends for a last carouse before going farming, when he fell ill and died of pneumonia, aged 69.

My Uncle Gerry was a different kind of optimist to Frank Wild, or Ernest Shackleton. His was a frail optimism, built on nothing, an optimism that takes the place of work and carries you only so far before something important runs out. His optimism was a snow bridge across a crevasse; sooner or later the glittering rime will break under your weight and you'll fall through and if you are lucky, you'll dangle from a harness attached to other people who will pull you back up again.

One day just before I was born, or perhaps just after, my Uncle Gerry decided he'd lost the game. He went to his car and led a hosepipe from the exhaust to the front seat and sat behind the wheel and started the engine. He was found the next morning with an empty brandy bottle beside him and a Louis L'Amour novel half-read on his lap. My father told me that. He also said: Gerry always had his priorities wrong. He should have finished the novel and only drunk half the bottle.

18. MUTINY

Be men, or be more than men. Be steady to your purpose and firm as a rock. This ice is not made of such stuff as your hearts may be; it is mutable and cannot withstand you if you say that it shall not.

VICTOR FRANKENSTEIN, RALLYING A CREW OF
MUTINOUS SAILORS IN THE POLAR SEA

Shackleton and Wild had scapegoated Orde-Lees as the Pessimist, and the carpenter Chippy McNish had taken his lead and had himself sneered at Orde-Lees as the Pessimist, but when the mutiny came, it came from Chippy McNish.

McNish was an odd character. He was grizzled and cantankerous and physically strong, but suffered loudly with haemorrhoids, which didn't sweeten his temperament. Everyone, including Shackleton and Alfred Lansing (who in 1959 wrote the first great book-length account of the expedition), seemed to think he was 56 or 57, and admired his physical stamina, but actually he was only 40.

McNish had been brooding for several days, since the death of Mrs Chippy. He knew she couldn't have gone with them, but our minds and hearts too frequently run on different tracks. Her death felt personal, a casual social violence performed on the powerless by the powerful. The personal feeling he most regularly expresses in his meagre diaries is an aggrieved animosity towards authority, especially the British government.

In thinking about the war in Europe, he hopes the Russians capture the Kaiser because they're sure to hang him, while the English government would bring him back and house him on a state pension at the expense of the English poor.

On the ice his cigarette makes him think of tobacco tax, and then the tax likely to be levied on his salary: 'I expect we will have to submit to have £2 S10. abducted from our wages after being out of the world for 2 years & received no benefits & they will say Briton is a Free Country.'

He looks out bleakly at the snows, and darkly opines that this is where the English government should be, 'for any good they ever done a working man or woman.'

The Russian Revolution won't happen for nearly two years, but you rather suspect it might find support in Chippy McNish.

Now, in the final days of 1915, the carpenter dropped his rope and told Worsley he refused to go on. He held that since the ship had sunk, he was no longer bound by his articles of passage and wasn't obliged to take orders. This trek was a waste of time, he said. It was tiring them unnecessarily, and they were hungry. They should go back to camp.

It was a dangerous moment. Chippy McNish wasn't the only one who thought this way about the march, or even the most vocal, but he was the first to take action. The others stood around, watching to see what Worsley would do. Shackleton was half a mile ahead, cutting the path, and Worsley was captain of the ship, but Worsley was not a disciplinarian or even a natural leader. He also secretly agreed about the value of the march, but that didn't matter: a mutiny couldn't be allowed to stand.

Worsley couldn't control the situation. Shackleton came striding back. The circle of men parted silently to allow him to stand before Chippy McNish.

He took McNish aside and explained that in a society, not everyone has to agree, but differences of opinion mustn't paralyse the whole. He wondered what Chippy McNish would do now? Go off on his own? He would be dead within days. He suggested that Chippy McNish take a moment to think things through before making his decision. He may also have quietly suggested that if it came to that, he would ask Frank Wild to shoot him.

Shackleton left McNish behind an ice hummock to gather his thoughts, and called the rest together and read out their articles of passage. The law was clear, he said. They were bound by the contract of employment until the termination of the voyage, and the voyage did not end with the loss of the ship. If the ship sank at sea and they were in the lifeboats, would the voyage have ended? Of course not. He expected every man to do his duty.

It was a good, firm speech, and it gave any formerly outspoken potential mutineers an excuse to obey his authority without loss of face. The officers later agreed that he had improvised some of the provisions of the contract, and invented some of the clauses. Necessity knows no law.

When the call came to march again, McNish silently took his position at the boat.

But the very next day, they came to another halt. It wasn't McNish this time, and it wasn't anyone else either. The ice was broken up ahead, and there were narrow leads of water running between the floes. Even the ice they stood on was suddenly uncertain, honeycombed and rotten with sea water, barely an inch thick. Men kept stepping into snow-covered holes, submerging to their waist. Five days of torture had brought them scarcely four kilometres, and there were 316 still ahead, but they couldn't go on, and they couldn't stay there. It was a terrible, ironic echo of the trench warfare in the European north: at savage cost they had gained feet and inches, and now they had to retreat and give them back again.

Chippy McNish had been right in everything he had said: Shackleton's decision to resume the march had been an error of judgment, and it hadn't paid off. They had left behind valuable food and equipment, their circumstances were materially worse, yet none of that mattered, because the men were still with him. Leadership isn't being right, or not all of the time. Leadership is getting people to agree that with you they can do better; that being wrong with you is better than being right without you.

They retreated and made a new camp. Shackleton said they would wait for the ice to improve, but the soot from the blubber stove, tracked across the ice, absorbed the sun and melted the floe beneath them. They had to retreat again, a kilometre back the way they came.

They made another camp on more solid ice, perhaps the fourteenth or fifteenth camp they had made since abandoning ship. They called it Patience Camp.

They would sit there and wait while the summer peaked and waned. They would sit there for three months.

19. THE PESSIMIST

You wait. Everyone has an Antarctic.
THOMAS PYNCHON

Going back to visit Aunty Molly went against my natural inclinations, which are to avoid intimacy and obligation. (Intimacy and obligation, I realise as I write that sentence, are troublingly synonymous in my mind.) But I did go back to see Aunt Molly, and that meant seeing Roy.

Roy, by way of explanation for why he was always home, told me that he was recovering. Recovering is a lovely word: who doesn't need to recover something we've lost? That isn't the recovery he meant, or maybe it is.

Sometimes, when Aunty Molly fell asleep or was awake but not quite there, I came out and sat in the lounge watching him build a model ship. We didn't have much to say. We were connected through adjacencies of genetics and maybe that should mean something but neither of us knew what. We felt like strangers occupying the same space but years apart.

The parts of a model ship were spread across a long low table and he sat on a couch somewhat too soft so that he sank down into it and had to lean forward between his knees to pick over the pieces and consult the instruction sheet under the table. He had tools and paraphernalia for model-building: a pair of bathroom tweezers, a magnifying glass with a white plastic rim, a pair of curved nail scissors to snip pieces from plastic frames. He was very careful and very slow. It wasn't loving, exactly, but it was patient. Perhaps that's the same thing.

When I was young I tried to build model aircraft kits – Spitfires, Heinkels, Wellingtons – but I squeezed out too much glue on the plastic pieces and they became bumpy and unattractive, and I confusedly attached fine struts and ailerons upside down, and whenever I saw this wasn't going to be a perfect Heinkel or Wellington, I gave up.

Roy was building an aircraft carrier, a vast model of USS *Nimitz*. It would take months to complete. It wasn't like a model aircraft, where you start at the tail or the fuselage and keep adding things till it's whole. It was too big and complex for that. It was modular: you had to construct this section then that section and have faith it would all connect and make sense in the end. Some sections would be hidden inside the superstructure – you wouldn't even see them when the ship was finished. Maybe you would *feel* they're there. Maybe that's art: the extra work that matters to no one but the person doing it.

The ship gave us something to talk about. He had made other ships, mainly naval: HMS *Hood*, *Ark Royal*,

Bismarck. I talked to him about the ships of the polar explorers. Small ships, made of wood: *Fram, Discovery, Terra Nova, Nimrod, Endurance.* I thought there must be models he could make.

Did they have sails? he wanted to know.

I told him they did. I said *Endurance* was a barquentine. I hoped he would ask what a barquentine is.

What's a barquentine, he asked.

'A barquentine,' I said nonchalantly, 'is a three-masted ship, with the forward mast square-rigged, while the main mast and the mizzen carry fore-and-aft sails, like a schooner.'

'What's a schooner?'

I wasn't exactly sure what a schooner was.

In time we spoke about other things. He told me he missed Kensington where he grew up. He remembered sunlight on windowsills and old faded matchboxes and the smell of those musty white net curtains and watching TV with his grandma and grampa after his parents left. He didn't remember my dad but that was okay, because I didn't remember his. He remembered playing in the street, and he said the streets were safe then and everyone was friends. That was not how I remembered Kensington, but everyone's home is their own.

Once I foolishly asked him if he'd been back. One thing we all know about home is you can't go back. Home isn't a place, it's not even only a time, it's a time made visible by being stitched into an idea of a place. At most it's a place *in* a time, before something important was lost.

I spoke to Roy about my father. I told him what I thought my dad was: a wanderer who washed up on the shores of an island and was stranded there, and the island was us, the island was me. I told him I was afraid that it was my fault, that I had kept him there, land-bound, unable to wander, that some are made to move and some to stay, and those who are forced to stay are weakened. An albatross on land will starve to death. I don't know why I said these things to Roy. Maybe I sensed we wouldn't be in each other's lives very long.

I told him that I was afraid that there was a part of me that was driven to move, maybe on my father's behalf, maybe on mine, that a part of me was driven to break good things and go to the South Pole.

'You want to go to the South Pole?' he asked.

No, I said, not the South Pole, but something like that.

I told him I was afraid I wasn't ever going to make anyone happy in the end, and if I wasn't going to make anyone happy in the end, why try? I told him I was frightened, because a man who doesn't trust himself finishes by punishing the people who do trust him.

Roy didn't look at me.

Another time I spoke to him about votive ships. In 15th-century coastal Europe there was a tradition of making a model ship and offering it to God or a saint, before or after a voyage, to ask for luck or to say thank you. You can still see them in churches in Brittany and Normandy, in the Nordic countries, in Germany and Spain.

Roy was attaching a piece with a pair of tweezers. 'You're married, right?' he said.

I said I was.

'Where's your wife?' he said.

I said she was at home.

'You've been coming here a lot lately,' he said.

Another time I told him about the Monastery of Archangel Michael Panormitis, on the Greek island of Symi. In the church of the monastery is a mosaic made with golden tesserae, tiny square tiles made of gold leaf compressed between glass, and when the sunlight touches them through the high windows the light mirrors and multiplies and flames out like shining from shook foil. I told him that it was beautiful, the light broken smaller, made myriad and thrown wider. There are two kinds of people, I told him: those who want to gather together the fragmented things of the world, and those who rejoice in seeing the single made multiple. I told him sometimes I'm one kind of person, sometimes I'm another.

I told Roy that Michael is the patron saint of sailors in the Dodecanese. In the monastery there's a collection of bottles that washed up on the shore of the island, containing written prayers to Michael. If you ask a favour of him, you must offer something in return. There's a small museum beside the chapel with models of ships and boats that have been brought by sailors or their relatives. Michael also likes strings of garlic, and loaves of bread, and for some reason brooms are also popular. He accepts IOUs in the form of pledges, but he's a scrupulous creditor: if you don't keep your promise, he'll let you know.

'How does he do that?' asked Roy.

He moved his head closer to the model, but I felt a weight behind the question. I felt that for Roy the subject of broken promises was an interesting one.

'I don't know,' I said. 'Shows up in your life and makes things go wrong, I suppose.'

Once, not on this occasion, Roy punched me. We were both standing at the time, and I could tell that on that day

153

he wasn't recovering as diligently as usual. He accused me of something that made no sense, and when I laughed at him he became angry and punched me in the face.

Fortunately, it's not as easy to punch someone as it looks on television. He punched me and it turned my head sideways but it didn't cloud my head, and we both stood there for a moment. He was scared by what he had done. I thought: so that's what it feels like to be punched in the face.

I'm sorry, he said, and started to cry.

It's all right, I said.

I knew this would happen, he said.

It's okay, I said.

In a way there's a bond when another man punches you in the face. You have shared something most people do not. If you are the one who was punched, it feels good to forgive. If you are the one who punched, it is always good to be forgiven, although being forgiven doesn't make it easier to forgive yourself. I also can't escape the thought that maybe I felt I deserved to be punched. Still, I didn't ever want him to punch me again.

There is a votive ship in New York City that interests me. The tradition of votive ships never really made it to America, but after the First World War, soldiers who had visited churches in Europe brought back the idea, and today there are a couple of votive ships in California and Iowa. There are also two in New York City, although at one point there were many more.

At St Paul's Episcopal Church in Carroll Gardens in Brooklyn, 172 years old in the year 2023, as many as a dozen ships once hung from the ceiling, bows pointed towards the altar. They were offered by grateful loved ones of soldiers returning alive and intact from the war. One was a three-masted ship with a steeply raked stern, green-and-white hull and a long bowsprit. It had previously been a childhood toy that sailed on the lake in Prospect Park. It was donated by three parish mothers whose sons were on USS *President Lincoln* when it was torpedoed by the submarine U-90, returning from Brest in 1918. The ship sank and the boys were in the sea for 26 hours but they survived.

The boats hung suspended from dedicated hooks in the rafters, until 1978 when someone stole them. At some point of the heist, the green boat fell and broke and was left behind. The church didn't have the heart to throw away the wreck of the green boat. It was stored on the shelf in a cleaning closet until 2010, when the rector had it restored and rehung from its original hook.

In the summer of 2021, as the Covid pandemic began to recede, the new rector of St Paul's wanted to commemorate the moment. There were more than enough plaques – the world is both shiny and tarnished with commemorative plaques, and St Paul's more than most. The Very Reverend William Ogburn looked aloft for inspiration and saw the green and white votive ship, sailing alone through the mote-dancing air, and thought: surely it has been alone long enough.

A woodworking parishioner made the three-masted barquentine, and included a tiny dog and a ginger cat – Mrs Chippy. They hung it from one of the original hooks, and it was blessed in November 2021. Three months later, *Endurance* was found.

I like the idea of the Brooklyn church as a ship, frozen in by the darkness of a bad time, offering a small beating heart of community. I like how the votive ship reminds us of the faith and optimism that sailors needed to go to sea in wooden boats, far from home, and believe that they would come home again.

I noticed that the aircraft carrier hadn't progressed much the last few times I'd been there. Roy still sat on the couch and looked at the instructions, but some tide was ebbing from him. We talked about the votive ships. He looked thoughtful. He said, 'The sails and the ropes are difficult. I don't know how to do that.'

There must be ways of learning, I suggested.

He thought about it, and in his eyes I saw that spark that comes when someone has the thought of trying something new. A leader would somehow fan that spark, point Roy in the direction of a bigger version of himself. But I'm not a leader.

His eyes flickered down the aircraft carrier, to the wall, to the floor, to me, and I watched helplessly as the ember cooled to something grey, to the fluttering film of soot on a fire grate that Coleridge called 'the stranger'.

'Maybe,' he said. He looked down to the aircraft carrier. 'Maybe I'll try it.'

I was away when Aunty Molly died. I had left my home because my marriage was ending. I was on an island in the Eastern Aegean called Ikaria, named after Icarus. There is a monument to Icarus on the pier in Agios Kyrikos, looking to the place in the sea where he fell from the sky and his circling father saw his wings upon the water. There is also a statue of Icarus in the tiny airport, which I think is an idea that wasn't perfectly thought through.

When I came back to Cape Town, I went to see Roy. I had bought him a model kit of *Endurance*. It was reasonably sized, 1:70 scale. It had lots of ropes and rigging, but I thought he could do it.

He was moving out of the house. The owner wanted to rent it to someone else, he said. Roy didn't mind. He said he'd been in Cape Town long enough. He thought it might be easier to recover somewhere else. Maybe he would go find his daughter. His daughter was also recovering somewhere, and maybe they would recover together. He didn't want to make any more ships. He hadn't finished the *Nimitz*; it was too big. He shouldn't have started something so big. He wondered if I could spare anything for relocation costs.

I asked Roy if he thought it would work this time, if he would stay recovered.

'Yes,' he said. 'I got it cracked this time. I got it beat. I just need to get away from here, and I'll be fine. Hundred per cent.'

You can't blame him: he didn't know me well enough to understand that I am not like the world, which demands optimism – not real optimism, but the script of optimism, the display of an empty optimism that lies to itself and isn't sober. It demands we make promises we can't necessarily keep. I didn't say so, but I thought Roy was beaten, and I think he thought so too.

I don't know where Roy went. I don't know where to reach him now. I know where he wanted to go. He wanted to go home.

20. THE END OF THE WORLD

*Never predict the end of the world. You're probably
wrong, and if you're right there won't be anyone
there to congratulate you.*

JOHN GREEN

We all suffer loss. We all ache for something that
was taken, that can't be had back.

Until relatively recently, part of the imaginative appeal
of Antarctica was the idea that, in a world of loss, it's
unchanging, and that time there, if it exists at all, is deep
and geologic.

There's enchantment in that thought and there's also
some science. A core sample drawn from deep in the east
Antarctic ice shelf glitters with compressed silvery bub-
bles of million-year-old air, preserved because the snows
that fall on the continent don't melt but accumulate, each
layer compressing the one below it to form 'firn', made of
compacted snow and ash and atmospheric particles of air.

With each year's snowfall the firn is pressed and squeezed and frozen until it becomes glacial ice. Melt the ice and you can inhale an inconceivable past, a time so long ago it's a different place.

Nothing decays in the Antarctic, and because it's not a human place, there's no human sense of things passing. It feels like there's no heat, so there's the illusion of no time. You can go to McMurdo Sound tomorrow, to Hut Point and Cape Royds, and see the hut that Scott built or the hut where Shackleton stayed. You can curl up and take a nap, as Sara Wheeler does at the end of *Terra Incognita*, on Scott's own bunk. Until the last few decades, the Antarctic presented itself to the imagination as a place where the river of time doesn't flow but freezes over, and is never subtracted from but only added to.

The Antarctic Treaty, signed in 1959, is a lovely attempt to make this dream of permanence real. It's a vision like Gene Roddenberry's utopian *Star Trek* future: the twelve countries whose scientists were involved on the continent agreed to declare the Antarctic a place of scientific collaboration, with no central authority, where military activity is banned and territorial claims suspended. There are 54 signatories to the treaty now, agreeing to keep it unchanging: no permanent structures, no unremoved waste, no foreign species, including dogs. Nowhere else in the world is so monitored for change and flux. The dream of the Antarctic is a promise of stasis: an Always Land, an Ever Land, a Never Land.

When Scott was dying in his tent on the ice, he wrote to his good friend J.M. Barrie. They had met six years earlier, introduced by Scott's wife Kathleen. Scott gave Barrie a copy of his book; Barrie invited Scott to a rehearsal of

Peter Pan. Barrie was delicate and fearful, a stay-at-home, a writer, but he declared that he wanted to join the next expedition, in order to know 'what it really feels like to be alive'. Scott and Kathleen named their son Peter, in honour of Peter Pan. Barrie was his godfather.

Peter Pan was first a play then a novel, both written by Barrie. In the first version, in 1904, Peter took Wendy and the Darling children away to the place where no one grows up, to the trebly emphatic Never Never Never Land. For the play's run – it ran and ran and ran – it became Never Never Land. By the time of the novel, in 1911, published while Scott was on the ice, it was just Neverland. Even for Peter Pan, eternity was getting shorter all the time.

(Young snow that has fallen and partly melted, refrozen and compacted, the intermediate stage before it becomes firn, is called névé. The snow Scott crunched across was névé. Neverland, at least on the surface, is also Névé Land.)

Peter Pan, the boy who never grew up, became the focus of the sunny Edwardian sentimentality about the boys it sent to war to be slaughtered. 'To die will be an awfully big adventure,' says Peter on Marooners' Rock. The golden boy Rupert Brooke was obsessed with the play and saw it ten times before he signed up, and wrote his sonnets, and died on a Greek island on his way to Gallipoli. As the war wore on and the death count climbed, the producers of the play quietly cut the line on Marooners' Rock.

To Barrie, Scott's death made him even more like Peter Pan. In a speech to the students of the University of St Andrews ten years later, Barrie said: 'When I think of Scott, I remember the strange alpine story of the youth who fell down a glacier and was lost, and of how a scientific companion who had accompanied him computed that his body would again appear at a certain place and date many years afterwards. When that time came round some of the survivors returned to the glacier, all old men now, and the body reappeared as young as on the day he left them. So Scott and his companions emerge out of the white immensities, always young.'

I used to imagine the same thing: that Scott and Bowers and Wilson are all still there, in their collapsed tent on the ice, beneath their cairn of snow, but of course that's not true. The tent would have sunk down under the accumulating weight of the snow, a little deeper each year, and drifted slowly northward. Glacial ice isn't frozen in place – it flows like cold lava, as much as 25 centimetres a day. It slides down from the high ground to the sea and makes an ice shelf, and keeps flowing until it breaks off in icebergs and drifts north and breaks further into bergy bits and growlers. It circles in the Weddell gyre or it drifts north until it melts. By one calculation, if Scott's tent stayed intact, it would have flowed into the ocean around 1980.

The truth of course is that nothing is unchanging. The Antarctic has always been changing, one way or the other, but we only noticed when the speed of change became visible in our human scale. Three billion years ago Antarctica was on the equator – some of it would have stuck into the northern hemisphere. It has only been over the South Pole for about 100 million years, and for much of that time it was covered with forests and ferns.

The cruel paradox of the Antarctic Treaty is that as hard as it tries to keep the Antarctic unchanging, all things in this world are connected, and the warming air of the tropics makes its way in air currents and sea currents to the shores of the south, and now the Antarctic is changing not because of what's happening there, but because of what's happening everywhere else.

Of course, we don't think about the Antarctic any more as an unchanging place. We have swung, as we do, entirely the other way: the Antarctic exists in the imagination today as a barometer of change, of melting sea ice and tragically calving glaciers. The loss of the Antarctic has become a synonym or a metonym for the loss of the world, and it is hard to think of that, so many of us don't. Others do, but in ways that don't always help: excess optimism, excess pessimism, denial, escape.

At the end of *Peter Pan*, Wendy chooses to leave Neverland in order to return home and grow up. Cruelly, of course, to grow up will mean one day to once more leave her home behind, to lose her parents, to grieve. Growing up is to make your terms with loss.

Peter Pan can't make that choice because he can't face that pain, so he's ultimately a pathetic figure, an eternal shadow tapping at the nursery window, looking in at other lives being led. Because what we learn with age is that life may be loss, but that without loss – without heat and the simple physics of heat moving down a gradient – there is no life, there is only the polar winter, the polar night, the heat death of the universe. If we didn't have loss, we wouldn't have anything at all.

Peter Pan dreams of escaping the pressing truth of loss: Elon Musk with his visions of escaping Earth's future by running away to Mars is the *real* Peter Pan of our age. Escape is tempting, but after escape, perhaps the most surprisingly seductive daydream is the apocalypse.

I don't know that we're closer to the apocalypse now than we were when I was young, but I do think people are more deeply invested in the idea that the world is ending.

For people campaigning to save the planet, it used to be that the biggest threats were denialists: people who, for psychological reasons or more cynically, had a stake in the empty optimism of saying we don't have to do anything, because everything will be okay. Nowadays it's unnecessary to deny the science: it's more effective to be a pessimist. In a 2021 survey of 20,000 people in 27 countries, fully a fifth of those under the age of 35 claimed to believe it's too late to stop the end of the world. Pessimism, as Shackleton knew, is a powerful brake on action. If it's too late to do anything, there's no point in doing anything.

There are people, some of them sincere people and not entirely fools, whose identity is invested in the apocalypse. Perhaps the best known is Guy McPherson, professor emeritus from the University of Arizona, who has gathered a sort of doomsday cult of self-proclaimed rationalists since insisting in 2016, more or less convincingly citing data, that we will all be dead by 2026. Less charismatically, it's difficult to pass many weeks now without being told that it's already too late to make the lower level of the target, established in the Paris Agreement, of keeping global warming to 1.5°C above pre-industrial levels. That may well be true, and perhaps they say it to frighten us into action, but we humans are odd things: a little anxiety is motivating, but too much fear paralyses us, then makes us mad.

I do not doubt their intentions or their good motivations, but when I think of McPherson, and the other smaller and more reasonable McPhersons, I think of Adrien de Gerlache on *Belgica*, locked away in his cabin, lugubriously assessing his chances at 100:1.

And then I think of Shackleton striding out with his ice saw, saying 'Follow me.'

I feel a certain sympathy with the pessimists because what, after all, is apocalyptic thinking, other than imagining a world free from the ache to go home? At the end of the world, there's no home to go to, the homes are all gone, the conditions for home have been erased. If home is time stitched to place, the apocalypse that wipes away space also wipes away time. An apocalypse seems almost attractive, because it allows us to stop worrying about it. If everything is lost, then there is no loss to worry about. If everything is lost, nothing is lost, because it has all started again. There is no responsibility to make things better, there is no adult reckoning with what has happened, and no responsibility to decide, in the light of that, how to be. The terrible, seductive appeal of catastrophic thinking is that it seems to offer what revolutions seem to offer: that eternal appeal – so especially appealing to the young – of a long, undifferentiated newness.

(It has become a kind of mantra that the problems of tomorrow will be solved, if they're to be solved, by today's young. This might be a mistake. The young are prone to excessive optimism and excessive pessimism. I often think of what Shackleton said to Frank Wild on their difficult march home across the Beardmore in 1909. Their two companions, Marshall and Adams, were younger than them and stronger than them and would beat them over a short distance, but endurance and stamina are the province of those with the miles already in their legs. Marshall and Adams' minds had let them down and they were unable to move. Wild and Shackleton had to go on alone to fetch back food for them from the nearest depot. As they shouldered their packs, Shackleton turned to Wild and said, 'Well, Frank, it's the old dog for the hard road, every time.')

It's appropriate to think about the end of the world, just as it was appropriate around our ancient campfires to think about Dinofelis. But predict it too much and we become attached to the rightness of our prediction. The danger with any danger is that if we live with it too long, we fall in love.

21. PATIENCE CAMP

To love, and bear, to hope till Hope creates
From its own wreck, the thing it contemplates
PERCY BYSSHE SHELLEY

At Patience Camp catastrophe was in the air. Shackleton wasn't sleeping. He worried about the drift and the wind, he worried about the food, he worried about McNish and Vincent. He worried about the unexpected.

One day as Orde-Lees walked from camp a leopard seal lunged from the water and onto the ice ahead of him. A leopard seal is not like other seals – it eats other seals. It has an outsized head and jaws and the smooth curved canines of a sabre-toothed cat. The majority of their interactions with humans are uneventful, but inflatable research boats in the Antarctic are fitted with puncture guards because of repeated attacks by leopard seals on the black pontoons.

In 1985 a leopard seal broke through a thin rind of sea ice in the Ross Sea to seize the leg of explorer Gareth Wood, and tried to pull him into the water. His companions finally drove it away by kicking it in the head with spiked crampons. In September 2021, in Cape Town, three spear fishermen fought a leopard seal for half an hour after it attacked them close to the seabed, biting through a 5mm wetsuit. In 2003 while Kirsty Brown of the British Antarctic Survey was snorkelling on the surface near the Antarctic Peninsula, a leopard seal surged from below and pulled her down to 70 metres. When her body was recovered there were more than 40 injuries around her head and neck.

The leopard seal came for Orde-Lees and he shouted for help and ran back the way he had come. Seals don't hunt people but this one did. It followed and Orde-Lees fell and scrambled up and slipped again and kept running. The leopard slid into the water and swam below the ice, following his shadow, and came out of a gap ahead of him.

Frank Wild came with his rifle and fired and hit it in the chest. It turned and came for him. Wild backpedalled and fired again and hit it again and it kept coming. After the third shot it stopped coming.

The leopard seal provided 450 kilograms of meat and enough blubber for two weeks. Its belly was full of fish. Some of the fish were already half digested, but there were 22 that were newly consumed, intact enough for Charlie Green to fry them for supper.

The men didn't recognize the fish. Antarctic fish are not like other fish. Channichthyidae have no haemoglobin at all – their blood is white, and they have an antifreeze molecule in their blood.

In Charlotte Brontë's *Jane Eyre*, Jane reads Thomas Bewick's *A History of British Birds*, in which he proposes that from below the polar ice there issue forth 'swarms of fishes, as if engendered in the clouds, and showered down like the rain, multiplied in an incomprehensible degree.'

Bewick was only imagining the great gusts of fish, but in 2021 researchers dragging an underwater camera in the Weddell discovered the largest nesting ground of any fish species ever discovered: some 60 million circular nests on the seabed, covering 240 square kilometres, each nest containing some 2,000 eggs and guarded by an adult Jonah's icefish.

They are curious fish, half beautiful, half bizarre, crocodile-headed and transparent, a shimmering ice blue. Their translucent flesh cooks to white and tastes of shrimp. Did the men eat Jonah's icefish from the belly of the sea leopard? Perhaps. Jonah's icefish is so called because the first specimen known to science was recovered intact from the belly of a whale.

After that Wild would kneel on the edge of ice floes, flapping his arms and imitating a penguin, and when leopard seals came lunging for him, he snatched up his rifle and threw himself back, giving himself time for a second and third shot. One was five metres long and had thirteen Adélie penguins in its belly.

Shackleton trusted Wild not to get himself killed but he was growing concerned for the others. His was a very specific optimism: the kind without magical thinking. He understood what lay ahead, the odds against his martingale, and he had no appetite for tempting fate.

Fresh meat was low, but the ice was crumbling so he banned the hunting parties from venturing far from camp, and banned the use of skis, as too great a temptation to foreign adventure. When Orde-Lees fell once too often in the water, he banned him from leaving camp at all. He fretted and scolded like a mother, like a father. They started calling him Old Cautious.

At the beginning of January he made another decision. The dogs consumed a seal a day, enough meat to feed all 28 men for half a week. The only way home would be in boats, and the dogs couldn't be in the boats. Shackleton ordered Wild to starting killing the dogs: Wild's dogs first, then McIlroy's and Marston's and Crean's. There were some stores of dog food that wouldn't be needed without the dogs. He told Green to add the dog food to the men's rations.

There was a four-day blow that pushed them north, over the Antarctic Circle. The gale drove the floe with the remains of Ocean Camp closer to them, so they fetched more food and clothing, and collected the *Stancomb Wills*. Marston's oil paints were lost, so McNish caulked her with seal blood and flour.

There was nothing to do but wait. They had read everything, spoken about everything. McNish had read the Bible from end to end. The wind dropped and the drift slowed. A sea mist snaked across the ice. Sea mists come from open water: the ice was beginning to break up.

The men discussed what they missed most: running streams and the colour green, bread and butter, apple pie and Devonshire cream, beer. Worsley dreamt of 'dewy wet grass and flowers on a spring morning in New Zealand or England'. One day they found a twig in a pile of old seaweed and burnt it and gathered round, aching with nostalgia for the land smell of a fire.

In February the rations were reduced. Winter was coming again. Solemnly, they shared out the last of the cheese. Orde-Lees searched the ice for two days for a morsel of cheese the size of a fingernail that he had dropped the week before. They used up all the toilet paper rolling cigarettes, and had to use broken hunks of ice instead.

Their tea ran out, their cocoa was all but out. They opened one of the final packets of flour and found it spoiled by salt water. 15 February was Shackleton's birthday but he refused to let them celebrate with extra food.

The wind came back up. A 55 km/hour wind will drop the temperature from -6°C to -28. Their eyes watered and the tears froze on the tips of their nose; when the icicle broke off it took a patch of skin with it. Reginald James diagnosed the camp with a new complaint of his invention: anemomania, or wind-madness. You were either obsessed with the wind direction and talked unceasingly about it, or you were driven to madness by others doing it.

A new danger arose. Icebergs were calving from the Larsen Ice Shelf, smashing through the floes. Ice floes move with the wind, but a 75-metre iceberg extends 600 metres underwater, and that vast keel catches currents independent of the wind, driving them through the pack ice like trains through Styrofoam, annihilating everything.

The Larsen shelf is one of the most productive calving grounds for bergs. In the winter of 2017 a giant flat-topped iceberg called A68 broke from the Larsen C shelf, just about adjacent to where the men were. A68 was 175 kilometres long and 50 kilometres wide. When icebergs become big enough, people start measuring them in units of Luxembourgs, as though that helps you to picture it. A68 was three times the size of Luxembourg.

It weighed one trillion tonnes. A trillion is a million multiplied by a million, if you can imagine that. I can't. At a certain point, as they leave our human scale of reference, big numbers are just words we say, like the social formulae of commiseration. Here is a helpful formulation: there are roughly 20 quadrillion square kilometres of ice in the Antarctic ice sheet, which means there is just about exactly one tonne of ice for every ant in the world.

A68 drifted towards South Georgia, melting as it went. At the height of its melting, it dropped more than 1.5 billion tonnes of fresh water into the ocean every day. One tonne of water is 1,000 litres. I cannot even really picture 1,000 litres, let alone multiply that by 1.5 billion. Does it help to say that 1.5 billion tonnes is 150 times the amount of water used daily by all UK citizens?

The bergs of February 1916 weren't the size of A68 but they were the size of city blocks, suburbs. They went careening past ahead and to the side and behind. At last, two bergs came straight for them, carving through the frozen ocean like a gigantic pair of dorsal fins.

The men watched them come. Shackleton leant calmly against a tent pole, smoking a cigarette, waiting to give the word. Run too soon, run the wrong way, and they might place themselves in the path. Run too late, and they might still be in camp as it was run over by a mountain. At the last minute the bergs sheared aside. Shackleton stubbed out his cigarette and suggested an early dinner.

On Leap Day, 29 February, they had a desultory feast and the last of the cocoa. From then on there would be just warm water with spoons of powdered milk. They were running out of blubber for the stove, so there was just one warm meal a day.

In early March a dozen Adélie penguins wandered into camp. They are handsome fellows, with black heads and beaks and shoulders and snowy undersides and pale rose feet. The men fell upon them gratefully. The next day twenty more wandered in, and then more the next day, and still more. They kept coming, like feathered lemmings waddling unto their blades. The camp was directly in the path of an Adélie migration.

Adélies are one of the most common penguins in Antarctica. They feed on krill, which they regurgitate for their chicks. Krill feeds a community of rust-coloured organisms found only on the underside of sea ice. Shackleton had noticed the organisms – he called them 'diatomaceous scum'. Lose the ice, you lose the scum, you lose the krill, you lose the things that eat the krill, including seals and whales and the Adélie penguins. Today, as the sea ice melts, Adélies have declined by 90% and Gentoo penguins have taken over. Gentoos don't need krill: they're like subway rats, they'll eat anything. They don't even like sea ice: they prefer uncovered rock. I mention the Gentoos simply to be able to say that west of the Antarctic Peninsula, there has been a Gentoofication of the neighbourhood.

The Weddell Sea is protected from the warm western currents by the peninsula, so sea ice is still high, and Adélie numbers seem stable. The sea ice of the Weddell Sea may be the last of the sea ice to melt, Antarctica's last stand. The ice that held Shackleton might one day be the last ice holding.

By the time the migration was over the men had taken more than 600 penguins. But Adélies are slender and stringy and don't yield much blubber: 40 penguins were the equivalent of one Weddell seal. Their skins are rich in subcutaneous oil so they could be burnt in the stove, but it took twenty skins to fuel the fire for a day. Still, the larder was full. That night they had stewed penguin heart, liver, eyes and toes, with a cup of water. It can't have been all bad – years later, Frank Hurley would name his first daughter Adelie.

The ice started breaking and the men were excited but also afraid. If it broke up too soon and they took to the boats without access to the open sea, they would have no chance in the clashing ice.

The drift seemed to be speeding up. They were rock-eting north, and they realised they were going to shoot straight past the nearest land. 'A single molecule in a gale of wind,' wrote Reg James in his journal, 'would have about the same chance of predicting where he was likely to finish up.'

On 9 March Orde-Lees woke up seasick. There was an oceanic swell beneath the ice. The pack rippled, loose plates of ice rattled, water squeezed up geyser-like between open cracks. There were eighteen seconds between swells, and with each swell the floe broke a little more.

Shackleton called lifeboat drills, although there was still no open water to be seen. Tempers were ragged. Hunger is bad for morale.

Two days later, the ice pack opened. There were ave-nues of dark water. At the other end of the lanes of water lay the open sea and a chance to survive, but if they went and the ice closed, they would be lost. The men wanted to go. They pointed to the water. Shackleton was a man of action, of doing and striving, who believed he could shape the future. Shackleton was an optimist, but not a blind optimist. Shackleton waited, and the ice closed again.

They were still alive, but they were hungry. Winter was coming and there were no more seals so rations were reduced again. The men became colder, unable to generate their own heat. Inside their tents the vapour from their breath formed clouds that fell to the ground as snow. They were almost out of blubber for the stove so they ate cold food and couldn't melt ice for drinking water. They put snow in tobacco tins and slept with them pressed against their bodies to melt them. A full can of snow yields a few tablespoons of water.

Two weeks later, Shackleton looked west in the morning and spotted the black volcanic rock of the Antarctic Peninsula. It was the first land they'd seen in sixteen months. It was their 139th day on the ice. Joinville Island was as close as a good day's row.

Shackleton stared and stared. Every part of him wanted to go, but the ice was broken and shattered. A different kind of optimist would have gone for it. Shackleton did not. It was like 9 January 1909, when he stood on the polar plateau, 150 kilometres from the South Pole, and told Frank Wild: 'We'll go back.'

Shackleton turned his head so that he wouldn't have to watch the land drifting past. The ice took them north, faster now, faster and faster, and now the Drake Passage lay ahead – the most murderous seas in the world. Their last hope was two tiny specks of land: Elephant Island and Clarence Island, a few kilometres apart, 200 km to the north.

They were desperate and dehydrated. The ice melted below them as they slept and they sank down into trenches like graves. A blizzard came up and the water froze in their mugs. There were twelve hours of darkness a day.

The men begged to return to Ocean Camp to find more food but Shackleton said it was too dangerous. A hunting party saw two seals and shot them and managed to bring back one but Shackleton called them back from the other because the ice was breaking. The men grew fractious. Greenstreet was so agitated during a heated exchange that he spilled his one precious cup of powdered milk per day into the snow. He stood looking at it, trying not to cry. Silently, Clark, Worsley, Macklin, Rickinson, Kerr, Orde-Lees and Blackborow poured some from their mugs into his.

On 27 March the ocean swell picked up again and their floe began to break. Cracks ran through the camp and the men fled to safety on the thicker side, and realised they had left the last stock of penguin meat on the other. They jumped across the widening crack to rescue it. The floe had once been a kilometre and a half across. It was now 180 metres.

They killed the last of the dogs and the last of the puppies. They would have been upset before, but now they were so hungry they salivated rather than wept. They cooked and ate them and each man insisted his own dog tasted best.

The floe broke up more. They saw Cape petrels and terns, a sign of the open sea. They saw a jellyfish in the gap between the ice. They saw a giant petrel, pure white with two black stripes across its wings. The wind blew from the north but the current drove them into the wind. 'Such a life,' wrote Frank Hurley, 'ages one.'

Ahead in the sea haze they spotted the bleak outline of Clarence Island. It was a bottom line: if they missed

Clarence Island, they would enter the Drake Passage and be destroyed. They were 109 km south of it, but now, cruelly, they were veering westwards, towards the open sea.

Still the pack would not open. An orca raised its head and eyed them. The pack would not open. Shackleton ordered the tents taken down and the boats loaded. The activity lifted their spirits. 'Given the barest opportunity of winning food and shelter,' he wrote, 'man can live and even find his laughter ringing true.' Still the pack didn't open.

The floe broke again, precisely across the patch of ice where Shackleton's tent had stood. Standing on one floe, he could look down at his feet and see the indentation made by his body and legs, then look across the widening water to the second floe, where last night his head had rested.

Now their floe was 45 metres across. The pack opened, then closed again. Then opened, then closed. Each time it opened, they wanted to go. Each time it closed, and their lives were saved. They ate standing up, watching the ice, watching the pack, watching Shackleton.

It was always a Sunday when things happened. At 1pm on Sunday 9 April 1916, the floe broke again and Shackleton gave the order. They had run out of time. There was no going back. As they rowed away, the ice began to close behind them.

PART 3

ENDURANCE

22. CAPTAIN BENGU

When I heard that *Endurance* was found, I flew to Cape Town from Athens via Addis Ababa to meet Captain Bengu.

It was the end of March 2022, the end of the polar season. The expedition had dispersed, ice pilot Freddie Ligthelm was back with his family, there was only a skeleton crew aboard and Captain Bengu was getting ready for his leave. Further south the ice was gathering but in Cape Town the sun was warm. I hired a car at the airport and drove to the Waterfront.

I drove down the access road to East Pier, and futzed about looking for the correct chain link gate. I found one that was padlocked and another that led to a pair of security guards sunning themselves on a step. They sent me to a third gate, which makes quite a lot of gates for a very small pier, and once you're through any of the gates you're in the same place you would have been had you come through any of the others.

SA Agulhas II seemed freshly painted: the white paint was very white and the cherry-red hull was very red. She was moored by thick-cabled rope to scuffed yellow bollards. There were gulls on the rooftops and on the dock beside the ship there was a small clutch of snowmobiles, looking dazed and defunct in the sun. It was Saturday afternoon and very quiet, except for the helicopters taking tourists on scenic flights.

Cape Town was still in some version of Covid lockdown – one of those intermediate stages when you could do normal things, but not in a normal way. I had been told to bring PCR tests and vaccination certificates. I walked down the dock and found a couple of cleaners eating lunch in the shade and said I was here to visit the ship. They called to someone and he called to someone but no one knew how to help. The gangway was open, leading up to the ship, but could I just walk up? I walked halfway up.

'Hello?'

There was a sound in the water below, a huffing and blowing from the gap between the wharf and the hull, like two competitive old men who have just swum a length underwater on a dare. I looked down through the slats of the gangplank and saw two shining black heads, the glitter of eyes and water on whiskers. Cape fur seals. *Arctocephalus*: bear-headed seals.

I walked all the way up to the hatchway.

'Hello?'

I couldn't just walk in, could I? It would be like walking onto the International Space Station uninvited.

'Hello? Can I come aboard? I'm coming aboard!'

I felt like the world's most diffident pirate.

Knowledge Bengu appeared in the hatchway. He wore a white t-shirt and jogging pants and grey trainers. He is very fit and trim for a man who spends so much time on a ship. His fingernails are neat and his handshake is vigorous and he looks at you curiously, with clear almond-shaped eyes.

'Welcome aboard,' he said.

He led me up to the bridge in purposeful bounds, two and sometimes three steps at a time. I had to trot to keep up. I was star-struck. It is like being shown around *Titanic*, not by Captain Smith but by James Cameron.

On the bridge he made us coffee. He apologised that the machine was decommissioned so we had to make do with instant coffee. No problem! I said. I prefer instant coffee! He looked at me thoughtfully, as a captain looks at a new recruit trying too hard to ingratiate himself.

He sat in the captain's chair and I sat on the chair beside him and we sipped our coffees. I wasn't sure how to start. I have spoken to remarkable people before, who have achieved remarkable things in the face of difficulties that would defeat you and me, and one thing is consistent: unless they're American, it's very hard for them to talk about how they do it.

For the most part, remarkable people can tell us the things we already know – you should work hard and pay attention to detail and stay positive, or whatever – but they can't describe the thing they have that makes them succeed where others fail. They can't tell you how, when the moment came, they weren't defeated but endured.

Knowledge Bengu was born in Umlazi, a black township south of Durban. There's an official list of notable citizens who were born in Umlazi, the usual roll-call of South African celebrity: musicians, politicians, soap actors, soccer players, activists. Knowledge Bengu isn't on the official list but he should be. At the age of 31 he was the first black ice pilot in the world. He is the master of *SA Agulhas II* and the man who took her into the Weddell Sea through ice and gyre, and placed her over the spot where they found *Endurance*.

It wasn't the first time people had tried to find *Endurance*. In 2001 Robert Ballard, who found *Titanic*, tried but failed to raise the finance, and in 2004 there was briefly a race between two new teams.

The first was led by David Mearns and his salvage company Blue Water Recoveries. Mearns had found HMS *Hood* in the Denmark Strait in 2001, at nearly the same depth as *Endurance*, and he had a knack for promotion. He borrowed Huberht Hudson's sextant from his grandson to use in the search, and signed an agreement with Shackleton's granddaughter Alexandra, granting him the right to retrieve Shackleton's effects, perhaps forgetting the wreck is protected as a Historic Site and Monument under the Antarctic Treaty, and can't be salvaged or even touched.

The second team was led by Jock Wishart and Jonathan Adams. Wishart had rowed the Atlantic and hiked to the Magnetic North Pole, and Adams had raised Henry VIII's warship, the *Mary Rose*, from the Solent.

In the well-worn tradition of the Antarctic, the two teams were at each other's throats. Mearns said Wishart and Adams were hostile and uncollaborative; Wishart and Adams said they were pure-minded scientists and that Mearns lacked ethics, much as Scott once said Shackleton lowered the tone of the noble Antarctic project.

There is something wearying about the constant rivalry that clings to the Antarctic story, so it doesn't sadden me that neither team made it. The first serious expedition was in 2019 under the banner of the Falklands Maritime Heritage Trust, led by polar geographer John Shears, with Mensun Bound as the Director of Exploration, and they came to Knowledge Bengu to be their captain.

Growing up, Mfanafuthi Knowledge Bengu had no interest in the Antarctic.

'Neither did Shackleton!' I told him. 'Nor Scott! Amundsen grew up dreaming of being a polar explorer, but Scott and Shackleton would happily have made their names doing something else.'

I found that more remarkable than he did, but that's because the most passionate sports fans are always at home on their sofa, the ones who can't do it, not the sportsmen who can.

Never mind ice, Knowledge had no particular interest in the sea. He was planning to be a gynaecologist but his neighbour was a bosun in the merchant marine, and was a big man in the neighbourhood. When he came home to Umlazi he needed two cars, one to carry all his baggage and gifts. Knowledge noticed that the ladies liked to listen to his stories of the sea.

Knowledge's neighbour had joined the merchant marine under apartheid, but he told Knowledge that times were changing. South Africa was democratic now. He could be an officer. There was a scholarship available. It was a way up.

I grew up on the Bluff and it's part of the story I tell myself that I worked my way off the Bluff like some kind of blue-collar hero, but I only call the Bluff working class when I talk to white people. I couldn't do that with Knowledge. Umlazi is the fourth biggest township in South Africa, a million inhabitants living about twenty minutes south of the Bluff, but I was a white boy growing up in the 1980s so in all my childhood I never once went to Umlazi. The only thing I knew about Umlazi was that our domestic worker came from there.

There are some things that I try not to remember, but when I do remember them, as I am remembering now, I feel a kind of panicked shame which burns my skin and makes me cold at the core. One of those things is being a seven-, eight-, nine-year-old child giving orders to an adult domestic worker, being a child and referring to my mother as 'the madam', and my father as 'the master'. Being ten years old when my father had died and thinking, *I am the master now*.

Knowledge Bengu's parents weren't domestic workers, and he doesn't frame his childhood as I embarrassingly frame mine, as a story of hardship overcome. He sees himself as lucky. His parents raised him with values and ambition and set him an example. His grandmother taught him to garden and cook, but she was also his high school class teacher.

She had been to a multiracial private school and used to boast about coming top of her class, ahead of the white girls. More was expected of him: he was expected to lead. 'If something went wrong in class, she blamed me,' he said. 'Even if she knew it was someone else, I had to learn to be responsible.'

It was a time of political activism, and Knowledge woke to dawn raids with policemen hunting his older brother. His grandmother swore at them in Zulu, then switched to English to show them she spoke it better than they did.

His grandmother taught him discipline. When he played in the street with his friends, he was always the first called home. 'Mfanafuthi!' she would call. 'Come put the rice on for supper! I'm hungry!'

Knowledge took the merchant marine scholarship and studied at the Technikon. He had worked in school while other kids were playing; now he worked while other students were drinking. 'I was serious,' he says. 'I wasn't there to joke around.' A classmate warned him that people thought he was stuck up. 'Where I'm going,' he replied, 'I don't expect to be liked.'

'You don't seem that serious now,' I said.

'These days I like to joke,' he agreed. He sipped his coffee. 'When the work's done.'

In the holidays he worked in his grandmother's vegetable garden. When he finished his cadetship there was no job so he went home and learnt to be a bricklayer.

I wanted to ask him about race. It's tricky, a white South African asking a black South African about race. The white South African doesn't want to diminish someone's achievements by bringing race into it. He doesn't want to diminish someone's achievements by leaving race out of it. He doesn't want to seem insensitive or oversensitive, to intrude or ignore. He doesn't want to make the moment all about himself.

'And, uh, and race?' I said. Knowledge Bengu looked at me calmly.

'Race,' he said.

'Mm,' I said.

'There weren't many black cadets when I joined,' he said.

'What was that like?'

He has a way of answering the question you asked, not the one you're clumsily implying.

'Well, I didn't know anyone there, black or white. It's like going to a new school – you're an outsider even if everyone is the same race as you.'

'Hard, though,' I said. 'Being the first. I would imagine.'

It's true, he said. At the Technikon, some lecturers were sceptical. The same at sea. Some officers were genuinely hostile – they saw in him the changing face of their country, the passing of their era. Others gave him a hard time just to test how he would handle it. 'Why are you here?' one asked. 'There's no Mandela out at sea.'

Alone, he thought: why *am* I here? There were many more obvious careers, and fortunes were being made far more easily. He watched black peers quit. But he thought of his father, who owned his own business and saw it fail, and tried again, and saw it fail, and kept on trying.

'The racism thing was an obstacle,' he said, 'but a minor obstacle. I don't mean minor compared to other obstacles, I mean *all* obstacles are minor. All obstacles, you can break through them.'

'How do you break through them?'

The better a leader is, the less they can explain it. They're like singers or actors or elite athletes: the more powerful a gift, the harder to reduce it to words. 'I turn reality into motivation,' he said.

I told Knowledge that I don't understand him. I can't grasp his focus and his drive, his ability to bend the world. I'm too pessimistic, I said. Not about the world but about myself. I am too easily discouraged and therefore easily defeated. He thought about that seriously, and said there would still be a place for me on his ship. A ship, he said, needs more than one kind of person.

It was such a kind thing to say, and so hopeful, that for a moment I couldn't speak because there were tears in my eyes.

In July 2012 he qualified as a captain and also became the first black ice pilot. A captain can take a ship most places, but only an ice pilot can take it into the ice.

You can qualify as a captain, then still wait for opportunities. You have to wait to be trusted. In March 2013 he was asked to be an officer on the *Agulhas II* on a voyage to Marion Island under his old captain, Dave Horn. Dave Horn was officially in retirement, but was asked to captain the voyage. Dave Horn took Knowledge aside and said: 'As far as I'm concerned, you're the captain. For this voyage, I am here but I am not here, and after this voyage it will just be you.' He said: 'Knowledge, you are the master now.'

Later that year, Knowledge took the ship to the Antarctic for the first time as master of *SA Agulhas II*. The weather was bad. There were ten-metre swells. The bow dug into the green ocean and the spray came all the way up to the bridge. He felt the ship flex and hunch beneath him, and rattle in the lull between the trough and the crest.

'How did you feel?'

'I felt calm.'

In the zone below the storms, he hit bad ice. It was old, ridged, compacted, multi-year ice. It closed around them. They were stuck for eighteen days.

I tried to imagine what that felt like, the pressure from inside, the pressure from outside, the voices. I asked him, and he just smiled and shrugged. 'The ice was bad that year.'

The ship drifted 80 kilometres before he could break free. How did he break free? He said something about swinging the crane for leverage and de-ballasting the water, but then he laughed. 'You don't tell the ice,' he said. 'The ice tells you.'

That year he was the South African Marine Safety Authority's Seafarer of the Year.

I was excited about the story of his first voyage alone in command to the bottom of the world. When you meet people who have done things you dream about, you try to persuade them of your own meanings, so I told him about something I'd read: how for Heroic Age explorers, Antarctica was a *katabasis*: a journey beyond the limits of experience, a voyage beyond life to the underworld.

In the classic katabasis, the hero has a guide. The Sibyl guides Aeneas through Hades. Virgil shows Dante through the Inferno. Odysseus goes into the underworld and asks the blind seer Tiresias how to get home. In the north, if you were wise, you asked indigenous people for Arctic advice but there were no indigenous people in the south, no guides to the Antarctic. It was unpeopled, a void, a blank page.

I told Knowledge this, and he laughed. He sipped coffee and looked at me and laughed some more. But a little later, talking about something else, he interrupted himself and said: 'When I went to look for *Endurance*, I had Shackleton and Worsley inside me, to show me which way to go.'

In 2017 John Shears and Mensun Bound discussed the expedition with Knowledge. Knowledge was bemused. The Weddell Sea seemed a mighty big place to go looking for something you couldn't even take home. He didn't think they'd find her. Worsley's coordinates for where she sank – 68' 39.30S, and 52' 26.30W – were guesses at best. Worsley hadn't seen the sun for two days before the ship went down so he couldn't take sextant readings. He was on a moving plane of ice below a grey lid of cloud, having to guess the current and the movement under the wind.

Using retro-projections of weather conditions and best guesses, they came up with a search grid of some 130 square nautical miles, but it's not as easy as steering there. Knowledge had to place the ship against an ice floe to let the drift take her where she needed to be, while also making sure she didn't get frozen in. It was navigation on a moving surface, predicting the future from the past and vice versa, wrestling with time.

The 2019 expedition sent a Rover AUV (autonomous underwater vehicle) over the search grids in pre-arranged lines, 70 metres above the sea bed, while the *Agulhas II* forced its way through 114 football pitches of ice to make periodic rendezvous with the Rover. (It could have been worse – it could have been a quarter of a Luxembourg.)

About halfway through, the Rover didn't turn up for a rendezvous. They fought to stay in position over line 7, with the sea ice pushing in, but it never arrived. Perhaps the AUV lost power and sank, or drifted away. Perhaps it self-aborted the mission and returned to the surface. Surfacing triggers satellite location, which is great in open sea but radio waves can't pass through water, so returning to the surface under the ice was like vanishing into a black hole.

They hunted for the Rover but the ice was thick and old and closing in. It was Knowledge's job to say: 'We can't be here any longer. We have to go home.'

Knowledge thought that was the last of *Endurance*, but in 2022 John Shears and Mensun Bound were back. They brought 50 tons of equipment, three winches, augers to drill through ice three metres thick. This time, they brought a new Sabertooth vehicle, manufactured by SAAB: an AUV hybrid that could operate autonomously, like the Rover, but could also be controlled by a fibre-optic tether. They weren't going to lose any more vehicles: a single tether was 25 km long.

There were twelve nationalities on board. They reached Antarctica late in the season and encountered the ice, but this time it was new ice. There had been warm summers in the previous years, so the pack was young and thin. The ice was weird, said Knowledge. It turned to powder as the ship pushed against it. There was hardly any splashing. None of them had ever seen that before.

They budgeted ten days of searching. The search block was 107 square nautical miles, 13.7 miles on its longest side. They searched 50% of the block, but it took longer than expected. They squinted at the sonar feed for hours at a time, judging the reflections from the seabed, looking for shadows upon shadows. They searched 75% of the grid. They were running out of time.

Knowledge was watching the ice. 'You don't worry about the ice in front of you. It's the ice behind you that catches you.' When it came stealing up behind, he would wedge into a floe and blast backwards with the propellers to keep it clear. They would back up and ram, back up and ram.

Towards the end of February the AUV found some-thing. The abyssal plain of the Weddell Sea is flat and there are occasional rocks that were once embedded in glaciers and dropped by melting icebergs, but these weren't rocks.

Knowledge Bengu and ice pilot Freddie Ligthelm both say this was the moment things changed. Before this, it was just another mission, but suddenly they both felt the rising thrill, the astonishing possibility that they might have found what had been lost.

They took a closer look. They switched modes on the Sabertooth to conduct a low-altitude, high-frequency pass, producing high-resolution sonar images. It wasn't a rock, or a shoal. They went back over.

It was debris from *Endurance*.

They went back over.

But it wasn't *Endurance*.

The disappointment was crushing. Knowledge wanted to find her. He felt that Worsley and Shackleton wanted her to be found. But their ten days were up. He discussed it with John and Mensun. He said they could stay a little longer. He would make the call at the end of February. If the ice was worse, they would evacuate.

Tension rose on board. People snapped at each other in half a dozen languages. February ended, but the ice was still okay. March began and they were still there. Five days into March, they had completed 30 dives with the primary vehicle, four hours each, sometimes eight. They were down to the last 13% of the search block. They were down to the final days.

On 5 March on the bridge, ice pilot Freddie Ligthelm noticed the AUV was off-course, investigating another anomaly. Previous anomalies had been flat, but this one stood three to four meters off the seabed.

John Shears and Mensun Bound were walking on the ice floe, but when they arrived back they were called to the bridge. The director of subsea operations, Nico Vincent, held out a cellphone. On the screen was a sonar image, like a pregnancy scan. 'Gentlemen,' he said, 'let me introduce you to the *Endurance*.'

Knowledge made the announcement over the PA system to the crew. He heard the cheers and shrieking through the ship. It was 100 years to the day since Shackleton was buried.

Before they came back to Cape Town, they made a detour to South Georgia, and walked the little curve of the bay and up the gentle slope to Shackleton's grave.

Mfanafuthi Knowledge Bengu stood before Shackleton and said: 'We've found your baby. We are here to present you with your baby.'

23. WHAT IS LARGE

Today there are many women on the ice, and they are researchers and captains and navigators and bosuns and Bosses, but in the Heroic Age, that bungling, bone-headed time that ended with Shackleton's last voyage, there were none.

There's a short story by Ursula K. Le Guin called 'Sur', Spanish for 'South'. It's set in the year before Scott and Amundsen reach the South Pole, and reveals that in fact a small group of women from Peru went there first. They kept it quiet because their husbands wouldn't approve, and also from a distaste for clamour and hullabaloo. One of their party is writing the account in order to place it in a leather trunk of mementoes in an attic, along with her daughter's christening dress and a silver rattle, in case one day it might be of interest to her grandchildren.

The ladies of the *Yelcho* expedition of 1909/10 require no fame, no glory, no reward of priority. They plant no flag, because what's the point in planting flags? They barely even leave their footprints behind. When they find Scott's hut from his earlier expedition, they tut over how messy it is, and reflect that 'housework, the art of the infinite, is no game for amateurs.' One of them thinks the only thing to do with such a tip is to burn it down, but more temperate opinions prevail.

Their trek has physical challenges but a lack of struggle. They are cooperative and loving. They do not build huts but hollow out ice caves in order to shelter within the environment. They discover the Beardmore Glacier and call it the Florence Nightingale. One of them gives birth: the first and I think the only birth on the continent so far.

They are not fixated on the end point. When two of them fall weak at 88 degrees south, a short walk from the Pole, they turn back without a qualm, wishing the others well. One of their friends turns back too. She wants to keep them company, and what fun would it be to reach the Pole without them? 'Achievement is smaller than men think,' writes the narrator. 'What is large is the sky, the earth, the sea, the soul.'

Admittedly they do seem to have good luck with the weather, but it occurs to me that a party of women might well have an easier time of it than men. Men have greater physical strength, but if you're not foolish enough to be man-hauling (and the term here is exact, because who but a very specific type of man thinks that's a good idea?) – if, say, you are on skis or dog sleds – then men would have no advantage at all. Women need to eat less than men, and statistically they are better at surviving extreme cold. Perhaps they are also less likely to be so infatuated with the virtues of suffering, finding it less of a novelty.

It's not that women didn't want to go to the Antarctic in real life. A group of women applied to *Endurance*, telling Frank Wild they had no experience, but would make up for it with application and seriousness. Frank Wild mentioned it to Shackleton, and Shackleton said no.

(Shackleton's criteria for selecting his party were obscure at best. None of his interviews lasted more than five minutes. His interview with Frank Worsley lasted 30 seconds. He had only four questions for Reginald James: How were his teeth? Did he have varicose veins? Was he good-tempered? Could he sing? He hired Leonard Hussey as the meteorologist because he found his face funny, and because he had just returned from the Sudan and it struck Shackleton as amusing to take someone from the desert straight to the South Pole. This weighed more than the fact that Hussey was in fact an anthropologist, and not a meteorologist at all.)

Marie Stopes wanted to join Scott's last expedition. Long before she became more closely identified with women's rights and family planning, Marie was a paleobotanist, and the first woman on the faculty of the University of Manchester. She met Scott at a party after his first voyage, and begged to join the next one. J.M. Barrie did the same thing, but he, being a man, loftily wanted to know what it truly was to feel alive. She wanted to test a scientific theory.

She was interested in Eduard Suess's idea of Gondwanaland – the notion that there was once one great connected southern landmass that gradually pulled tectonically apart into continents – and she thought pale-obotany was the way to prove it.

She had a particular interest in *Glossopteris* – seed ferns from the Permian era, extinct since the Triassic Period, but whose fossils have been found in India, Africa and South America. If there was *Glossopteris* in Antarctica, it would prove finally that there had once been a supercontinent over the equator, and that what is now the farthest-flung south had been part of it. She worked on Scott all evening, begging to be allowed to come along and look for *Glossopteris*.

Scott, of course, said no – he was in some ways an unconventional Edwardian, but not *that* unconventional – but he finally agreed to bring back rocks for her to examine. When the search party found his tent in November 1912, they found the three dead bodies with their diaries and papers and Scott's final 'Message to the Public'. And they found a sled laden down with 16 kilograms of gathered rocks. Even under pressure of scurvy and starvation, all the way back from the Pole, they hauled Marie Stopes' rocks, and the rocks contained the *Glossopteris* she had predicted.

We know now that Antarctica wasn't just part of Gondwanaland, it was the hub to which the spokes of India and Africa, South America and Australia were attached. In the world, and the history of the world, and Antarctica in particular, and the stories we tell about it, everything is connected.

But for the most part the Antarctic story offers women a choice between Emily Shackleton and Kathleen Scott: versions of the wives who waved their husbands goodbye and waited for them to come home.

In Beryl Bainbridge's *The Birthday Boys*, Scott's wife Kathleen is by far the most interesting character: insouciant, irreverent, sexy, a little scandalous. The novel only really springs to life when she is present. Beryl Bainbridge never really liked women, but she liked Kathleen Scott, or perhaps she *was* Kathleen Scott: Kathleen Scott never really liked women either.

Kathleen was an artist, born to a wealthy and conventional family but orphaned aged ten. She studied in Paris under Rodin and won a medal at the Paris salon. She was friendly with Picasso and George Bernard Shaw. She sculpted Florence Nightingale, Edward VIII, Captain Smith of the *Titanic*. She specialised in male busts and occasionally in life-sized naked male forms. She met Scott at a lunch at the home of the sister of Aubrey Beardsley and they were married in 1908. Less than two years later he left for the Pole.

She was a great traveller, sometimes with friends like Isadora Duncan, sometimes solo. She visited the Sahara and Marseilles, Greece and Macedonia and Cuba. In 1913, when Scott was expected to emerge from Antarctica, she decided to meet him in New Zealand. She left Liverpool for New York, then went by train to New Orleans and El Paso, then went camping in Mexico before sailing from California to Tahiti and onwards.

At least one historian has claimed that she might have slept with the Norwegian explorer Fridtjof Nansen while Scott was on the ice. Another asserts she had a red-hot summer of passion with the Australian explorer Douglas Mawson in London in 1916. For a while she was recognised as the foremost female English sculptor before Barbara Hepworth, but in time, to the public imagination, even though she remarried, she became simply Scott's widow.

Kathleen's maiden name – Bruce – is the same as my mother's maiden name, but there's not much family resemblance. My mother reminds me more of Emily Shackleton.

Emily was slightly older than Kathleen Scott, with roots deeper in the Victorian era. Comparatively few of her personal letters survive, and if she kept a journal or a diary, I haven't found it. We know she was slim and lively and had a good singing voice, and that she loved another man when Shackleton met her (he became a banker, and later would be one of the men Shackleton asked for money for the expedition). Emily was raised by her father to like literature and poetry, which may have been an error on his part, because it made her susceptible to the charms of a romancer like Shackleton.

He was employed by the Union-Castle line when they met, and had spent his twenties at sea. His blue-grey eyes sparkled like the sun on the Solent and romance blew off him like spray from the waves. He could recite stanzas and stanzas of verse, memorised in his cabin on stormy nights off Valparaíso and Malabar and Tierra del Fuego. His smile held all the mysteries of the Strait of Malacca.

Their shared favourite poem was 'Prospice' by Robert Browning, which begins like a polar explorer's manifesto:

Fear death? – to feel the fog in my throat,
The mist in my face,
When the snows begin, and the blasts denote

I am nearing the place,
The power of the night, the press of the storm,
The post of the foe;
Where he stands, the Arch Fear in a visible form,
Yet the strong man must go ...

It also includes the line, 'I was ever a fighter, so – one fight more, the best and the last!' They used the word 'Prospice' in their letters as code to each other, an encouragement, a secret bond.

Her father's disapproval may have enhanced Shackleton's glamour. By force of letter and personality, he prevailed over his rival. Emily was 36 and Shackleton 29 when her father died and they married. She was left a small private income. She would need it.

When a memorial cross was raised to Scott, overlooking McMurdo Sound, the explorer Apsley Cherry-Garrard selected the epitaph, and chose the final line from Tennyson's 'Ulysses': 'To strive, to seek, to find, and not to yield.'

It's a wonderful line – although an ironic one, in the context of the poem, and of course you'd have to say that Scott did, ultimately, yield – but it's Shackleton who more clearly embodies Tennyson's Ulysses, or Odysseus, who spent years pining for home, struggling to reach it, finding ways to delay arrival, then no sooner arriving than itching to be off again:

How dull it is to pause, to make an end,
To rust unburnish'd, not to shine in use!

The first letter he wrote to Emily from each ship, at the beginning of each voyage, declared how much he missed her, and that she was the north star guiding him home, and that once returned he would never leave again. But Shackleton's ardour thrived on distance. He was no good at home, or as a husband. Soon she must have seen the pattern: the end of all his exploring was not to arrive where he started and to know the place for the first time, but to arrive home and set straight out again, to London or to Norway or to the South Pole, where he could once again safely long for home. Longing is better than having; it keeps the game going longer.

When *Endurance* set sail, they had three children. Edward was three, Cecily was eight, Raymond was nine. The marriage was under strain. Shackleton was late to join *Endurance* in Buenos Aires because he was mending a quarrel with Emily. She had resumed her friendship with the banker, a fact that irked Shackleton to the point that he wrote to her invoking the sacred bonds and trust of marriage. If Emily was tempted to write back, invoking the sacred bonds and trust of marriage and mentioning his various friendships with Elspeth Beardmore (the wife of one of his first backers), or Rosa Lynd, the American actress, or Elizabeth Dawson-Lambton, or Isabel Donaldson, or Hope Paterson, she appears not to have sent it.

There has been so much written about Shackleton: books and biographies and learned articles and television series. He left letters and diaries and two books of his own. And yet there's no *terra* more *incognita* and impenetrable than the human personality. We don't know him, not really. We tell ourselves we do, especially if we are writing about him, but we do not. When I write about people I've actually known, I'm guessing, at best. I'm describing a mask, or perhaps creating one. That's also true when I write about myself. How much less reachable is Emily Shackleton, née Dorman, who left so little of herself behind.

When I think about Emily, I remember what Francis Spufford wrote: that the masculine heroism of the polar explorers was subtly different to the contemporary heroisms in Tennyson and Walter Scott and Kipling. Antarctic heroism demanded a particular set of virtues – patience, resignation, stoic optimism – more usually associated with the women of the era than the men. The ice forced men to wait, to suffer and be patient, much as the domestic world did for women, and it demanded a cooperative and sensitive attachment, a mutual attentiveness and care, to the men who endure beside you.

The polar explorers' stories are filled with this kind of tenderness: in *The Worst Journey in the World*, Apsley Cherry-Garrard describes how they crawled into each other's sleeping bags and buried their feet and hands inside each other's clothing and armpits to keep each other warm; in *The Home of the Blizzard*, the Australian explorer Douglas Mawson describes how each day he carefully wiped and cleaned Xavier Mertz, who had diarrhoea from eating too much dog liver.

And then there's Shackleton. When they were beset in the ice, Orde-Lees threw out his back while shovelling snow and Shackleton put him up in his own cabin because it was warmer there, and warmth helps sciatica. He brought him mugs of tea. He slept on his own floor so that Orde-Lees could use the bed to recover. Just think of Shackleton waking his men with coffee on the ice, and how peevish Wild was when they took it for granted. Shackleton achieved greatness as an Antarctic leader partly because he paid constant, anxious, *loving* attention to the psychological and emotional needs of his companions. Scott, the naval man, whose leadership consisted of giving orders, did not.

This is one more way of casting the difference between Shackleton and Scott: on the ice, Scott was more of a Victorian husband; Shackleton more of a Victorian wife.

I think often of Emily raising three children by herself, as good as widowed even while her husband was alive, while his financial mismanagement sank her deeper and deeper in peril. When he didn't return from his final expedition, he left her with the equivalent of £1.5 million of debt.

Emily Shackleton understood very well the power of the stories we tell ourselves. In an interview with an American journalist, she said: 'I don't believe in fairy tales. I think fairy tales are to be blamed for half the misery in the world. I never let my children read "and they were married and lived happily ever after".'

After my father's death, my mother did not remarry. She worked long hours teaching at a government primary school and studying for extra qualifications because it would mean a slight increase in salary. She sold our house and moved us to a series of ever less expensive rented houses. She had two children. She had no pension, no savings, no inheritance, no help. I can't imagine how lonely she was, and how afraid. I don't know how she did it, and kept on doing it.

Emily Shackleton never came home to tickertape and her name isn't in the pantheon of heroes but to me she's a hero because I remember waking in the night, hearing a sound from my mother's bedroom. I remember tiptoeing down the corridor in the dark to stand very still outside her door, listening to my mother cry with her face buried in her pillow so that we wouldn't hear.

24. IN THE BOATS

Three boats on a grey sea in the white sea mist, with white ice closing from the white. One boat in front with a man standing tall in the prow. Another following the grey shadow of the leader. The third boat falling behind, the men rowing painfully with their elbows above their shoulders, working the oars over the raised wooden sides.

In front: the *James Caird* with Shackleton in command, seven metres long and two metres wide, a double-sided whaleboat made of Baltic pine planking over a frame of American elm and English oak, laden with eleven men and crates and boxes of food and equipment. On board with Shackleton: Frank Wild, Leonard Hussey, Charlie Green the cook, the cheerful Irish sailor Timothy McCarthy. The scientists Robert Clark and Reg James and James Wordie. The troublemakers Chippy McNish and John Vincent. Shackleton chose the *James Caird* because she was lighter than the other boats so less seaworthy in heavy swells. He chose the scientists for his crew because they were the least physically helpful. He chose McNish and Vincent to keep them under his eye.

The *Dudley Docker* and the *Stancomb Wills* were cutters: heavy square-sterned boats made of solid oak, half a metre shorter than the *James Caird*, half a metre narrower, designed for hunting bottlenose whales. There were three benches on each cutter and a post in the bow for attaching the harpoon rope.

On board the *Dudley Docker*: Captain Frank Worsley in command. Lionel Greenstreet the first officer and a seasick Orde-Lees. Dr Macklin and Alfred Cheetham the bosun. The artist George Marston, the second engineer Alexander Kerr, the two crewmen Tom McLeod and Ernest Holness.

Aboard the *Stancomb Wills*: the navigator Huberht Hudson in command. Second officer Tom Crean, chief engineer Lewis Rickinson, and Dr McIlroy. The three sailors, Walter How, William Bakewell and William Stephenson, and the stowaway Perce Blackborow.

The sledge hanging from the back of the *Dudley Docker* tangled in the ice and had to be cut away. There were clouds of birds over the open water – terns and skuas and petrels – and they rowed with their heads lowered to keep the droppings from their faces.

They were in the Bransfield Strait, a treacherous area connecting the Weddell Sea to the Drake Passage, murderous to small boats. It was prone to cross seas, the most dangerous sailing conditions, when the current runs one way and the wind the other, throwing up violent blocks of sheer water.

They picked through the ice pack, trying to head north-west. Just at the edge they found themselves in a tide rip, a current thrown up from the ocean floor, driving the ice ahead of it, a roaring freeway of ice moving so fast the floes threw up a bow wave. They bent their backs and rowed perpendicular until their hands cracked and bled, but they broke out of the rip and the ice rushed past them like a fleet of warships.

The men were shaking. They wanted to shelter and rest on one of the bergs, but Shackleton refused. Icebergs look stable, and they are, until suddenly they're not. They melt under the surface at different rates, and in a moment the balance can shift and the whole thing can flip and turn turtle. The men wanted to take the risk. Shackleton was not looking for more risk.

They rowed on another ten kilometres and found a long, flat floe, well positioned side-on to the swell. They pulled up the boats and made camp. The men were exhausted and fell instantly asleep but Shackleton lay awake. At 11pm he stepped out of the tent and saw that the floe had swung end-on to the swell. As he watched, the swell ran along the length of the floe and its spine bulged upwards then broke, and a crack ran horizontally across, through their camp, directly beneath one of the tents. He saw the crack pull apart and the tent collapse. He shouted and ran. In the dark water he saw something pale.

The stoker Ernie Holness was asleep when the crack opened beneath him. He dreamt he was falling. He reached out with his arms like a man on a cross and clung to the two sides, trying to hold them together, but they pulled apart and he swung his left arm across beside his right. His sleeping bag fell off and into the water. His legs were in the water, and then his body. He couldn't hold on. He was in the water.

There is a crater on the moon, on the edge of the Sea of Fecundity, named after Joseph-René Bellot, who was standing on sea ice in the Wellington Channel in 1852 when it opened. He fell through without a word and vanished for ever in perfect silence.

Shackleton threw himself to the edge of the ice and reached down and seized Ernie Holness and pulled him from the black sea onto the floe as the two edges clashed together. Shackleton said: Are you all right? Yes, said Holness, wet through and shaking, but I've lost my tobacco.

They marched him around the rest of the night to keep him warm, his clothes freezing and cracking with every step.

You should be grateful you're alive, Wild told him.

'So I am,' grumbled Holness, 'but that doesn't bring my tobacco back.'

The dazed men gathered on one half of the floe but it cracked again. Shackleton sent them jumping one by one across the gap as it widened. He was last across but by the time it was his turn it was too wide, and he was stranded on a tiny floe, drifting away. They threw him a rope and he seized the end and they tried to pull the two pieces together but the ocean was too strong and they had to let the rope drop. They watched him move away and he watched them as he went, drifting into the cold and the dark like a space walker whose tether has snapped. 'For a moment,' he wrote, 'my piece of rocking floe was the loneliest place in the world.'

The men thought he was lost, but Wild ran to one of the boats and shouted and swore until it was launched and they managed to reach him in the darkness. Shackleton stepped back onto the floe with his men as though nothing had happened.

The next morning, he told them the boats were too heavy for the high seas, and they must leave things behind. He didn't know what they would need, but he had to decide what they wouldn't take. Sometimes I tremble to think of the pressure Shackleton was under: the remorseless pressure, unceasing as sea ice, to keep making decisions. At every moment of every day, he had to decide what to do, how to do it, where to go, when to stop.

They left behind ice tools, a sledging harness, some spare wood, some cooking utensils, two pairs of skis, and their only box of dried vegetables – 26 kilograms of Knorr's dehydrated vegetables, enough for 52 servings for all the men. Imagine the nerve it took to say: let's leave some food behind. Imagine doing it in such a way that the men don't see your doubt. They left the vegetables behind and sailed off into the mist.

The *James Caird* might have been less seaworthy, but it was faster than the other two, and sailed more easily into the wind. It had to hold back and wait so they wouldn't be separated. The *Stancomb Wills* kept turning sideways against the running sea, in danger of foundering or being pushed back against the ice.

They made it into the open ocean. They had been dreaming for months of deliverance from the ice, an open horizon, free travel under their own power, but a great many tears are shed over answered prayers. Instantly they were drenched by great gusts of spray that froze in the icy winds; the sea opened up in swells and chop that had them hanging seasick over the side.

The head-on wind was too violent, so they heeled around to head back into the pack and moored to a floe in the shelter of a big, beautiful blue berg, near enough to the edge that they could escape in the morning. Blue ice is hard glacial ice that shouldn't break, but Shackleton was wary and they tried to sleep in the boats, tethered to the berg. The wind and sea smashed the boats against each other, jolting them awake. A pack of orcas circled, assessing them for food. In later years some men still woke from troubled sleep, seeing those white throats against the black water, the glitter of their eyes.

The men had been 36 hours without sleeping, shoulders knotted, backs in spasm, hands torn and bleeding. They had to sleep, so he ordered them back onto the ice.

And yet, in their exhaustion, some *still* made diary entries before sleeping. When you are writing in a notebook in pencil in the extreme cold, you turn your head to exhale so that your breath doesn't create an icy film on the page. Frank Hurley wrote: 'Pray god we will remain entire throughout the night.'

But despite appearances, the floe wasn't safe. It was rotten below the waterline and kept breaking through the night. A gale howled and in the morning they found it had pushed them into the centre of the pack.

They stood astonished at the centre of a chaotic fallen world of ice and bergs, all of it rising and lurching and churning under rollers ten metres high. Nothing was still; all was ice, but nothing was frozen. There were mountains of ice above them, valleys of ice below, Alps and Himalayas tumbling like toy blocks, and they were upon one of those blocks. As the rollers passed below them they were lifted and dropped in a terror of booming and

shouting. If they hadn't yet experienced the awe and terror of the sublime – the beauty of that which can destroy
you – they experienced it now. In juddering pencil Macklin
scribbled down the lines of Tennyson's 'Morte d'Arthur':

> I never saw
> Nor shall see, here or elsewhere, till I die,
> Not though I live three lives of mortal men,
> So great a miracle

Because their floe-berg was bigger than those around it,
it moved more slowly, and other floes and bergs smashed
ceaselessly into its sides. The floe was breaking up under
the collisions, in danger of shearing off horizontally.
Morning and day passed. Night was approaching. Shackleton kept watch for gaps in the ice. The sea was washing
over the floe, threatening to sweep away the boats, freezing in rivulets. All eyes watched Shackleton.

Silently they watched, and silently he stood, hour after
hour, scanning the sea, eyes burning, jaw tense from the
strain. 'I do not think,' he wrote later, 'I had ever before
felt the anxiety that belongs to leadership quite so keenly.'

The berg would not last another night, and nor would
they, but with a little over two hours of daylight left, a
pool of water opened. Shackleton nodded, and said 'Go',
and they launched the boats. The *James Caird* tipped on
her side and nearly capsized. The edge of the floe on which
Shackleton was standing see-sawed and he fell toward
the water but the men beside him caught his jacket. They
were away.

They stared up in befuddlement at the icebergs as
they passed between them. Shackleton describes one with

the head and face of a dinosaur. He said the men's eyes were hungry for patterns and figures – living forms that would give some meaning to the ice: 'People living under civilised conditions may scarcely realise how quickly the mind weaves curious imaginings like firelight fancies.'

They took the measure of the wind and decided to head south-west for King George Island. They tied the boats together and rowed. They strained their eyes into the snow and wind to watch for ice.

That night they tied up to another floe and Green carried his stove onto the ice to make supper but the wind and the sea came up, and Shackleton called him back. Stephenson slipped into the sea, up to his thighs. It was enough: Shackleton decided they were done with ice. They would never be trapped again; they wouldn't again leave the boats unless it be on land. He ordered the metal poles from the tents jettisoned to make more space.

No one slept that night, rolling and jolting at the bottom of their boats, the wind cutting through their jackets, the sleet covering them centimetres deep. The killer whales blew and surfaced around them, flipping over small floes. They worried the white bottoms of the boats looked like ice. They worried an orca might go over a rope connecting them. The fear wasn't that the rope would break but that the whale's weight would pull two boats under. One man in each boat kept watch with an axe, ready to cut the rope.

The next day there was sun and Worsley could finally take a reading. He realised that although they'd been sailing west, an undetectable current had pushed them a full degree and a half of longitude back east, and also back south. It was devastating. When Shackleton pulled alongside, Worsley called him into the *Dudley Docker* and they conferred in low voices.

Shackleton calmly announced they would choose a different destination: Hope Bay, 200 km away on the Antarctic Peninsula. All their effort so far had been wasted, but Shackleton gave no sign of dismay. When the old mark went to ground, he simply switched the goal, and made the game bigger.

They still hadn't slept. Whenever a moment of rest seemed possible, the loose ice would gather around. They would find a leeward shelter behind a berg and tether themselves, but the wind would switch and drive them against the ice.

The moon rose in a clear sky, but again there was no sleep. It was achingly cold. Ice formed on the oars, doubling their weight, trebling their thickness, and two of them were lost. The sea froze with a sound like fat sizzling. Snow crackled as it fell on the ice. They huddled for warmth. The spray froze on the boats and the ice weighed them down in the water. The men's clothes froze stiff, and they tried to sit very still, because any movement brought naked skin in contact with frozen cloth, but they were cold and they shivered and the shivering made it worse and kept them awake.

Some of the men were declining. They had no warm food, no warm drink. They had been five days in the boat, and hadn't slept in at least 48 hours. As their bodies weakened, their minds did too. On the *Dudley Docker*, Huberht Hudson was unresponsive. He had a bad salt water sore on a buttock and his hands were frostbitten and he stared at the sea with unseeing eyes.

The next day the wind changed again, and Shackleton and Worsley again conferred, then announced they would change again, and run for Elephant Island in the South Shetlands, 160 km north-west. Each day the target moved, but at least there was a target.

As they switched to the north-west a jagged piece of ice that couldn't be poled away in time struck the *James Caird* and tore open a hole in the planking. They were lucky it was above the waterline, and that they had left so much weight behind.

A gale came up in the afternoon and lashed the boats, water pooling on the bottom and freezing. The men lay themselves over barrels and crates to prevent the water getting inside and spoiling their food. They picked ice off each other's backs and arms. Hussey somehow lost his mittens and Shackleton offered him his own. Hussey refused. Shackleton had been standing for five days at the stern of the *James Caird*, where everyone could see him and take heart, and he needed any protection he could get. But Shackleton threatened to throw his mittens in the sea if Hussey didn't take them.

They saw an apocalyptic scene: sheets of flat pancake ice, littered with dead fish, killed by the snap icy current. Birds swarmed on the fish, rising like steam and falling like white rain, tearing the flesh and scattering the ice with silver scales.

They broke from the ice into open sea again, blue and emerald water. The men were stunned by the infinity of it, the lack of close horizon. Shackleton thought of the Ancient Mariner and sang aloud:

Alone, alone, all, all alone,
Alone on a wide, wide sea.

They were in a series of swells so huge it was like sailing up a hill a kilometre long, going over the peak and descending to a valley, losing sight of the boats in front or behind. They made sea anchors, three oars lashed together with a piece of sail stretched over them, to work as a brake and hold the bow up into the wind.

Shackleton was afraid of many things now, but he was most afraid of the boats separating. The *Stancomb Wills* needed support because Hudson wasn't a leader any more, and they all needed Worsley's skills as a navigator. And most of all: if the other boats weren't beside him, Shackleton wouldn't be able to take them home.

The men had been eating uncooked dog pemmican and it gave them diarrhoea. They lowered their trousers and hung over the sides. Wild said that half the men were out of their minds, helpless and hopeless, and that Shackleton treated them and cared for them 'like babes in arms, and all mothers will understand what I mean.'

Then the wind came up. In cold seas it's the wind that does the damage. A 35 km/hour wind can drop an ambient temperature of -6°C to a windchill of -25°.

Shackleton doubted they would survive the night.

25. MOM

Last year I went to Devon, where George Bovey came from. Bovey Tracey is on the edge of Dartmoor. 'Bovey' comes from the river that runs through it; 'Tracey' from a lord of the manor, William de Tracy, one of the knights who murdered Thomas à Becket in Canterbury Cathedral.

There's a stone arch called Cromwell's Arch standing halfway up the high street, marking the day Oliver Cromwell and his roundheads marched in and caught the officers of Lord Wentworth's regiment playing cards at an inn. The officers escaped by throwing silver coins over their shoulders as they fled, but they lost the next day at the Battle of Bovey Heath. Neither Cromwell nor his men ever marched through Cromwell's Arch – it's just a piece of old priory – but the people of Bovey know a story when they see it.

I don't know what I wanted from Bovey Tracey. Some sort of clue, I suppose.

'I'm from here, you know,' I said to the barman in The Bell.

He looked at me with eyes that would just as soon murder Thomas à Becket as not.

'Yeh,' he said, 'we all are.'

Although my people rose from the oozing banks of the River Bovey, they soon scattered to surrounding towns. I stayed a month in Buckfastleigh, half a day's walk away, where there are Boveys in the graveyard, Boveys on plaques in the church. Nearby was a war memorial to some heroic Bovey who fought in the Boer War.

Every morning of that December 2021 I walked up the 197 steep stone steps from the damp village in the damp river valley to the ruined Holy Trinity church. In the graveyard a Bovey sarcophagus faces the mausoleum of Richard Cabell, the evillest man in Devon. On the day he died in 1677, fiends and fire-breathing black dogs ran vengeful across the moorlands. He inspired Conan Doyle's novel *The Hound of the Baskervilles*.

The stone steps up to the churchyard are very old, and are grooved with horizontal lines so that you don't slip when it's wet, which it always is. Halfway up there are two steps one after the other where the grooves are vertical. It was once customary to stop on these steps and make a wish. Each day I stopped on the first and made a wish, then on the second and made another. The first wish was about the people close to me. The second wish was about home.

While I was in Devon, wondering what I was looking for, my mother called me. We don't call very often. We are both shy, even with each other. She is shyer than I am. She said she had moved to England. This was surprising.

My mother is 81, and has emphysema and had Covid twice. She has cancer. She has two replaced knees and one replaced hip and is waiting for a cataract operation. She has never lived anywhere except South Africa, and has scarcely left the country, even on holidays. Her father had been English, but she had only ever been to England once before in all her life and hadn't much liked it. She is also, as I've said, very shy, and all of this made the news quite surprising, but my sister and her wife recently moved to England, and they have a little girl who my mother loves very much, and her own mother had recently died and left some money in her will, so my mother did what she needed to do about residency permissions and packed up her house and sold her furniture and ordered a moving company and flew to England during Covid times and waited in a quarantine hotel and now she's a resident of a ground-floor flat in a small retirement block in Tunbridge Wells.

'You didn't tell me you were moving,' I said.

'I didn't want to bother you,' she said. 'I know you're busy.'

I told this to Jo. I had met Jo in an unusual time, under unexpected circumstances, and I was in love with her. She was in love with me too, and we were good together, but it was sad because I didn't think we could be together. I had already broken one good thing in my life. I had obviously broken many things before I broke my marriage, but the marriage was something that I had promised not to break, and when I broke it, that had an effect.

I was older than most people when I married, because I wanted to be old enough to be able to make a promise and keep it. When I married, it was a statement of faith:

that I could make a promise and keep it, come what may. But then I didn't.

And now I was with Jo, and it was something good, but what if I broke it again? I watched for signs that I was tarnishing a good thing, and I found them, and it made me think it was pointless to go on. If this was a game I could only lose, maybe it was kinder to stop playing.

It was sad, because it was good between us, but it would be worse if I stayed. Is there anything sadder than breaking something beautiful? I apologise for saying all this: I know I sound like I'm seventeen years old.

I went to visit. When I arrived it was the jubilee and my mother said she wanted to go to London to see the Queen. I warned her there was a slight possibility we would go to London and not see the Queen, that the Queen might be somewhere we weren't, or that there might be people in the way. She recognised this as a possibility, but she wanted to feel the atmosphere.

I personally did not want to go into London on the Queen's jubilee. I do not like crowds, and I suspected there would be a crowd, but my mother had never before, in all my life, expressed a desire to do something. She doesn't like to be inconvenient.

We emerged from Charing Cross station. The streets were lined with flags, and with people dressed in flags, and wearing flag hats. Many people were English and many were not. We arrived early, so there was still some space in Trafalgar Square as we shuffled through and up the Mall and through some side streets, but the space was closing all the time, people were pushing in like pack ice. No matter where we went, there were people, and they were all going in the opposite direction to us, because they had already been where we were going and had discovered it was no good.

My mother wombled along behind me, staring around, squinting up at bunting. She wanted atmosphere, and this was atmosphere. We made our way back across Trafalgar Square and it had filled up. We were like a pair of goats passing through a python. At one point the crowd took us in the wrong direction, and I think my mother covered many metres without her feet touching the ground. Something happened in the distance and there was a roar and everyone waved their flags.

We realised we were not going to see the Queen. We found a pub in Soho and she had a cider and I had a pint of ale. We looked at the families walking by. It felt nice, the way it might have felt when Elizabeth was crowned and my mother was ten years old, sitting in her dormitory at boarding school, listening on the radio.

I mentioned a friend of mine who has cancer. My mom sipped her cider. Outside a sleeping child was draped over his father's shoulders. She said, your father had cancer.

'No, he didn't,' I said.

'Yes, he did.'

'No, he had a stroke.'

'Before that, though. He had cancer. They gave him six months to live.'

My mom, I thought, is very surprising. I asked her when he had cancer.

'When I was pregnant with you,' she said. 'They weren't sure what would happen first: you would come, or he would go.'

The Red Arrows flew overhead.

When she was three months pregnant with me, and they had been married for two months, my father was diagnosed with terminal cancer. The doctors said he had six months to live.

My father was working as a sales representative and had very little money in the bank. He went home and told my mother. They sat on the floral-patterned furniture that I have seen in photographs, and took stock of the situation. I don't know what he thought, exactly, because he didn't keep any journals or diaries, and he didn't write any letters I've ever seen, and anyway I know now that diaries and journals and letters don't really show you what happens in someone's head. Words aren't good at explaining things like that, and when you do think you understand the words that people use, that's probably a sign that you're wrong.

So I don't know what he felt, but this is what he did: he finished thinking and then he stood up and took his jacket and walked to the next-door neighbours. He knocked on their door and told them that he noticed they didn't have burglar bars on their windows. This was 1971, when not everyone in South Africa had burglar bars. People – white people – felt safe then, like they owned the place.

My dad offered to make them burglar bars, for a reasonable price. I don't know what his sales pitch was, but he could talk. To be a salesman, you must be an optimist. My dad took an order, then went to the next house, and the next house.

He knocked on every door up our side of the street, taking orders for burglar bars. Then he came home and called a friend and asked if he could borrow his welding kit to make burglar bars. His friend asked him if he knew how to make burglar bars, and my dad said, as well as lending him his welding kit, could he also come over and show my dad how to use it?

My mom and I caught the train out of London and from the window of the train we saw the dome of St Paul's. At Tunbridge Wells we walked down from the station. There was a pub called The White Bear on the High Street. I hoped it would have a stuffed polar bear in a corner, but I suppose the days of stuffed polar bears are gone. We sat in the beer garden and I ordered her another cider and a pint for myself.

My dad made burglar bars. He heated and bent iron rods and then cooled them in a bucket of cold water with a hiss. He made diamond patterns and welded them together. He painted them in undercoat and then in white or black paint, according to your preference. He installed them and was paid, and then he went to the other side of the street and started knocking on doors.

My dad gave all the money to my mother so that she would have money when he was dead. He worked in the day selling motor oil, then he came home and welded late into the night.

I asked my mom how he was during this time. Was he sad? Was he angry?

She thought about it. 'No,' she said, 'he was busy.'

Did he say anything about it?

She thought. She said she couldn't remember anything specific from that time, but sometimes when things went wrong, he would shrug and say: 'It's not the end of the world.'

The doctors had told him there was nothing more they could do for him, so he didn't bother to go back to the hospital. He didn't speak about dying, or what would happen next. He didn't mope or stare at the ceiling, wondering why he was so unlucky. His previous mark had gone to ground, so he shaped himself to a new one. He just wanted to stick around and see me. Six months to live; six months before I arrived. It would be tight.

Five months came and my dad was still there. Six months, and my mother gave birth. My dad wasn't at her bedside – it wasn't very common in those days, and I am not trying to persuade anyone that he was some kind of modern man – but he was at the hospital, and when she was released, he drove us home.

He kept making burglar bars and security gates. I was one month old, two months old, three months, four. He wasn't dead yet, my dad. He found more work. He worked in security. Five years later my sister was born. A year after that, he bought his first house and gave my mom her first home.

What happened to the cancer, I asked her, sitting in the garden of The White Bear in Tunbridge Wells.

I don't know, she said. I think it went away.

She looked at the next table. There was a couple with a dog under their table, a sort of sheepdog with matted white hair. Why would you have a dog like that, my mother wondered. They must be so difficult to keep clean. You have to wash them all the time.

It's not my mom's fault that she's shy. When she was five years old, her father left home. He didn't pack a bag or take anything, he just left. It is not for me to pass judgement on a man leaving his home. I have done it, and it hurts. It hurts everyone and if you do it properly, it hurts you as much as anyone, but it hurts the people you leave, and the hurting takes a long time.

When her father left, her mother sent my mother to boarding school. The boarding school was in the same city as her home. My mother, I remind you, was five. She was allowed home four times a year, on school holidays. While my five-year-old mother was at boarding school my grandmother burnt all photos of her father. Then she sold the house.

The first time my mom returned home from school, it was to a different home, with different furniture. Her father had never existed – he was never mentioned again. My mother was the one artefact of the marriage her mother couldn't expunge, but at least she only had to see her during the holidays. My mother, I have said, is very shy. All my life she has been loving and supportive but she is very shy. She doesn't want to bother anyone. She doesn't want to get in the way.

At school she was very good at sport. She played tennis and cricket, and hockey for her province. She studied to be a teacher and became one. She was posted to Durban, and in a boarding house she met one of the other boarders, an unattached man with a moustache and an optimistic attitude. Soon they married and eight months later I was born, and five years later my sister was. I think my mother wanted a home, and I hope she found one with me and my father and my sister. I hope so.

Even after my father died, my grandmother never forgave my mother for marrying him. She never helped with money or with love.

My grandmother died last year, aged 104. I hadn't spoken to her in twenty years, but my mother had.

Ten years ago my mother moved from Durban to Cape Town, to live fifteen minutes away from my grandmother. She went to her house every day to sit with her and listen to her complain and to shop for her. At least now she was allowed into the house. Children become parents to their parents, but I wish that time could somehow be made to run in more than one direction, so that my grandmother could have learnt from my mother how to be a mother, and so my mother could have had a mother when she needed one.

'How did you do it, ma?' I asked her, in the beer garden of The White Bear.

She looked at me with surprise. Do what?

All of it, I said. Keep us going. Look after us. How did you keep doing it?

She looked uncomfortable. I also realise it's a question that can't really adequately be answered.

'I don't know,' she said. She looked at the dog again. 'He's quite sweet though,' she said.

I didn't know how to ask what I wanted to ask. I knew some of the words, but I couldn't think of an order to put them in.

'It must have been hard,' I said. 'All alone.'

She looked uncomfortable again. 'You don't normally ask so many questions,' she said.

'I do,' I said. 'I ask all the time.'

'Yes,' she said, and what she said next made my skin flush hot and made me cold at the core with shame, 'but it's usually about your father.'

26. IN THE BOATS II

It was a bad night. The temperature plummeted. They held each other and hugged each other and pounded on each other's arms and legs and backs, hoping for pain, because when you stop feeling pain you know you're dying.

One thing they couldn't understand: why did they need to urinate so much? They were thirsty and their mouths were dry, yet they had to pee all the time, non-stop, all night.

Not everyone freezes to death at the same temperature. A core temperature of 25°C will usually do it, but the lowest temperature recorded in an adult who survived is 16°. Women are more resilient than men, and children are more resilient than adults: in 1994 a two-year-old girl in western Canada wandered out of her home in a snowstorm and was found the next morning, curled up and hugging her knees, her core temperature less than 14°. She survived.

Cold is more dangerous after exertion. Vigorous activity – like man-hauling, say, or hours of rowing on the open ocean – can generate ten times more heat than the body at rest. Your core temperature might climb to 38°, even in the extreme cold, and your capillaries will dilate to carry heat from your core and disperse it in the air. That continues when you suddenly stop exercising, before the sensors in the skin get a chance to reverse the process. It might take several minutes for your core to drop to 37°, but then it speeds up.

At 36° your capillaries constrict again and you shiver a little. The temperature control centre in your hypothalamus triggers autonomic responses.

At 35° you shiver heavily. You're at mild hypothermia, and hovering on the threshold of normalcy – below this, the cascade of responses becomes faster. With every 1.5° drop in body temperature now, the metabolic rate in your brain drops about 5%. Your thinking becomes slower, more fuzzy. You're distracted by things you can't quite remember. There was something you needed to do, but whatever it was, it doesn't feel so urgent.

Under 34°, you've forgotten what urgency is. Time is something elsewhere. Heat is going and time is standing still.

Drop another degree down, and you stop caring about any of it.

At 31° you no longer know you're in trouble. You've stopped shivering. Your blood has thickened. Your metabolic rate has dropped 25%. You're only aware of one thing: you need to urinate.

When the men on the boats stopped rowing, their capillaries were dilated wide. When their bodies suddenly realised they were cold again, their capillaries constricted. There was suddenly more blood than capillary volume to accommodate it, so the excess was forced inwards, and their kidneys were working overtime to process it.

The urination was a danger sign. Half a degree colder, and they might not recognise the face beside them. They might not remember their own names. At 30° the hallucinations start, and the irregular heartbeat. Below that is the deep solitude of space, the vast and roofless universe where there is only starlight and cold.

The men fought to survive. They got angry. They cursed the weather and the night, the spray, the salt, the cold, each other. On the *Dudley Docker* they cursed Orde-Lees, who was not, I regret to say, behaving well.

Orde-Lees was not a good sailor. He was constantly seasick and begging to be excused his turn to row, saying he didn't know how. When he was forced to row his ineptitude was instant, falling out of rhythm, smashing the fingers of Kerr, seated behind him.

On the long cold night, he behaved even worse. There was only one complete pair of oilskins and he commandeered them, curling up at the prow, groaning with seasickness. They kicked at him and threatened him. There was nearly a fight but George Marston swallowed his fury and snatched up the tiller, bellowing work songs at the top of his voice. It seemed to ease the pressure.

It's easy to blame Thomas Orde-Lees. He behaved, without question, poorly. But a community is made up of people who do not always behave well, all the time. In order to survive, or even to thrive, a community need not be made of Shackletons or Marstons or Worsleys or Wilds. Communities do not exist just at a single moment or a single place. If it survives long enough, there's also a place for the Orde-Leeses and Chippy McNishes.

The next morning, Greenstreet's feet were tallow-white with frostbite. The flesh froze and ice crystals formed between his cells, drawing out water and blocking the blood supply. Without saying a word, Orde-Lees began to massage Greenstreet's feet, rubbing the blood back into them, then opening his shirt and placing them against his chest to warm them with his body.

There was no Orde-Lees aboard the *Stancomb Wills*. The boy Perce Blackborow had decided to wear his leather boots, to preserve his finneskos from the sea water. By the time the sun came up, he couldn't feel his feet. They removed his boots and looked away. It was a matter of time before gangrene took hold. Even if he lived, he would never walk again. He was twenty years old.

Shackleton brought the *James Caird* alongside and spoke to Blackborow. Blackborow was his favourite. Shackleton told him he would live. He would still learn to read and write. He would die an old man in his own bed. He told him that soon they would reach Elephant Island, where no human had ever stepped, and he promised Blackborow that he would be the first on Elephant Island. He would go down in history. Blackborow smiled, and nodded, but he couldn't find the words to reply.

They had survived the night but they were still in trouble. They were weak and exhausted and at least two of them had lost their senses. And they were dying of dehydration. There was no fresh water, and no way to melt the ice. Shackleton had them chew strips of raw seal meat and swallow the blood, but the meat was salty and made the thirst even worse.

They spent another night in the open. They knew they must be getting close to Elephant Island, and were terrified of overshooting in the darkness. The *Stancomb Wills* was wallowing and leaderless and Shackleton bound her tight to the *James Caird*. Watches were posted through the night to break off ice to stop the weight taking her under. The *Dudley Docker* lay off to windward, invisible in the night.

Shackleton hadn't slept in days. For twelve hours at a time he held his position, upright and visible. On the *Dudley Docker*, Worsley hadn't slept either. He sat at the tiller, exhausted, keeping her head-on to the wind, but the long trick was telling: his head started to sag, he no longer responded to questions. Finally they persuaded him to let Greenstreet take the tiller, but Worsley's limbs were frozen too stiff to straighten. He toppled sideways and lay curled, asleep before Greenstreet could take the tiller from his hands.

On the *James Caird*, they persuaded Shackleton to rest, but he lay in a delirium, worrying about the *Dudley Docker*, snapping awake to ask where she was. Don't worry, I can see her, Wild murmured. She's right there, don't worry. She's fine. She's right there.

In the hour before dawn, Frank Wild shouted that he could see land. They woke and stared into the grey dark but there was nothing. Their hearts sank: now Wild's mind was going too.

The sun came up through a deep salmon mist that turned golden with the day, and ahead of them was an island. Shackleton blinked and shook his head and it was still there. Two days without readings, two days of guesswork and dead reckoning in the dark and through gales and the Bransfield current, and Worsley had brought them directly to these black specks of rock.

Shackleton grinned at the men. They had aged ten years. They hadn't slept. Their faces were mottled with frostbite, and carved by hunger like scrimshaw. Their bodies were covered in saltwater boils that issued a grey discharge. They grinned back.

Shackleton turned to shout to the other boats, and stopped. The *Stancomb Wills* was still there, lashed alongside, but *Dudley Docker* and Worsley and the other seven men were gone.

On the *Dudley Docker*, that night, Worsley lay comatose while Greenstreet tried to navigate the blank darkness. On the horizon were flashes and blinks that might have been the reflection on the clouds of moonlight off the ice caps of an island. They tried to steer towards it. They had lost the *James Caird* and they felt very alone.

Without Worsley at the tiller it was hard to keep the *Docker* straight. She slewed side-on to the sea and the waves broke over the side. The water was warmer than the air, but it kept coming. It was eight inches deep and the boat was settling and wallowing, and the water was still coming. Worsley was so exhausted he didn't wake, and they had to lift his head to stop him drowning. Orde-Lees took a bucket and bailed. All his idleness had been in preparation for this moment. He bailed and bailed without stopping, hours and hours and hours without end. He saved their lives.

In the morning they saw the island away to port but no sign of the other boats. They were scared and hungry and tired and they had been 48 hours with nothing to drink. They sipped sea water from their hands. Holness tried to untie the knot on their sea anchor but his frozen fingers wouldn't work and the boat bucked and knocked out two of his teeth against the anchor. He wept, and the tears froze in his beard.

They made the lee of the island, and the wind vanished as they came beneath her cliffs. Dominican gulls wheeled down the face of the stone. A slender glacier had calved, and the sea was awash with small fragments and hand-sized blocks, and the men cried in relief as they scooped them up and sucked them for water.

The *Stancomb Wills* and the *James Caird* had circled the island too, looking for a place to land. There was nothing leeward, and as they rounded the head and came into the wind the surf was high and white against sheer cliff. They saw one small inlet but it was too exposed, and breakers raked the opening. They pushed on. Shackleton was trying not to worry about the *Dudley Docker*. Worsley was a good captain. He would find the island.

But the further they went, the more he worried that the island was a false friend. They had nearly circled it, and there was nowhere to land. The charts were no good – there were no charts. No one had ever been close enough to map her. They saw narrow beaches at the heads of glaciers, where ice fell and crushed anything beneath. If there was nowhere to land, they would have to try run against the wind to Clarence Island. He didn't think they would survive that.

Wild had been at the tiller more than 24 hours without a break. And then Shackleton said: There's a beach.

They steered toward the beach. The beach was in a wide bay, partly sheltered from the rollers. They called it Table Bay, because it reminded them of Cape Town.

There was a reef in front, too high and jagged for the *James Caird* to cross it, but the *Stancomb Wills* was shallow in the draw so they unloaded onto her until the *Caird* became light enough to be hauled across the rocky shelf. As she crossed, they heard a shout and looked to see the *Dudley Docker* coming around the headland.

They reached the shallows and Shackleton shouted to hold back. He had promised that Blackborow would be the first man on Elephant Island. He made Blackborow get off, but his frostbitten feet wouldn't hold him and he collapsed on the shingle and Shackleton and Bakewell had to drag him up the beach.

It took them four hours to get everyone ashore, and all the goods. The beach was 30 metres wide, 15 metres deep. They had been in the boats for seven days. It was the first land they'd felt in 497 days.

Rickinson, once on shore, dropped with a heart attack.

27. ELEPHANT ISLAND

They staggered around like drunkards, like dreamers. Some men crumpled, some danced. They pressed their faces into the beach, they let pebbles trickle between their fingers like misers with a hoard of gold.

Shackleton was like a proud father watching his children on Christmas morning. He stood smiling at them, and Wild came ashore and stood beside him.

While the men collected their wits and hunted seals and gathered eggs from birds' nests, breaking them directly into their mouths, Shackleton looked around. The beach ended in a vertical cliff that rose 250 metres straight up to a ledge, and then straight up again. He looked at the base of the cliffs, then looked back at the sea. He didn't say anything.

They made Rickinson comfortable and monitored his heart. They wrapped Blackborow's ruined feet in blankets and canvas. They lit the stove and drank warm milk and ate fresh seal steaks. They ate and ate. Their stomachs had shrunk but they forced down the food like children at a party. Then they climbed into their damp bags and slept with a gratitude so profoundly physical it was almost spiritual. The skies were clear and the moon washed them and they lay upon land that couldn't break or open up or take them away. They woke in the night and stretched out and touched rock and stone and smiled and went back to sleep.

The release from the pressure made them domestic. They cherished small tasks. They dried socks that had been wet for weeks. They gathered limpets from the rocks. They melted ice and washed the salt from their eyes. They washed clothes and hung them on washing lines. They rubbed rusty needles shiny on stones and darned their clothes. They lay back and looked at the sky.

But the next day Shackleton said they couldn't stay.

He had allowed them a night to relax before saying so, but the beach was open to storms from the sea, and there was no escape by land. There was tidewrack at the base of the cliff, and signs of falling boulders. They had been lucky to arrive in good weather, but good weather doesn't last long in the Antarctic. When the ocean swept the beach, they might manage to climb above the high-water mark, but their food would be lost and their boats would be smashed.

He sent Frank Wild with four men in the *Stancomb Wills* to scout for safer harbour.

They were away for nine hours, and night was dropping when they returned. They had been all the way up the coast and found only one place: a partly exposed spit of strand eleven kilometres to the west.

It is crushing to imagine them packing again, girding themselves again, pushing the boats into the sea.

They went back out over the reef and the wind came up and kept coming. It became a hurricane. The *Dudley Docker* was taken as it rounded the outside of a jagged rock and nearly swept away to sea. Greenstreet lost a mitten and his hand was frostbitten. When they finally reached shore, the men killed a seal and cut it open and he put his hand in its guts to defrost.

Their new shelter was a slender peninsula of Elephant Island and they called it Cape Wild. The beach was sheltered from the open seas, but exposed to the wind, and the wind was the worst they'd experienced.

A blizzard trapped them for five days. It whipped away clothing and cooking pots and canvas and boots. It ripped open a tent, and the men from the tent had to sleep in the boats with rags of canvas pulled over their heads. A surge tide rushed up the beach and they made camp again on the highest ground possible. It was a penguin rookery. There is no describing the smell of a penguin rookery. They slept on decades of frozen penguin waste, an evil fermentation of fish and filth and ammonia and rot. Under the heat of their bodies they sank into a foul melting yellow mush of urine and shit.

After all the horror to reach land, they couldn't make sense of this new suffering; their systems shut down. Shackleton mentions using 'drastic means' to get some of the men to work. Wild says some of them had to be driven to work 'none too gently'. Hurley says some of the sailors conducted themselves 'in a manner unworthy of gentlemen and British sailors'.

What happened? We don't know, there's a veil of silence over some aspects of the time on Elephant Island, but we can guess the behaviour wasn't always good.

Some people find this disappointing – it tarnishes the narrative of brave men, bravely enduring – but I find it encouraging. We sometimes fret today that we lack our former mettle and temper, that we have not now that strength that in old times moved heaven and earth. We look around at our allies and our enemies and ourselves, and sigh that we're no longer cut out to do difficult things. But perhaps we are not so different today, after all. What we are, we are, and probably always have been. Even in that more stoic time, even in a Heroic Age, not everyone behaved well all the time. And yet they endured.

On the fifth day of the blizzard Shackleton and Wild agreed they wouldn't last the winter. Shackleton told the men he would sail for help.

There were three choices. South America was closest: 800 kilometres north-west. Port Stanley in the Falklands was a little further: 900 kilometres due north. But the winds and the currents in the Drake Passage run east and the only hope was to have them from behind, and that meant the farthest destination: South Georgia, nearly 1,500 kilometres north-east, a microscopic nib point on the map of the world.

Reaching South Georgia would mean at least two weeks in an open boat in the world's worst seas under leaden skies without navigational sightings, in order to somehow hit a target barely 40 kilometres across.

Shackleton took five men, and the men he chose says much about him.

Of course he had to take Frank Worsley, the best navigator among them, and everyone expected him to take Frank Wild. Wild was his right hand, his best friend, the only man he truly trusted. But Shackleton was leaving

22 men on the island, and Wild was the only one besides Shackleton who could keep them alive.

Instead of Wild, he took Tom Crean. Crean was a tough Irishman. Once someone gave him a cup of cocoa made with curry powder to see how he would react, and he drank it down without noticing. He had been on Scott's last expedition, and the only time anyone saw Crean weep was when he wasn't selected for the final fatal march to the Pole.

Shackleton wanted to leave Crean on the island to help Wild, but Wild knew Shackleton would need Crean, because he was also taking the two troublemakers, John Vincent and Chippy McNish. McNish and Vincent were a danger wherever they were, but Shackleton made sure the danger was always close to him.

Finally, Shackleton chose able seaman Timothy McCarthy. We haven't met McCarthy before because he didn't write a diary, and never caused trouble. But Shackleton liked him immensely: he was cheerful, popular, a good sailor and a good worker. And he was an Irishman from Cork.

They worked through the blizzard to load the *James Caird*. McNish cannibalised wood from the other boats to make decking and to raise the sides even further. They melted ice for two barrels of drinking water, and gathered rocks for ballast. They stretched canvas over the decking and McNish lashed the mast from *Stanford Wills* along the bottom to strengthen the keel and prevent her 'hogging', or buckling in the sea: what Formula 1 drivers call porpoising.

She looked good, but Shackleton worried that the canvas-covered decking was like stage scenery: a mask of solidity that would fold under pressure.

While they waited for the weather, Orde-Lees recorded a 'magnificent golden sunset, a great pale green-yellow disc settling in a mass of golden fire. Later the crescent moon shows up. Venus close to the moon. Many huge bergs appear pale violet and pink, the sea a deep indigo and snow peaks behind are first golden then aglow with alpengluhn.'

There is something beautiful about this, as beautiful as the sunset itself. Why does Orde-Lees record it? He isn't writing a book, or taking notes for a lecture; he merely wants to preserve something beautiful. He is hungry, afraid, his life is in peril, yet he is looking at the world and saying: This is beautiful. There will be other sunsets, sunsets after sunsets unto infinity, world without end, but *this one* matters, because I was here, and I saw it, and I do not want it to be lost.

I want to record Orde-Lees' recording of his sunset, because it is like a hand-print on a cave wall. We give beauty to the world by seeing it and loving it and saying 'this is beautiful'. The world doesn't need us in order to exist, but it needs us in order to be beautiful, just as we need it in order to be purveyors of beauty. Through loving the world, we love ourselves into finer being. Neither of us, neither us nor the world, must be lost.

They were going to launch on Sunday but the sea was too fierce. On Monday 24 April 1916, they were able to go. Shackleton left a letter for Wild, giving instructions and signing off: 'Convey my love to my people and tell them I did my best.'

They struggled to launch in the high surf, and Vincent and McNish fell into the sea. Hurley took pictures of them in the water. Vincent refused to change his wet clothes, leading some to suspect he had stolen items concealed under his clothing. No one was unhappy to see the back of John Vincent.

Finally the *James Caird* was taken out across the reef, and the *Stancomb Wills* brought her ballast and food. On the shingled shore, the men cheered them away and heard distant cheers come back. Wild saw tears in the eyes of the men around him. They watched the oars move the tiny boat on the immense grey water, into the grey haze. They watched them disappear.

28. THE INFINITE GAME

....

A player of an infinite game may lose the resources or the will to keep playing and drop out. But the game continues.
SIMON SINEK

....

Oliver Goldsmith was an Anglo-Irish writer and a friend of Samuel Johnson, and is probably best known today for his novel *The Vicar of Wakefield*, or his play *She Stoops to Conquer*, or the children's story of Little Goody Two-Shoes. He coined the expression 'a citizen of the world'. Goldsmith was impetuous and improvident but sweet-natured and life-loving and had many friends. He also had a most cavalier attitude to money.

He devised a simple system for debt: large debts were outside of his control and sphere of influence so he ignored them, but when smaller bills arrived he placed them in a hat. Whenever he had a windfall, he would go to the hat, draw some lucky winners and settle them, in the order that they were drawn, until the windfall was depleted. Then the hat went back on the shelf. Whenever a creditor came complaining about late payment, he would sit them down and show them the hat and explain the elegance and scrupulous fairness of the system. 'But any more complaints from you, sir,' he would conclude sternly, 'and you are out of the game!'

The philosopher James A. Carse doesn't make a distinction between optimists and pessimists, but between two different kinds of games. He says that there are finite games and there are infinite games, and in every human endeavour, we are playing one or the other.

Sports and board games are obviously finite games – they have rules and boundaries and a set arena, and their goal is to find a winner and a loser. You play a finite game in order to win it, and when it's won or lost, it's over, and you can start another. But a game does not need to be finite or infinite in its essence – it depends on how it's played. We can convert a finite game into an infinite one, and vice versa, depending on how we play.

An infinite game is not played to be won or lost. The goal of an infinite game is that the game never ends. If an infinite game is in danger of being won, the rules must change to expand it or bring in more players, or to do whatever it takes to make sure there is no winner.

Carse says the rules of a finite game are like the rules of debate: this is the order of speech, this is how long you must speak, these are the criteria by which you will win or lose. The rules of an infinite game are like the grammar of a living language: they evolve to keep allowing people to communicate, to make and exchange meaning. Finite players play within boundaries; infinite players play with boundaries.

I think the tragedy of Scott is that he was a finite player playing a finite game. His goal was to be first to the Pole. Losing the Pole meant losing the game, and losing is very dangerous on the polar plateau.

Shackleton was playing a series of finite games – he also wanted to be first to the South Pole – but he was an infinite player. He turned back from the Pole in a way that was unthinkable to a person for whom the Pole was the point. The point for Shackleton was to keep playing.

I spent much of my life thinking my father had lost some kind of game of life. To me he was a man stranded by fate, by illness, by time running out. I saw him as someone who hadn't been to the places he wanted to go, hadn't done the things he wanted to do, who was curtailed by circumstance and bad luck. That's not how he saw himself.

'A man must shape himself to a new mark the moment the old one goes to ground,' said Shackleton on the ice, and that's what happened when my dad received that diagnosis.

But as I sat there in The White Bear, I realised my mother was right: she's been there all along, in front of me, showing the same endurance, but I prefer to look past her. I fixate on my dad because he's safely lost. He's in the past and can't come back, and it's easier to be sad about what's gone than to be open to what's here.

In a finite game, the past is safe, because it has a meaning and the meaning doesn't change. But in an infinite game, we are surprised all the time, by the present and therefore by the past. Infinite players, says James Carse, do not regard the past as having a permanently established outcome, or being over and fixed in meaning. Infinite players are playful, as opposed to serious.

Being playful doesn't mean being frivolous – it means being open to surprise. To be serious is to live in dread of surprise – it is to push for a specified conclusion, to write your own strategic script and to do whatever you can to see it realised, in just the way you planned it. Surprise disrupts that script. If you are committed to seriousness, then a surprise in the present casts doubts on your understanding of the past – what you thought was true has not led to the expected present. Serious players of finite games are tempted, under such circumstances, to ignore the parts of the present that don't align with the meaning they have given the past. But playfulness is to consider that the present has meaning and consequences of its own, and can be surprising.

Infinite play is a triumph of the future over the past, since infinite players do not consider the past to be finished. By being available to possibility, to surprise, they are saying they have no way of knowing what was begun in the past: I thought it was *that*, but it turns out it was *this*, and may yet change again. Playfulness is to allow possibility.

With each surprise the past reveals in itself a new beginning. In as much as the future is always surprising, the past is always changing.

In 2015 the Paris Agreement gave the world a target: to keep the level of global warming to less than 2°C – preferably 1.5° – above pre-industrial levels. It's good to have targets. Without targets, it's hard to know where you're going. When you set out on the ice you want to know if you're heading for Joinville Island or Deception, for Elephant Island or Paulet.

In April 2022 the United Nations Intergovernmental Panel on Climate Change issued its third report in six months, saying it was unlikely that the world would make its 1.5° target. If we are playing a finite game, the set goal being 1.5°, we may be said to have lost. But if we are playing an infinite game, the goal being to survive and keep playing, keep playing forever, forever together, world without end, then we are only just beginning.

Life is expansion and multiplication, a dazzling scatter of light, an infinity of brightness and surprise, and although much is lost along the way, not merely does more abide, more is added: delight is added, insight and wisdom are added, beauty and bravery are added. I suppose what I am trying to say, and sometimes struggle in my day-to-day life to remember, is that the world is a trembling threshold of possibility, of conjunctions and contradictions, of opposite things that can be true at the same time. We are doomed and we are not. We can go home and we can't. The past is over and the past is still changing. Lost things are lost, and lost things come back.

My father played an infinite game and he played it as long as he could, and he wanted the game to go on after he died. He would be very sad to think it had ended now. It hasn't. I know he was on Shackleton's expedition.

29. TO SOUTH GEORGIA

Even the slightest collision with the smallest shard of sea ice could stave them, so they had to get north as soon as possible, out of the ice zone, then turn east for South Georgia. They had one compass and it was erratic, so when night fell they steered by the stars.

While the others slept, Shackleton and Worsley smoked and spoke. Worsley tried to roll the cigarettes but his fingers were frozen and Shackleton took over. Worsley had never known him so unguarded. It was the first time – the last time – he glimpsed the face beneath the mask.

They looked at the Southern Cross hanging overhead and Shackleton wondered about their chances. He worried about the men left behind. Worsley tried to convince Shackleton of his faith in him, but Shackleton was tired. There was a lull in their conversation, then Shackleton said: 'Do you know, I know absolutely nothing about boat sailing?'

Worsley laughed, and after a while Shackleton laughed with him.

They cleared the ice pack, and the wind picked up. They were entering the Drake Passage, a salt-slashed highway through an almost permanent low-pressure zone, with gale-force winds driving non-stop around the world with no landmass to break their charge, pushing the ocean clockwise beneath them, producing waves, 'greybeards', of terrible majesty, 30 metres high, traveling 60 kilometres per hour. A greybeard might be three kilometres long from crest to crest. The *James Caird* would climb a wave in a gale then drop into a trough so deep her sails hung limp as dry laundry in the horse latitudes. Charles Darwin saw greybeards from the *Beagle* in a storm off Tierra del Fuego and wrote in a letter home that he dreamt for a week about shipwreck and drowning and the end of the world.

Green water broke over them without cease. The navigational books and logarithm books and star almanacs were soaked, the pages swelled, turned to pulp. They had to pump continuously almost from the start. The pump was light and the bottom of the boat was curved, so while one man pumped another held it steady with his bare hands. You couldn't do it for longer than five minutes at a time.

At night, if you weren't on duty you slept at the head of the boat, under the decking, on the ballast rocks. The rocks were jagged and dug into your flesh and bruised your bones. It was claustrophobic – there wasn't enough space between the rocks and the decking to roll over from your back to your stomach, or your stomach to your back. When the boat pitched you were thrown up against the decking, down against the rocks. The boat pitched all the time. It bucked, it jerked, it never stopped.

Here's something I think about: Crean was the cook and had to work the primus stove. Their food was a dehydrated meat protein that had to be hydrated in melted ice water. To light the primus he had to sit bent double under the decking, out of the wind. But the nozzle of the primus was easily choked by dirt and soot, and must be cleaned by inserting a thin metal pricker – like the pin of a brooch – into the tiny hole. Obviously they had lived through worse, and there was worse still yet to come, but when I think about the challenges of the human condition, I often imagine sitting bent double and seasick in the dark on a wild sea, in a wooden boat moving three directions at once, threading a needle while your friends wait, knowing if you can't get it threaded, no one can eat.

After three days they were still heading north, but it started to rain, steady and cold, and the wind reversed to become an icy headwind.

After four days their legs were swollen and white from the constant wet, aching from lack of use. The chafing was even worse. Beneath a Burberry gabardine overall, they wore wool: woollen trousers and underwear and socks, thick woollen sweaters, knitted woollen helmets tucked in at the neck. The wool soaked up water and rubbed against the skin. The skin came away and sores opened underneath.

Shackleton's sciatica came back. Even more than it requires warmth, sciatica requires you to lie prone on your back and relax your muscles and be very still. I have had sciatica. I have had sciatica lying in a carpeted house that did not move. I cannot imagine having sciatica in a small boat in the Drake Passage.

After five days the sun appeared. It was visible for less than a minute, but long enough for Worsley to snatch a reading with his sextant. They had covered 380 kilometres, a third of the way.

They passed the flotsam of a wrecked ship. It was the first human trace they had seen in more than a year. What do you think when you see such a thing? My Uncle Jim, who lived to 102, read the obituaries every day. He said it was sad to see people die, especially people he knew. Then he added: 'But it's also motivation.'

When it became colder, the spray froze on the canvas over the decking, making a waterproof carapace of ice. It was the first time in days they weren't getting drenched. Shackleton lashed the helm and they slept for five hours, the most in a week. When they woke the boat was caked in ice a foot deep and had settled four inches lower into the sea. Without McNish's raised sides, they would have foundered and sunk. They hacked off the ice with axes and knives.

There were unexpected tortures. The constant wet made the hairs moult from their reindeer hide sleeping bags. The fine, stiff, heavy hairs went everywhere. They covered their bodies and the boat, the drinking water, the food. They clogged the pump and the nozzle of the primus. The men woke under the decking, choking. In a spoonful of food, thought Worsley, there was an equal amount of food and hair.

To take Shackleton's mind off his back pain, Worsley told him the joke about the Irishman whose friend found his wife in bed with sciatica. 'Well?' demanded Pat. 'Did you kill the Oitalian divvil?'

Worsley claimed this made Shackleton laugh. Shackleton didn't record the joke in his book, but you can almost hear him chuckle as he remembers the occasion Worsley picked up a hot cooker with frostbitten hands, yelped with pain, juggled and dropped it, tried to pick it up again, yelping again. There's nothing, Shackleton writes, to make a man laugh so much and so heartily as misfortune to a friend.

They had been using a sea anchor to give the boat stability, but ice formed on the rope and frayed it, and the rope broke, leaving them rolling and bobbing worse than ever. McNish and Vincent were in decline. Vincent was the youngest and physically the strongest, but he was a passenger, helpless. He could scarcely brace himself against the movement of the boat, flopping and lolling like a poorly-stuffed mannequin. The others fed him and forced water on him and kept him alive. Whenever Shackleton became concerned at one of their conditions, he ordered hot milk to be served to all, pretending he needed it himself.

At noon on the last day of April a wandering albatross appeared overhead. They decided it was a she. They envied her stillness, the way she hung above the violence of the sea. She stayed for hours and Worsley estimated she could fly to South Georgia in half a day. She was gorgeous, but Shackleton thought she was too stately, too aloof. He preferred the friendly Cape petrels. His idea of beauty was messy and warm, not carved in marble. They considered shooting her for food, but they had enough to eat.

McCarthy made up for Vincent and McNish. He was energetic, irrepressible, always ready with a joke. On the morning of the tenth day, Shackleton emerged from the decking. The mist-rain swirled, and a wave slapped the side and drenched McCarthy where he sat in the stern. Shackleton opened his mouth to commiserate but McCarthy beamed and said, 'Good morning, sir! It's a grand day!' With such companions, mused Shackleton, all things are bearable.

They were halfway to South Georgia when the sea eased and the sun came out. In the sudden brightness they were startled at each other's appearance. Their faces were black with blubber soot, their bodies pruned and white. They had lost patches of flesh to frostbite and their knees scraped bloody by the rocks, but the sun felt kind on their flesh and if only you could sit very still, wrote Worsley, and not come in contact with parts of your clothing that were still frozen, 'life was worth living.'

Worsley's spirits, never low, rose even further. He fondly recorded snippets of the ongoing colloquy between Crean and Shackleton, that ebbed and flowed in affectionate grumbles like an old married couple.

'Go to sleep, Crean, and don't be clucking like an old hen.'

'Boss, I can't eat these reindeer hairs any more. I'll have an inside on me like a billygoat's neck.'

Some time after midnight on 5 May, Shackleton was on night watch and felt something wrong. He looked to port, then starboard, then to stern, and saw something inexplicable: a streak of lightness in the sky, like the opening of the heavens for judgment. But it wasn't the heavens, it was the crest of a gigantic wave. It was the biggest wave Shackleton had seen in 26 years at sea. He shouted to the men to get out from the decking. He tried to run with the wave but it caught them and drove them before it and lifted them and the peak of it toppled and poured down over them as it passed onwards and left them knee-deep and staggering in its wake. It was inexplicable to Shackleton, a prodigy, one of God's mysterious works in the deep.

With daylight, Shackleton noticed his own patience running out. It was enough now. Enough waiting, enough striving, enough enduring. He felt himself grow angry; he felt the fight in his muscles. Finally he lost his temper with a little bob-tailed bird that was darting about the boat. He stood roaring and shaking his fist at it, like Captain Haddock in a Tintin comic, until he came to himself and sat, shamefaced.

But still the sea was wide and the horizon was empty. To take an accurate reading you measure the distance from the perimeter of the sun to the horizon, but the sun was a dissolving lozenge in the haze with no centre or boundaries. He guessed at the centre and the perimeter, took reading after reading in the hope they would average out.

He thought they were close to their destination. He optimistically gave himself a margin of error of 15 kilometres. They had to hit South Georgia on the first approach, because if they missed, the winds would be too strong for them to turn and beat their way back. The next land was Cape Town, 5,000 kilometres away.

They had finished their first barrel of water and opened the second to discover it had been fouled by seawater and reindeer hairs. They were down to half a cup of brackish water a day, strained through cloth, and the salt from the brack drove them half mad with thirst. The fog came down again, and they were half afraid of missing the island, half afraid of smashing straight into it.

The first sign they saw was a strand of floating kelp. Then they saw a cormorant. You can use birds as yardsticks to measure distance from land: frigatebirds might roam 120 kilometres out to sea, terns seldom more than 35. In the Pacific this skill has a name – *etakidimaan* – and no islander is a navigator without mastering it. Noah's dove and his raven were both tools of *etakidimaan*. Worsley had mastered it too. He knew cormorants seldom venture more than 25 kilometres from land.

Around noon the fog parted and McCarthy gave a cry. Just for a moment through the fog, dead ahead, they saw a face of sullen black rock, crowned with snow. They had been sailing for nearly 20 days, using best guesses and hope, and Worsley had brought them directly to that place like a pigeon flying home. Then the mist closed up again.

Shackleton was the only one who spoke.

'We've done it,' he said.

But they hadn't done it yet.

On his second voyage in 1775 Captain Cook named South Georgia after George III, the mad king, but without much enthusiasm, calling it 'a land doomed by nature, whose horrible and savage aspect I have not words to describe.' He claimed it and kept going: nothing he saw tempted him to stop. But Cook only saw South Georgia from the north. It was horrible in the north, but far worse in the south.

The men made for a kind of natural harbour, but they realised they were being driven in by blind rollers that didn't pass under the boat but seized it and carried it with them. Ahead was the sound of water crashing against rocks. They could reach land in less than an hour, but they would be pulverised if they did. They had to stand off and wait another terrible night.

The last of their water, the bottom of the salty barrel. With the darkness another gale picked up. The gale drove them towards the rocks so they were forced to turn and run to sea. It blew all night, and all the next morning. When it dropped they were wrapped in fog and couldn't see the sun, couldn't see the island.

As the day wore on, they heard a sound growing louder, a deep booming bass, and realised it was the waves on the rocks. The waves rose around them and the wind strengthened. The fog parted and showed them the island. They had been driven back again, closer than before, at the point where the long rollers of the open sea shorten and gather speed to become the combers that rush on to become the breakers that would shatter them on the land.

They turned and tried to beat into the wind but made no headway. The wind became a hurricane. The sea under such winds turns white as milk. The waves are white, white spray is driven from their peaks, the walls and troughs are white. They tacked and bailed out water for hours but they were going nowhere. The wind and sea were driving them against the barren broken jawbone of Annenkov Island, ten kilometres off shore. Worsley believed it was all over. He thought about the diary he'd been keeping ever since the ice, wrapped in oilcloth inside his sleeping bag, and thought savagely that it would be lost, and no one would ever know how close they'd come. What a waste it was.

Later they couldn't explain how they missed the island. Perhaps the wind veered to the south-west. Perhaps they caught the edge of a side current, or some hidden eddy from the rebound of waves from an unseen reef, but at the last moment they jagged sideways and passed so close they had to lean back and crane their necks to see the upper peaks. As they cleared the island the wind dropped, as though defeated.

Later they learnt that in the hurricane they just survived, a 500-ton steamer foundered and was lost with all hands.

It wasn't yet over. They turned and went back and around Cape Demidov and toward King Haakon Bay in the east, but the wind reversed yet again and blew them back out. They tacked in, again and again, four times they came back but they couldn't get in. They were exhausted, they were mad with desperation. They couldn't face another night at sea. Worsley turned down the coast, doubled back and tried to slip in behind the wind, but before they could reach the bay, they spotted a cove.

The cove was protected by a reef like a jaw of blackened teeth. They saw a gap, too narrow to sail. They rowed in, scraping sides against rock. They made the shore and Shackleton jumped out and held the bow to prevent her being pulled back. At the last, nearly tragedy: his foot with its worn finnesko slipped on a wet boulder and he fell toward the boiling sea, but a sharp rock caught his jacket and held him up.

Shackleton turned to Worsley, and then to Crean and McCarthy, and then to Vincent and McNish.

He shook each of their hands in turn.

It was 5pm on 10 May 1916. They had been in the *James Caird* for seventeen days. They were back on the island they had left 522 days earlier.

But it still wasn't over.

30. AN EXTREMELY BRIEF DIGRESSION ABOUT A MIDGE

Life is incalculable.

The voyage of the *Belgica* resulted in one scientific discovery: the only animal that lives full-time on land in the Antarctic.

Belgica antarctica is found only at the tip of the Antarctic Peninsula. It's a black flightless midge, usually 3mm long, although some giants reach 6mm. The winds are so brutal where it lives that evolution took away its wings to save it from the world. It lives up to two years in larval form, buried in the dirt, and then only a few summers' days in its adult state when the temperature is just perfectly right, between 0°C and -10°.

Belgica antarctica can't live anywhere else. It can't survive temperatures warmer than freezing, or lower than -15°. It exists purely to exist in the Antarctic, and because if it didn't exist there, nothing would.

On the ice, enjoying a supper of dog pemmican and seal hoosh and penguin toe, Shackleton mused that in order to survive, the yaks of the Himalayas can eat only a certain kind of grass, at a certain kind of altitude, but humans can get used to anything, anywhere, faster than we think.

Humans can do anything, so long as we can tell ourselves a story about it.

31. THE HERO WITH A
THOUSAND FACES

We have a sense of when a story should be over, when the hero's journey is complete and they have learnt what they need to learn, when they have met themselves and known themselves and conquered the shadow. But sometimes life exceeds storytelling.

While the men were shaking hands on the shingled shore, the surf pounded the *James Caird*. It tore off and carried away her rudder. They unloaded the boat but were too weak to pull her up onto the beach, so they tied her to a rock. They had to sleep, but they couldn't risk losing the boat, so they kept watch in one-hour shifts.

Tom Crean was on watch at 2am when a high sea came up and snapped the mooring. He shouted and ran to the boat and tried to hold her but the sea pulled her, and pulled him with it. He was up to his knees in the sea, up to his waist, and still shouting. Finally Shackleton woke. With all hands holding on they could stop her going out, but they weren't strong enough to pull her in.

They removed her decking and broke down her sides to make her lighter, and waited for what Shackleton called 'Byron's great ninth wave'. In the lore of the sea, the ninth wave of a set is the strongest, the one that will drown you. Shackleton's stock of poetry was deep, but I've found no mention of the ninth wave in Byron. Perhaps he was thinking of 'Milton', by Longfellow:

> And the ninth wave, slow gathering fold by fold
> All its loose-flowing garments into one,
> Plunges upon the shore ...

Or perhaps more likely 'The Coming of Arthur', in Tennyson's *Idylls of the King*:

> Wave after wave, each mightier than the last,
> Till last, a ninth one, gathering half the deep
> And full of voices, slowly rose and plunged
> Roaring, and all the wave was in a flame.

The ninth wave is the one to fear, but Shackleton's ninth wave is more like the one in the painting by the Russian Romantic, Ivan Aivazosky: a group of shipwrecked survivors cling to the shattered cross-tree of a mast. They have barely survived the savage night, and the ninth wave builds over them, but through the green glass of its crest is the golden light of sunrise, and resurrection, and hope.

The stories we tell ourselves, true or not, are always real. We make meaning from the stories, and they determine which lives we live. The ninth wave broke and pushed the boat on the shore, and the men lay at the fire and slept.

They slept for twelve hours. Shackleton dreamt they were on the sea again, under the great wave that reached to the sky, and he woke screaming to warn them. Worsley's sleeping bag was too close to the flames and caught fire, but the burning in his feet just felt like frost-bite and he rolled over and went back to sleep. The movement smothered the flames.

In the morning they found an albatross nest on a cliff. They killed the bird and its chicks and ate them. Shackleton wrote that the bones of the chicks, not fully formed, melted in their mouths. 'Each time we ate one, we felt a little less remorseful.' He hatched a scheme with Worsley to introduce albatross chicks to the gourmets of Europe. How much should they charge for so fine a treat? They settled on £50 apiece.

They gathered their strength but the journey wasn't over. They needed to reach the whaling stations in Stromness Bay on the north-east coast, on the other side of the island. They couldn't sail there – the rudder was gone, and without her decking and planking she wouldn't make it. The charts of South Georgia only included the outline, and not even all of that. The interior was unknown. Beyond the coast was a shark-toothed range of sheer black mountains, capped with ice and snow, rising from a foggy chaos of valleys and broken moraine. No one had entered the interior or even tried.

Shackleton told them he would cross the island and fetch help.

But there was no way into the interior off the beach: the cliffs were again too sheer. That day, picking through flotsam and tidewrack, Worsley stared at something on the beach, wedged between two boulders. It was difficult to believe. He walked back into camp carrying the rudder from the *James Caird*. The southern ocean had taken it away, and then it had brought it back.

Hugging the shore with the jury-rigged rudder they made the head of the bay and found a friendly gravelled beach, backed with a steep cliff that was just about climbable.

They pulled up the boat for the last time, and turned it over to make a shelter. They called it Peggotty Camp, after the poor but honest family in *David Copperfield* who make their home in a converted boat at Yarmouth. Shackleton said he would go with Worsley and Crean.

Vincent lay beside the fire in a stupor, but McCarthy helped them prepare, and McNish took screws from the boat and fixed them through the soles of their boots as cleats to grip the ice. They packed a small pot and three days' food, a tiny primus, fifteen metres of rope, a half-box of matches and the carpenter's small hand adze – similar to an axe, but with a curved blade at a right angle to the handle. They took no sleeping bags: they wouldn't have time to sleep. If they were caught by weather at altitude, they would die. They needed speed and luck. Worsley brought his diary.

At 3am on 19 May, the sky finally cleared and there was a full moon. McNish walked them to the foot of the cliff. They passed a sea graveyard, where the tides washed up the flotsam of wrecks. There were carved teak prows, fragments of figureheads, broken oars, splinters of decks. Each wreck once held men like them, the heroes of stories that would never be told.

As they climbed the cliff a light fog came over, lit from behind by the moon. Nothing seemed real. Their fingers cramped as they climbed. Their boots slipped and the screws grated against stone.

At the top they stopped to look down at the beach and the wide sea. They shook each other's hands. They started the walk.

The first thing they did was go wrong. They were on an uneven ridge but they saw a lake shimmering in a valley below them so they went down to the lake to walk north along its level shore, but at the bottom of the valley they realised it wasn't a lake, it was the sea. They had come down into the next bay on the coast. They had to climb back up again. It took two hours.

They followed the central plateau north but the way ahead was blocked by a barrier line of mountains, a row of peaks like the knuckles of a clenched fist. There were three possible passes through, between the knuckles, and no way of deciding between them. They chose the ice slope on the left.

It took hours to climb, Shackleton leading, cutting steps with the adze. It grew colder and they gasped for air in the altitude. At the top they peered over the edge. There was no way down the other side. They went agonisingly back down and tracked across to climb again to the next pass, up a second ice slope steeper than the first. Again they peered over the edge. Again there was no way down.

They were Sisyphus, three ragged Sisyphi, rolling their fate up a ghastly hill with no slope on the other side. They went back down and looked to the last pass between the last peaks. There was no reason to believe the universe was so ordered or so lucky that there would be a way across. They started up again.

The third slope was the steepest, and took longest. They had left Peggotty Camp at 3am, and had been climbing all day and now it was growing dark. It was too cold to spend the night up there. A cold mist rose. Their heads ached with altitude.

They reached the final gap, and an ice ridge so narrow that Shackleton sat with one leg on either side of it. It was steep on the other side, but not as steep as the others. Behind them the mist turned to fog, and climbed the slope towards them. They swung their legs over the edge.

Shackleton took the lead again, hacking steps and slots into the hard blue ice. The adze was becoming blunt, his arms were getting weak, the ice was hard as marble. It was agonisingly slow. Night was falling. Finally, he carved out a platform wide enough to stand side by side, and they climbed down to join him.

They saw that below the platform the ice slope became almost sheer. They couldn't carve steps to get down. Up on the ridge the fog had reached the top and it came over and dropped to find them. They couldn't go back.

Shackleton said: We'll slide.

You would laugh at it in a movie. They couldn't see below if there were rocks, or crevasses, or if the slope would end and drop them into space. Indiana Jones might throw himself down an ice slope into misty nothing, but no one in real life, and certainly not Old Cautious, who had spent the last year eliminating every unnecessary risk.

Shackleton said: If we slide, we might die. If we do nothing, we will.

They coiled up the rope to make mats. Shackleton went in front. Worsley locked his legs around Shackleton's waist and his arms around Shackleton's neck, and Crean did the same to Worsley, three tobogganers without a toboggan.

The drop squeezed the air from their lungs. Someone screamed. They dropped and perhaps they wouldn't ever stop dropping. The slope eased. It levelled off. Instead of a rock, they hit a snowbank. They lay there, and gasped, and laughed. They couldn't stop laughing. They had come down 300 metres in a minute. They looked up and as they looked, their ledge disappeared in the fog.

They walked on over the glacier. It was night, and they watched their feet, fearful of crevasses, but the moon rose and its glow etched shadows on the snowfield, throwing every contour into relief. They saw the crevasses and steered around them. Then they looked ahead and there were mountains.

Their legs weren't legs any more, their bodies weren't bodies. They were just torn woollen suits, stuffed with sand and wet cement. They trudged up the snowy slope into the mountains.

*

As the *James Caird* pulled away from Elephant Island and vanished in the grey, one of the men said bitterly, 'That's the last we'll see of them.'

Wild nearly knocked him down with a rock. No one was to doubt. The Boss would come back for them.

The wind was a torment, a scour, so they excavated an ice cave in the glacier above the shore, but their body heat melted the ice and swamped them with water. Instead they made a kind of hut of the two remaining boats, upside down and lashed together, the gaps filled with rocks and rags and guano. Some men slept on the floor, others on the narrow shelves made by the benches. Hurley said it held them all 'snugly though sardiniously'.

But it was filthy. The blubber stove coated everything in oil and soot. It was so dingy and so dirty you couldn't see an item on the ground. Frank Wild lost the pipe that Rudyard Kipling had given him, and hunted for weeks but never found it.

To leave the shelter at night you stepped on sleeping bodies and heads, and once you were outside the night was a black maelstrom of flying ice and stones, with a wind strong enough to knock you down, so they kept a large empty can in the hut as a urinal. Whoever brought it within two inches of the top had to empty it, so you would listen to someone using it and judge the water level by the sound. If it sounded too full, you held it in till morning. Sometimes a man of low character would stealthily fill the can and slip back to bed, leaving the next poor schmuck to discover that he must empty it before he could use it.

It wasn't until eight days after the boat had left – the day the *James Caird* reached South Georgia – that the sun came out and the men could partly dry their sleeping bags. But it was a brief reprieve. They were in the last days of summer.

They talked about food. Each night Marston read out a recipe from a penny cookbook, only one per night, to make them last. They craved carbohydrates: jams, breads, porridge, cake, milk, eggs, honey. Wild wanted apple pudding and cream. Reg James wanted syrup pudding. They agreed they would shoot the first man back in civilisation who offered them meat. Harold Nicolson once said: 'No

Edwardian meal was complete without ptarmigan.' No one on Elephant Island craved ptarmigan.

On 10 May Frank Hurley gathered them for a group portrait. In the picture they stare out at the camera, bulky in wool, their faces closed, some of them blank. They were in a bad way. They had styes and ulcers and frostbite. Hudson lay wordless. Blackborow's feet were getting worse.

Hurley described the red clouds of sunrise in the still bay, the violet snowy slopes, the ice of the mountain turning pea green, black rock like japanned lacquer, veneered with gold.

As the weeks stretched, they began to discuss why help was so long coming. They debated every possibility but one. If someone started to suggest that Shackleton hadn't made it, they were shunned as someone unclean, sullying something sacred.

On 25 May, it was a month and a day since the *James Caird* had left. The daylight was short, the clouds were constant. The sea was icing up.

*

They climbed through the night. Worsley wrote that now more than ever they behaved beautifully with each other. 'Never,' he says, 'is etiquette and good form more carefully observed than by experienced travellers who find themselves in a tight place.'

After midnight the ground began to drop and they walked down to the sea. They had been walking for 24 hours. They remembered Stromness Bay from the voyage out, and pointed out familiar landmarks: There, Mutton Island! See, I remember these rocks!

It took an hour to descend, stumbling, weak with relief. At the bottom would be Stromness Bay, then a flat walk to the whaling station, to food and sleep and help. Then they reached a glacier.

They were so tired, they didn't realise at first what was wrong. Then they remembered: there are no glaciers in Stromness Bay. They had come down the wrong slope into an uninhabited bay. The sights they recognised they had not recognised at all. Their minds had made the meaning, formed the patterns of what they longed to see. They walked two hours back up again.

They sat down to rest. Crean and Worsley fell asleep. Shackleton closed his eyes, just for a second, and felt himself sinking, and made himself open them again. This is how you fail at the last. This is how you freeze to death. He watched the others sleep for five minutes, digging a sharp stone into his palm to stay awake, then shook them and said they'd been asleep for half an hour. They stood, and their joints were so stiff that for a while they walked with bent knees.

The night passed and in the grey dawn Shackleton was hacking ice steps on a slope when he heard a sound like a steam whistle. It was 6.30am.

He went down to Crean and Worsley and said what he had heard. He was worried he was hallucinating, but at 6.30am didn't they blow a steam whistle at the whaling station to muster the men? And again at 7am to start the workday? They climbed up and waited for 7am. And there it came again. It was the first sound they had heard from the human world since December 1914.

They went tethered down an ice precipice, Shackleton first, carving steps and handholds. The tether was a fiction – Worsley had the upper end of the rope, but it was fastened to nothing and he had no grip or foothold. Any slip would take them all down. They walked a kilometre down into a valley and a kilometre up the other side. It took six and a half hours. At 1.30pm they made the ridge and looked at the Huvik rocks and the Stromness whaling station, 800 metres below. They turned and looked at each other, like stout Cortez and his men, silent on a peak in Darien.

They shook hands.

'Let's go down,' said Shackleton.

The ridge was like the wet side of a glass bowl. If you slipped, nothing would slow your fall. They could have slid down in a minute, but Shackleton said no. This was a risk they didn't need to take. It took more than an hour to work around the ridge to find a stream of snow melt carving out a narrow ravine. They waded down it.

A little after 3pm the stream ended in a waterfall, with a perpendicular drop of ten metres. They remembered the rope. They tied one end to a boulder and lowered themselves down through the frigid water. First Crean, then Shackleton, then Worsley. They left the rope hanging where it was.

They were less than two kilometres from the whaling station. They had been walking 36 hours without sleep. Suddenly they became self-conscious about their appearance. Worsley found four rusty safety pins he'd been hoarding in his pocket since the ice, and pinned up some tears in his trousers, although Shackleton thought the repairs only accentuated the shabbiness. There was a small settlement around the whaling station, a few mean streets with wooden houses. Two small children looked up from their game and saw three stumbling men coming in from the mountains, bearded and blackened and ragged, bones jutting, hair like horses, eyes showing white. The children ran screaming.

The station foreman Mathias Andersen heard the screams and saw the three men shuffling in. The leader asked for Anton Andersen the manager, but he was no longer there. He had been replaced by Thoralf Sorlle. They were led to Sorlle's house.

All they carried out of the Antarctic was the adze, Worsley's diary, the cooker and their ragged clothes. But Shackleton said they had more besides:

'We had pierced the veneer of outside things. ... We had seen God in His splendours, heard the text that Nature renders. We had reached the naked soul of man.'

Sorlle came to his front door and said: 'Who the hell are you?'

The man on his doorstep said: 'I'm Shackleton.'

Sorlle stared.

Shackleton said: 'When was the war over?'

Sorlle answered: 'The war is not over. The world has gone mad.'

32. THE MEN LEFT BEHIND

*I do not wish to belittle success with the pride
that apes humility.*
ERNEST SHACKLETON

That night a gale came up. It rattled the windows and shook the mountains. If they'd left six hours later, if they'd been six hours slower, they would be dead.

In the morning Worsley went on the whale catcher *Samson* to rescue McCarthy and Vincent and McNish. It had been two days since he left, but he'd had a bath and shave and they didn't recognise him. The gale blew down from the mountains and kept them at sea for two days.

When they were together again, the Norwegian whalers held a reception for them at the station clubhouse. In a small wooden room thick with cigar smoke they listened to Shackleton tell the story. The Norwegians were grizzled ancient mariners of the south, who made their lives in these waters and were indifferent to ordinary danger, but they listened and then came up one by one to look each man in the eye and shake his hand. Of all the honours he ever received, said Sir Ernest Shackleton, none meant more than that night.

Shackleton arranged for the whaler *Southern Sky* to take him to Elephant Island to fetch the men. He had slept that first night, but he would not sleep well again until he brought them home. They left within 72 hours. As they approached Elephant Island, they encountered the ice pack. It was thick ice, up from the Weddell Sea. After two weeks, *Southern Sky* had to turn back.

He tried again, with *Instituto de Pesca No. 1*, a borrowed Uruguayan survey vessel. It ran into pack ice and Shackleton tried to persuade the captain to push on through, but the ice damaged it and they had to retreat.

Shackleton chartered the *Emma*, a wooden schooner. She ran into a storm and then the ice came up. She couldn't come within 200 km of Elephant Island.

The triumphant final act was becoming a nightmare from which Shackleton couldn't wake. Months had passed and his men were still on the island. They were starving and the winter was closing in.

He went to Port Stanley in the Falklands and wrote cables begging the British government to send an ice-vessel. He couldn't understand the lack of urgency. Finally, they replied they would send *Discovery*, the ship that first took Scott south in 1901. It felt like a deliberate insult. Scott's ship was old now, in poor repair. It would take weeks to arrive. The government wanted to humiliate him: Shackleton would be permitted to accompany the rescue mission as a passenger only, under the authority of the captain. They instructed him to wait in Port Stanley for *Discovery*.

Worsley said this was when Shackleton truly aged. His wavy hair turned grey. He took his first drink in three years, a whiskey, and it took him badly. He drank more. He visibly shrank. His muscles lost tone and his body sagged. A light inside him started to dim.

The main street of Port Stanley is two kilometres long. On one end of the street is the slaughterhouse, and the other the graveyard. Shackleton imagined spending months pacing the street from the slaughterhouse to the graveyard.

He turned to the government of Chile, and begged them for help.

*

On 15 June Macklin and McIlroy took the toes off Blackborow's left foot. The foot was rotting and they wanted to do it sooner but the weather had been too cold for the chloroform to vaporise. When the time came they made the hut as clean as they could. Greenstreet lay in his bunk in the upper level and watched. Wild observed. The rest of the men retreated to the ice cave and cut each other's hair.

McIlroy applied the chloroform, then amputated the toes, dropping them one by one in a metal cup. He peeled away the skin from the foot. Greenstreet had to look away. He saw Wild watching perfectly calmly, neither flinching nor blinking. The doctors noticed too. 'Wild is a hard case,' wrote Macklin.

The procedure took 55 minutes and Greenstreet wrote that Blackborow behaved splendidly. 'When he came to, he was as cheerful as anything and started joking directly.'

For his part, Orde-Lees fretted at how much chloroform they used, and how little was left. He gloomily mused that if his own leg should need amputation, it would have to be without anaesthetic. It was a grim prospect, although he did concede that it was an unlikely one, as there was nothing actually wrong with his leg.

Besides food, the men worried about tobacco. In July it ran out. McLeod removed the sennegrass insulation from his boots and smoked that. One man smoked penguin feathers. One broke his wooden pipe into chips and smoked them in the bowl of a second pipe. Bakewell dug for four days to find a coat he had left outside with half a plug of tobacco in the pocket. It was buried under ten metres of snow, so wet it took three days to dry it out beside the fire. No one had helped him dig, but he shared it around.

They surrendered the unwinnable fight against dirt. It was impossible to become dirtier: the new dirt found no purchase on the dirt already there. They were dirt itself, the quintessence of dirt, they were returned to the primordial dirt from which they'd sprung. Hurley worried they were reverting in other ways too. He wrote that he was heart-sick of having to kill every bird or mammal that came ashore.

In August they began to quietly discuss the possibility that Shackleton wasn't coming back.

There appears to have been an agreement not to reveal the fullest details of those months, but years later Orde-Lees' daughter Zoe said her father confided there had been a lottery for who would be eaten first, and that he was the one selected. Orde-Lees had dark suspicions that the lottery may have been rigged.

There's a suggestion that Hussey wrote to Orde-Lees in the 1950s to confess this to him. Hussey wrote elsewhere that Wild was the prime mover, and that when food was dwindling, Wild broached the subject with him on a walk: 'We'll take that so-and-so Orde-Lees out on the hill and shoot him and eat him.'

It's unclear if this was a true memory, or how serious Wild might have been, but Hussey said he watched Wild eating pieces of raw seal or penguin, and was convinced Wild could do anything he needed to do.

Certainly, Wild held them together. He was forceful and unflagging and cheerful. It was four months since the *James Caird* left on a three-week voyage, and no one still believed they'd survived. No one but Wild. Every day that the bay was clear of ice, Wild rose and packed his gear and told them: Get ready. Today's the day The Boss comes back.

Finally, on 29 August, Wild decided to prepare the *Dudley Docker*. He would try to reach Deception Island.

The next day it was clear but cold. The men gathered limpets at low tide. Marston went up to the lookout point to fetch a pencil he'd left there. The men were in the shelter, eating boiled seal backbone, when they heard him running. They laughed: Marston had realised he was late for lunch.

He burst in, eyes bulging, gasping for breath. He finally managed: 'Should we put up a flag?'

They looked at him, puzzled.

Then he realised he'd forgotten to say. 'There's a ship,' he said.

They scrambled to get out but the door was too narrow so they smashed their way through the wall. James was in a such a hurry he put his boots on the wrong feet. Macklin ran up to the oar they used as a flagpole. He took off his warm jacket and tried to run it up the oar as a flag, but the halliard jammed halfway up.

Standing at the bow of the Chilean tug *Yelcho*, looking anxiously through binoculars, Shackleton saw the jacket at half-mast and went pale. He thought it meant a death in camp.

The men waved and shouted. They saw a stocky figure climbing down into a small boat. It was only a distant silhouette, but they knew that silhouette. Someone said: 'Thank God The Boss is safe.'

Wild wrote that when he recognised Shackleton, 'I felt jolly near blubbing for a bit, and could not speak for several minutes.'

Wild waved the boat in through the reef but it couldn't land for the ice blocking the beach. Shackleton stood in the bow and shouted: 'Are you all well?'

They said they were.

He threw them two packets. One was tobacco, the other cigarettes.

Wild invited Shackleton ashore. He wanted to show him their hut, and how they had arranged things. He wanted Shackleton to see how well they had done. Shackleton smiled and said no, let's rather go home.

Pandemonium in camp. Men running around packing, whooping. Walter How broke open a tin of biscuits they'd been cherishing, but they were too excited to eat. Perce Blackborow lay footless in the hut, begging to know what was happening. Macklin lifted him onto his shoulders and carried him to see The Boss.

They jumped on the boat and were ferried to the *Yelcho*. As the boat left for the last time, a figure came running and yelling. Orde-Lees had been waiting for Shackleton at the hut, to give him a tour and show him how well they'd managed. Wild and Orde-Lees alike: we all want our father's approval.

As *Yelcho* pulled away, Macklin saw his jacket flapping from the flagpole. He wondered how long it would survive, the ragged evidence of that brief spark of civilisation in this inhuman place. He thought of it fraying and unravelling under the eyes of the gulls and cormorants, beneath the shadow of the albatross, its slow decay while the ice rose and fell, and the seas pushed and pulled, while the snow fell and only the world endured.

Humans are funny things. We are contradictory, irrational, we make no sense. We are quite wonderful. Hurley stood at a different rail and watched the island recede. He felt ... he felt ... heartbroken. 'I could scarce repress feelings of sadness to leave forever the land that has rained on us its bounty and salvation.'

He was sad to be leaving home.

33. AFTERMATH

....

The world is changing and soon the machine will be of more importance than the body, and it's tremendous luck to have been born into the last few seconds of an epoch in which man is still required to stand up and be counted.

BIRDIE BOWERS, IN BERYL BAINBRIDGE'S
THE BIRTHDAY BOYS

....

The world they had left was no longer there.

They couldn't grasp the scale of the war news: Ypres and Gallipoli, chemicals and tanks, submarines and aircraft, bombs falling from the skies onto cities. When they left, war was still waged with horses. In less than 30 years there would be a nuclear bomb.

Aboard the *Yelcho*, Shackleton tried to prepare them: the daily list of the war dead was no longer called the casualty list, now it was called the Roll of Honour. England was dazed, half-crazed, with death.

By dying, Scott had finally won. In a time of apocalypse, he was fashionable; he spoke to a generation of men falling like blades of grass, desperate to find a way of making their own deaths meaningful.

In *Peter Pan*, Wendy tells the Lost Boys: 'I have a message to you from your real mothers, and it is this: "We hope our sons will die like English gentlemen".' Scott's 'Last Message to the Public' was reproduced and distributed in the trenches, where young men read it to prepare for their own glory. They wrote letters of gratitude to Kathleen Scott, whose husband had shown them how to die.

Scott had lost more men in one season, including himself, than all the Antarctic expeditions of the 20th century. Shackleton had lost no one. He had brought them all back alive. No single death had been countenanced or considered acceptable: they were all of them precious, even the cowards, even the shirkers, the slack-jawed, the mutineers. He strained his sinews and his muscles and his heart for them all. The story of Shackleton is the story that human agency can make a difference, that human effort is worth it and even the tiniest survival matters, even in the face of extinction. But that wasn't the mood of the moment. There was no fashion for men who went into the world instead of to war, and then had the bad taste to survive.

At Buenos Aires train station, Shackleton said goodbye – he was going east, to rescue the other half of his expedition, the ones who on the barque *Aurora* had gone to the Ross Sea and trekked to the Beardmore glacier to leave depots of food for the men who were expecting to cross the continent. The *Aurora* party had run into problems too. *Aurora* was iced in and drifted helplessly for six months, stranding the shore party on the ice shelf. Three people had died, including *Aurora*'s captain. Seven men were still marooned on the ice and needing rescue, including Frank Wild's younger brother Ernest.

All the members of *Endurance* were there to see Shackleton off, except Blackborow, who was in hospital in Punta Arenas, charming the local ladies, and Hudson, who had already shipped off to war. Orde-Lees had already obtained a commission in the Royal Flying Corps. His ambitions in the ice were satisfied: the sky was calling him now. The train pulled out and the men waved Shackleton away. They would never gather again.

Almost all of them joined the war straight away. The first to die was the cheerful boy, the one Shackleton said was the best of them all. Timothy McCarthy was 28 and seated at his gun on Friday 16 March 1917, when the SS *Narragansett* was torpedoed off the coast of Ireland. It was less than seven months since the men were rescued from Elephant Island.

The second to die was Alfred Cheetham, cheerful and popular, who Frank Worsley described as 'a pirate to his fingertips'. He drowned when his minesweeper was torpedoed off the River Humber, a few weeks before the Armistice. He was 51 years old, and left behind thirteen children.

Frank Hurley went to Ypres as a war photographer, and James Wordie went to France with the Royal Field Artillery and was wounded at Armentières. Leonard Hussey went straight to the front and served in 'every big battle from Dixmude to St Quentin'.

Alexander Macklin won the Military Cross for bravery while tending the wounded under fire on the Italian front. McIlroy went to Ypres and was wounded. He recovered, and accompanied Frank Wild on a military mission to Spitsbergen in northern Norway, where he nearly died after falling down a crevasse.

Walter How joined the Merchant Navy. He won two medals for bravery and survived but lost an eye.

Frank Worsley captained a Q-ship and became known as Depth Charge Bill. He destroyed at least three enemy submarines. He was at the helm when PC 61 rammed and sank the German U-boat UC-33. He was awarded the Distinguished Service Order, and stayed on after the war to fight the Bolsheviks in Archangel.

Shackleton rescued his men from the Ross Sea. They were stunned to see him on the deck of the rescue ship – they had been expecting him to come staggering out of the frozen continent behind them. When everyone was safely on land and he was free to turn his attention to the world and the war, Shackleton was desperate to join up, but he couldn't fight because he wouldn't pass a medical. He scrounged for deployments that might suit his skills. He was sent to Buenos Aires to coordinate propaganda in South America, and tried unsuccessfully to persuade Chile to enter the war. He was sent to Spitsbergen on a secret mission to establish an English military presence, then to Murmansk in northern Russia to assist in operations against the Bolsheviks.

After the war, he was asked to recommend his men for the Polar Medal. He recommended everyone except John Vincent and Chippy McNish, and the sailors Stephenson and Holness. It's unclear what Holness and Stephenson did to deserve exclusion. Presumably Wild had stories to tell from Elephant Island.

Shackleton was broke. He signed over the royalties for *South*, his memoir of the expedition, to pay outstanding debt. He took to the lecture circuit, but people's minds were still on the war, and the Spanish flu, and the world so recently lost. He was a relic, defunct, and the lecture halls were half full. He languished; he was lost. 'I have a curious nature,' he mused to Emily, 'and I have tried to analyse it, without much success.'

There was only one future for Shackleton. He was Tennyson's Ulysses, his Odysseus back from the struggle but looking out through that arch where gleams that untravelled world whose margins fade for ever.

In 1920, he contacted Frank Wild. My purpose holds, he said, to sail beyond the sunset, and the baths of all the stars, until I die. He didn't say it in those words. He said: will you come south with me again?

Frank Wild was in East Africa, with McIlroy. They had bought land in Nyasaland together, and were ready to farm when a barefoot runner arrived with the message from England. At Shackleton's call, Wild laid down his ploughshare and McIlroy went too. After everything that everyone had been through, Charlie Green the cook also returned, and so did Hussey with his banjo. Dr Macklin came, and Alexander Kerr and Tom McLeod. Some of them still hadn't been paid for their time on *Endurance*. Worsley came back as skipper.

Somehow, with sympathetic donations, they secured the *Quest*, a wide-beamed, underpowered vessel that had previously hunted seals. The intentions for the expedition were vague. There was talk about circumnavigating Antarctica. There was talk about charting one of the shores of the Weddell Sea. There was talk of stopping off on the way back to hunt the buried treasure of Captain Kidd. None of that mattered, says Caroline Alexander: they were going in search of yesterday.

I think that's true. But I also think Shackleton was going home.

In Rio he had a heart attack, but refused to be examined.

Quest sailed from Rio to South Georgia. At Grytviken, Shackleton and Worsley leant on the railing, pointing to familiar sights, the mountains and ridges they had walked. The men gathered to hear their stories. His diary entries are gentle, nostalgic. He is happy to be back. He remembers it all fondly, even the familiar smell of dead whale.

They went ashore in Grytviken, greeted old friends, walked in the hills where once Hurley had lugged his camera to photograph *Endurance* at anchor. Shackleton sat watching the gulls and the terns. He seemed very present and very complete. He returned to his cabin and wrote in his diary. He wrote with pleasure about the day, how peaceful it was, the loveliness of the sun-shining world. He finished the entry: 'In the darkening twilight I saw a lone star hover gem-like above the bay.'

He closed his diary and turned off the light and went to sleep. At 2am Dr Macklin was woken in his cabin next door. Shackleton was in pain. Macklin found a whiskey bottle beside the bed, the stub of a cigar in an ashtray. Macklin told him he needed to change his ways.

'You're always wanting me to give up things,' grumbled Shackleton. The last thing he said was: 'What do you want me to give up now?'

He died around 2.20am on 5 January of a massive heart attack. He was 47 years old.

Macklin performed the autopsy on his leader. He opened him and looked at that mighty heart. He diagnosed it as weakened with disease, pulled apart by care and exertion.

Wild said he would take *Quest* to complete Shackleton's last voyage, and Hussey set out to take the body to England, but Emily sent a message that met him at Montevideo. She said Shackleton didn't belong in England, under grass and hedgerows and soft rain. He belonged in the savage beautiful wild, in the south, at home. So Hussey took The Boss back to South Georgia.

The funeral service was held in the Whaler's Church, a black-steepled single-nave wooden church of vertical boards painted the snowy white of an albatross' throat. There is a memorial cross at the mouth of the Grytviken bay, on a rocky height called Hope Point.

He was buried in the graveyard, among the Norwegian whalers. The graveyard is ten minutes' walk around the little bay from the church, up a gentle rise from the water. Leonard Hussey only knew how to play six songs. One of them was 'It's a Long Way to Tipperary'. He had tried unsuccessfully to master 'The Wearing of the Green', but as they laid Shackleton to rest, Hussey played Brahms' Lullaby on his banjo.

In winter the snows cover the graveyard and all that stands clear is the square-edged slender granite stone, carved in front with his name and dates and a nine-pointed star, and on the reverse with a line from the poem 'The Statue and the Bust', by Robert Browning:

I hold that a man should strive to the uttermost for his life's set prize.'

I don't know who chose it but it's a terrible quote, unmelodious, inappropriate, quarried unsympathetically from a second-rate poem. Shackleton had no set prize. He did not have his heart set on being first to the Pole, or the first to cross the Antarctic. For him life wasn't set, it was something to explore, an unending cascade of horizons to meet and see and go beyond. When he bought his ship, it was named *Polaris*, but he removed the name and gave it the new name *Endurance*. 'Through endurance we conquer': his goal wasn't the pole star or even to conquer. It was endurance itself.

EPILOGUE

Seated on a grey sandstone rock halfway up Table Mountain, with an old pair of oversized binoculars in a scuffed hard leather case, you can watch *SA Agulhas II* leave her berth on her latest mission and head out past Robben Island and turn to head south. On a grey day her red hull is the brightest thing between a grey sea and the grey vast skies. As she passes beyond the outer breakwater a spinner dolphin jumps from the water, small and black, performing a barrel roll in the grey air, a pinwheel of joyous cold water. To the right, further away in the liquid distance, diagonally beneath a break in the clouds, a patch of sunlight lies on the sea and turns it silver, and the air above it is gold.

The Atlantic stretches far south and it stretches wide. The binoculars I am holding belonged to my father and for many years I thought they were lost until I found them in a dusty box in a dusty garage. He used them to look at birds, at clouds, at oil tankers passing in the Indian Ocean, at neighbours and weather and the moon.

I think of the people on board the ship, ordinary people, thoughtless and thoughtful people, hard-working people and idlers, going out to the far part of the world to do their jobs, to learn, to repair, to supply, to escape, to rescue. I think of all the men and women who have been to the sea in ships, and the men and women who have stayed behind and thought of them, remembered them, sung them into our human eternity.

We think we can see the future, we are afraid we can see the future, but we cannot see the future. We can barely see the past. The present stretches out like the ocean, moving, changeable, not exactly the same over there as it is over here.

Endurance has come back to us, not as she went down but as however we choose to read her. By the terms of the Antarctic Treaty she can't be exhumed or excavated, and there is a transcendent beauty in that: there is no closure to her, there is no reducing her to money or museums. She lies pristine in the wild world, a molecule of the changing past gleaming in the present. She reminds us, if we allow her to, that humans have done extraordinary things and still do and will do again, things so unlikely and so marvellous that we might without embarrassment call them miracles. She reminds us that miracles are things that can be performed by human beings, flawed human beings in impossible situations.

Endurance is a symbol of failure, or she is part of an ongoing and infinite story of survival, a stage in an infinite game that we must find a way of playing joyfully, with commitment, with love. I sat on the rock on the mountain and watched the red ship sail across the grey sea toward the silver light and toward the obscure horizon, and I thought about my own future. It is not solipsism to think about your own story. All we are is an infinite collection of our own and each other's stories.

The world is filled with cruel beauties and indifferent kindnesses, and with dreams and forgotten things and bad luck and good. The world is still filled with surprise. *Endurance* belongs to the ice and the ocean and the world, and she reminds us that it's a small-minded impertinence to declare that everything is lost, and everything is already known. It's an impertinence to say the world has already ended, it's an impertinence to say that I cannot change, or love, or make someone happy. It's an impertinence to give in to the past. The world mustn't end, and it won't end.

The red speck of the ship moves south and into the hazy curvature of the planet, towards the winds and the ice, where showers of gannets fall from the sky like rain. As I watch her go I feel a swelling in my heart. I want to turn around and shout and point and say, 'Look! Look! She's going to Antarctica! She found *Endurance*!'

She reminds us that the world is still as extraordinary as we have always felt it to be, that there is still human magic in it, transmutation and transformations. Time and the world do not only take from us – they also give something back, and what we do with it is up to us. If I were to bet – and why not? What have I got to lose? – I'd bet on us.

*

On a Friday afternoon in a small village in the Karoo during lockdown, in front of two witnesses and a police sergeant wearing a mask, I promised Jo I would trust the future rather than the past. I think I can keep the promise, but the important thing is making it. It's something to aim for.

Jo and I don't have a house. We don't even have a country. She has English citizenship and I have South African, and we live neither one place nor the other, nor anywhere else in particular. We move around every month or two months. The longest we have stayed somewhere is 100 days. It feels as though anything is possible, both in the future and the past.

I asked her if she missed having a home. She said she didn't know what I was talking about.

APPENDIX 1
Things Coming Back

In 2020 it felt as though things were being taken away. We lost people, places, the fabric of our lives. Some lost faith. If *Endurance* has something for us, it's the reminder that things are not only lost. Sometimes they come back.

1. Shackleton's last cabin

The *Quest* was bought by a Norwegian sailor named Ludolf Schjelderup. He had it refitted at the Rognan shipyard, where the yard-owner – a man named Johan Drage – removed the deckhouse that had been installed as Shackleton's private cabin. It was pitch pine on a steel frame, and there was a bunk stretching the length of the cabin. Shackleton died in that bunk. There were drawers beneath the bunk and a single porthole above. There was a small washstand, and shelves with books.

Johan Drage took the cabin on a horse-drawn carriage to his farm at Saltdal, 200 kilometres north of the Arctic Circle, where it became a playhouse for his daughters. In the Second World War it was involved in a heavy gun battle between German soldiers and Allied soldiers who tried to shelter behind it.

In 2022 it was being used as a garden shed by Ulfe Bakker, Johan Drage's great-grandson. One night an Irishman from Cork named Eugene Furlong was drinking in a pub on the Lofoten islands when he heard some locals talking about the Shackleton cabin. Sven Habermann, a conservator of historical objects based in Connemara, travelled to Norway to verify it. It is cold in the Arctic. There are no insects to eat the wood, and no fungal activity. Habermann found that 90% of the cabin was still original. The original wallpaper was still on the ceiling. The bunk was still there.

Ulfe Bakker donated the cabin to the Shackleton Society. It was taken by truck to Ireland to be restored in Letterfrack, Galway. It is owned by the Athy Heritage Centre Museum in County Kildare, and I cannot wait to visit it.

2. Frank Wild

Frank Wild died in Krugersdorp and was cremated, and his ashes disappeared. A little over ten years ago a journalist named Angie Butler tried to track them down. She knew his second wife was a South African named Beatrice 'Trix' Rowbotham, so she tried the Rowbothams in the Johannesburg telephone directory and found a June Rowbotham, the daughter-in-law of Trix's brother Benjamin, who had inherited all Trix's papers and letters, including Wild's memoirs and his diary of the 1909 trek with Shackleton to farthest south.

Angie Butler recruited the help of Alan Buff, a former regional manager of Parks and Cemeteries, a kind of grave whisperer, who had found the 90-year-old lost grave of Enoch Sontonga, the composer of *Nkosi Sikelel' iAfrika*. In January 2011, Alan Buff found Frank Wild's ashes in a green wooden box, hidden in a dusty niche in the columbarium beneath the chapel in the Braamfontein crematorium in Johannesburg.

Seventy-two years after his death, Wild's ashes were taken to South Georgia and buried in the graveyard, on the right-hand side of his Boss. His great-nephew Brian flew from Australia to be there. Alexandra Shackleton, Ernest's granddaughter, helped carry the ashes from the church to the graveyard. Brian's mother Joy was too frail to make it, but she remembered the family stories about Frank. 'He lived for the journey, not the prize', she said.

3. The Bible
When Shackleton made his grand gesture, tearing the pages from Queen Alexandra's Bible and dropping it on the ice, the men were impressed but one of them was troubled. Tom McLeod was a strict Presbyterian. He was the one who thought penguins contained the souls of drowned sailors. He had served in the Boer War and had been to Antarctica before, on Scott's *Terra Nova* expedition, where he won the Polar Medal.

Tom McLeod went to sea at age thirteen and was illiterate, but he thought it bad luck to leave a Bible behind. He quietly retrieved it, and kept it safe on the ice and in the boats and on Elephant Island. After the rescue, he was taken in by the Maclean family in Punta Arenas, and gave them the Bible in thanks. In 1971, Commander Burley of the Joint Services expedition to Elephant Island was giving a talk in Buenos Aires. Afterwards he was approached by one of the Maclean family, who presented him with the Bible. It's now in the possession of the Royal Geographical Society.

4. The stone
In 1937 a young sailor named Joseph Collis was serving on HMS *Ajax* when she stopped at South Geor-

gia. He paid his respects at Shackleton's grave and picked up a small piece of green granite as a keepsake. He kept it for 75 years, and lived to a fine old age of 95. But the green stone nagged at him: we can't just carry off pieces of the world. Just before he died in 2012, he asked his son Malcolm to return it. Malcolm Collis contacted the government of South Georgia. He handed the stone to a representative of the Royal Navy in Fareham, and it was flown to the South Atlantic under the care of Warrant Officer Andy Welch. He kept it two months in his care, then passed it along to the first ship heading to South Georgia: HMS *Protector*, a Portsmouth-based ice patrol vessel. In April 2013, the commanding officer of HMS *Protector*, Captain Rhett Hatcher, brought the stone home and placed it on Shackleton's grave.

5. The South Georgia pipit

The South Georgia pipit, *Anthus antarcticus*, is the size of a sparrow, dark brown and streaked with dusty gold. It's the southernmost songbird in the world. It builds nests on the ground from tussock grass and sea debris and sings in chirping phrases that repeat. Shackleton heard pipits in 1916, and again when he returned in 1922, but there weren't as many the second time. The South Georgia pipit exists nowhere in the world but South Georgia, and it very nearly doesn't exist there either.

The Norwegian whalers brought rats and reindeer to the island. The reindeer were deliberate but the rats were not. The rats spread, eating the eggs from pipit nests. By the middle of the century, there was only pipit song in the areas behind the ice, where the rats couldn't reach. By the

1980s and 1990s, beneath the calling of the seals and the gulls, there was silence.

Many conservationists thought it too late to save the pipit. There is always someone who thinks it's too late to do something, but they tried anyway. By 2015, all 6,700 reindeer had been eradicated. In 2018 the island was declared rat-free. Today, walk up from the beach and into the tussock grass, and all around you, you will hear the song of the pipits.

APPENDIX 2

Later Years

The *James Caird*

The *James Caird* ended up in the possession of John Quiller Rowett, an old schoolfriend of Shackleton's at Dulwich, who funded the *Quest* expedition. In 1924, not knowing what to do with it, he donated it to the school, who also didn't know what to do with it. They kept it in a shed with the lawnmowers. In 1944 German bombs fell and damaged the shed. In 1967 a pupil at Dulwich College, Howard Hope, agitated for its preservation and it was given into the care of the National Maritime Museum. In 1985 it was returned to Dulwich College and placed in a new location in the North Cloister, on a bed of stones gathered from South Georgia and, for some reason, Aberystwyth. Now it's the centrepiece of the James Caird Society (established 1994), whose dinners are held before it.

Frank Worsley (Captain)

After the *Quest* expedition, and his exploits in the war, Worsley hadn't had enough of adventure. He became co-leader of an Arctic expedition, where he was suspected of deliberately trying to get stuck in the ice. In 1934 he went treasure-hunting in the Pacific and in the atolls of the Cocos (Keeling) Islands in the Indian Ocean. In the Second World War he lied about his age and was given command of a ship, but was removed when it was discovered that he was nearly 70. He died the next year of lung cancer, aged nearly 71.

Lionel Greenstreet (First Officer)

Greenstreet arrived home and like many of the others, married quickly. He married Mille Muir in 1917 in Surrey. In the Second World War, aged 50, he served on rescue tugs in the Atlantic. He retired to Devon, where he became a widower but married again in 1955. In 1964 the newspapers mistakenly reported his death, to his great amusement. He was 89 when he did die. It was 1979, and he was the last of the survivors to go.

Thomas Crean (Second Officer)

On his return Crean married his childhood sweetheart Nell, who was 36. He was 40. Shackleton asked him to join the *Quest* expedition but Nell persuaded him that his polar days were done. He bought a pub in Anascaul in Ireland and called it the South Pole Inn. It serves a decent pint to this day. Crean led a disciplined life, working in the pub and his garden, walking his dogs Toby and Fido down to Dingle Bay every evening. He never spoke about his experiences in the south, not to friends or family or customers in the pub. He died in 1938, aged 61, of a perforated appendix, and was buried in a tomb which he had built himself.

Robert Clark (Biologist)

Clark served on a minesweeper during the war, and afterwards took up a job at a fishery research station in his home town of Aberdeen. He had always been very quiet, not to say dour, and he lived quietly and wrote research papers on herring larvae and haddock. He was respected in his community for his skill at football and cricket. He died in 1950, aged 68.

George Marston (Artist)

Marston was the portliest man on the ice, and some suspected he might be the laziest too. He collaborated with Frank Hurley on a number of painting and photographic composites but after that he fades somewhat from history. He died in 1940, aged 58, of coronary thrombosis.

Charlie Green (Cook)

Charlie Green had an unfortunate expedition, even by the standards of *Endurance*. When he signed on in Buenos Aires, he sent a letter to his parents telling them he was still alive and informing them where he was going, but the mail ship was torpedoed and the letter was lost and they never knew where he was. When he returned after the rescue, he found that his girlfriend had married and his parents had cashed in his life insurance policy. Green moved to Hull and resumed life as a ship's cook. Occasionally in later years he gave very entertaining but wildly inaccurate lectures about *Endurance*. He died in 1974, aged 86, of peritonitis.

Huberht (sic) T. Hudson (Navigator)

Hudson recovered from his nervous breakdown on Elephant Island, but his health was permanently impaired. His hands were ruined from frostbite, which also caused necrosis of the bone in his lower back. He served in the

Second World War as a commodore of convoys, and died in June 1942, aged 55.

(James Francis) Frank Hurley (Photographer)

After the war Hurley went on photographic expeditions to Papua New Guinea and Tasmania, and in the Second World War he went to Palestine. He married a beautiful Spanish-French opera singer ten days after meeting her, and they had three children, one of whom he named Adelie. In the 1950s he became a publicity photographer for the Australian tourism board. On 15 January 1962, he came home from work complaining of feeling unwell. It was unusual for him to complain. He refused to let his family call a doctor. He sat in his favourite easy chair all night and the next morning, grimly fighting the old enemy. He died at noon the next day, aged 76.

Leonard Hussey (Meteorologist)

Hussey served in two world wars – winning an OBE in the second, flying for the RAF. He had been an anthropologist and an archaeologist when he joined *Endurance* as a meteorologist, and later he became a medical doctor. He became a keen scoutmaster, and a president of the Antarctic Club, and the London Banjo Club. His banjo, signed by the members of the expedition, is in the possession of the Royal Maritime Museum. He lectured diligently about *Endurance*, and handed over his papers and slideshows to a younger friend and fellow scoutmaster, Ralph Gullett, imploring him to keep the memory of *Endurance* alive. He married but never had children. He died in 1964, aged 72.

Appendix 2

Reginald James (Physicist)

Reginald James was a brilliant academic, and became an expert in X-ray crystallography. He married in 1936 and emigrated to South Africa in 1937, where he took a chair of physics at the University of Cape Town and became vice-chancellor. He died in 1964, aged 73.

Alexander Macklin (Surgeon)

After the *Quest* expedition, Macklin settled in Aberdeen, where he became head of Student Health Services at the university. He stayed in touch with Jock Wordie and they met occasionally to discuss work and the old days. He became an important historian of the expedition and of Shackleton's later life. He died in 1967, aged 77.

Dr James A. McIlroy (Surgeon)

In Spitsbergen during the First World War, he fell down a crevasse and was also stalked by a polar bear. In the Second World War he was aboard a vessel that was torpedoed and sank, and he had to endure a second voyage on the open sea in an open boat – five days off the coast of West Africa – before being rescued by Vichy forces and imprisoned in a concentration camp. Along with Frank Wild, he founded a treasure-hunting society. He was a ship's surgeon into his old age and died a bachelor but with girlfriends to the end. He died in 1968, aged 88.

Henry 'Chippy' McNish (Carpenter)

McNish returned to sea for a while, then retired and lived with his son and daughter-in-law. One day he announced he was going to New Zealand, claiming he had a job there. He vanished, and a few days later a horse-drawn cart arrived for his sea chest, and they never saw or heard from him again. He fetched up in Wellington, living rough on the docks and sleeping under a tarpaulin in the wharf sheds. He claimed his health had been permanently affected by the journey in the *James Caird* and refused to shake hands on account of the pain. In later life he became obsessed with the fate of Mrs Chippy, dwelling on it in every conversation. He never forgave Shackleton for her death. He died in 1930, in Wellington's Ohiro rest home, and is buried in Karori cemetery. His grave was unmarked for 30 years. He was a pauper and left only one item: his diary. In 2004, after a public appeal and subscription, his grave was tidied and tended, and a bronze statue of Mrs Chippy was placed at the foot of his grave.

Thomas Orde-Lees (Motor expert and store-keeper)

Orde-Lees served on the Western Front in the Balloon Corps, and after joining the Royal Flying Corps became obsessed with parachuting, and promoting the parachute as safety equipment for pilots. He was opposed by senior officers, who felt they might dilute pilots' fighting spirit, and also that they might be unsafe.

Orde-Lees parachuted off Tower Bridge into the Thames to demonstrate how effective it was, and was placed on the panel that finally approved the adoption of the parachute as standard gear. After the war he resigned his commission rather than face a court-martial for his role in running a parachuting course for women, sponsored by the *Daily Mail*. He went to Japan to teach parachuting to the Japanese Air Force. He married a Japanese woman and settled down, working as a foreign correspondent for *The Times*. For twenty years he read the English news on the radio in Japan. He was one of the first non-Japanese-born men to climb Mount Fuji in winter.

In 1941, when war broke out, he and his family reluctantly relocated to Wellington in New Zealand, where he may have worked as a spy for the British government. His mental health declined in later life, and he died in 1958, aged 81, confined to a mental hospital, suffering with dementia. He is buried in Karori cemetery, ironically just a few graves over from his old nemesis Chippy McNish.

James Wordie (Geologist)

Wordie, who started out as a geologist but found very little to do geologically on the ice, turned his attention to glaciology. He was involved in numerous expeditions to the Arctic, and became the elder statesman of British exploration. In the Second World War he worked for Naval Intelligence. He remained friends with Alexander Macklin, and in time became Sir James Wordie, president of the Royal Geographical Society, and helped plan the first ascent of Everest by Edmund Hillary and Tenzing Norgay. While chairman of the committee of management at the Scott Polar Research Institute, he assisted Vivian Fuchs' first ever crossing of the Antarctic continent – the original goal of the *Endurance* expedition. He was master of St John's College, Cambridge. He died in 1962, aged 72.

Perce Blackborow (Stowaway)

After his return Blackborow worked on the Newport docks with his father. He remained cheerful and good-natured and stayed in touch with How and Bakewell, and their descendants stay in touch to this day. He taught himself to walk without a limp and never mentioned the amputation nor the circumstances around it. He died in 1949, aged 54, of a heart condition and chronic bronchitis.

William Lincoln Bakewell (Able Seaman)

Bakewell had quite a life even before joining *Endurance* in Buenos Aires. He ran away from home, aged eleven, and became a farmhand, a boxcar rider, and a rancher. Shackleton called him one of the nicest and best-educated of the hands, and a superior sailor. After the rescue he stayed on in Patagonia for a year, farming sheep. Subsequent jobs included merchant seaman, railroad switchman and farmer. In the Second World War he was twice on ships that were torpedoed and sunk – making a total of four ships that sank beneath him. In 1945 he settled in Dukes, Michigan, where he raised a daughter. In 1964 he was invited to England to celebrate the 50th anniversary of the departure of the expedition. His neighbours in Michigan had no idea why their elderly friend should be included in the celebration of an English polar expedition: he had never mentioned his former life, thinking they wouldn't be interested. He died in 1969, aged 81.

Walter How (Able Seaman)

Shackleton asked How to join the *Quest* expedition, and he intended to go but at the last moment stayed behind to take care of his ailing father. Shackleton had special admiration for How, calling him 'a man among men'. His sight was failing after a landmine incident during the war, but he became an amateur painter and a builder of ships in bottles, including *Endurance*. He went to great lengths to stay in touch with his old shipmates, especially Bakewell and Greenstreet. He, Green and Greenstreet were the last three left, and in 1970 they attended a ceremony for the commissioning of HMS *Endurance*. He died in 1972, aged 87, of cancer.

Ernest Holness (Able Seaman and Second Stoker)

Holness, like Stephenson, hasn't left much trace of his life. On his return he married a Hull girl named Lillian Bettles and went back to the North Sea trawlers. The man who was rescued from the sea by Shackleton when the ice broke beneath him died in 1924, aged 31, when he was washed overboard in a storm off the Faroe Islands.

Tom McLeod (Able Seaman)

McLeod, the Presbyterian who saved Queen Alexandra's Bible, moved to Canada and became a fisherman, then a school caretaker and a nightwatchman. He never married, although he wanted to, because he said he could never afford to buy a house. He died aged 91 in a rest home in Canada. He was not the last of the survivors to die – that was Greenstreet – but he lived to be the oldest. The headstone of his grave in Cataraqui cemetery in Kingston, Ontario tells his story, but manages to misspell both his name and Shackleton's.

William Stephenson (Senior Stoker)

We know very little about Stephenson except that he was from Yorkshire and worked the Hull trawlers. None of the men wrote much about him in their diaries, and whatever caused Shackleton to exclude him from the Polar

Medal has generously gone unrecorded. He died of cancer in a hospital in Hull, aged 64, in 1953.

Lewis Rickinson (Chief Engineer)
Rickinson recovered from his heart attack on Elephant Island, and served in both wars. On his return from the Antarctic he married Marjorie Snell and had a son and a daughter. He became a naval architect and consulting engineer. He died of lung cancer in 1945, aged 62, while serving in the navy.

Alexander Kerr (Second Engineer)
Kerr was 23 when he returned (the youngest other than Blackborow) and married his sweetheart Lilian. They had two children, Jack and Eileen. After the *Quest* expedition, he continued with the merchant service and worked on tugs around the City of London until his retirement. He refused any postings or promotions that would take him away from home. After retirement he set himself up as a wholesaler. He was a founder member of the British Antarctic Club, and died in December 1964, on the 50th anniversary of the expedition, aged 71.

John Vincent (Seaman)
Vincent by some accounts lost an upper lip on the voyage of the *James Caird*, after it stuck to the frozen rim of a metal mug. He was on a ship torpedoed in the Mediterranean in the last months of the war but survived. He worked for a while as a pilot for the Finnish government, and was offered a permanent position as a fishing instructor but his wife didn't want to live in Finland, persuading him to move back to Grimsby. They had five sons and

four daughters and he died of pneumonia in the Naval Hospital in Grimsby in 1941, aged 56.

These were the names of some of the dogs:
Rugby, Amundsen, Red, Hercules, Slobbers, Caruso, Splitlip, Satan, Painful, Bob, Shakespeare, Peter, Bummer, Smuts, Blot, Spider, Smooch, Smoocher and Jerry.

SOURCES USED

List of books used

The Endurance: Shackleton's Legendary Expedition, Caroline Alexander, Bloomsbury Publishing, 1999

The Birthday Boys, Beryl Bainbridge, Gerald Duckworth & Co., 1991

The Quest for Frank Wild (including his original memoirs), Angie Butler, Jackleberry Press, 2011

Alone, Richard E. Byrd, G.P. Putnam's Sons, New York, 1938

Six Memos for the New Millennium (Charles Eliot Norton Lectures), Italo Calvino, Harvard University Press, 1988

Fine and Infinite Games, James A. Carse, Simon & Schuster, 1986

The Songlines, Bruce Chatwin, Penguin, 1988

The Worst Journey in the World, Apsley Cherry-Garrard, Carroll & Graf, 1989

Flaws in the Ice: In Search of Douglas Mawson, David Day, Scribe, 2013

Wind, Sand and Stars, Antoine de Saint-Exupéry, HarperCollins, originally published 1943

Short Life in a Strange World: Birth to Death in 42 Panels, Toby Ferris, 4th Estate, 2020

Race to the Pole, Ranulph Fiennes, Hyperion, 2005

Mad, Bad and Dangerous to Know, Ranulph Fiennes, Hodder & Stoughton, 1987

The Third Man Factor, John Geiger, Viking Canada, 2009

Herzog on Herzog: Conversations with Paul Cronin, Farrar, Straus & Giroux, 2003 otilightal lddhoughtent

Shackleton, Roland Huntford, Hodder & Stoughton, 1985

The Last Place on Earth: Scott and Amundsen's Race to the South Pole, revised and updated, Roland Huntford, Modern Library, 1999

Race for the South Pole: The Expedition Diaries of Scott and Amundsen, Roland Huntford, Continuum, 2010

Endurance – A Year in Space, a Lifetime of Discovery, Scott Kelly with Margaret Lazarus Dean, Alfred A. Knopf, 2017

Endurance: Shackleton's Incredible Voyage, Alfred Lansing, Hodder & Stoughton, 1959; Weidenfeld & Nicholson, 2000

The Home of the Blizzard, Douglas Mawson, Palgrave Macmillan, 1998

The Biology of Human Survival: Life and Death in Extreme Environments, Claude A. Piantadosi, Oxford University Press, 2003

V, Thomas Pynchon, Harper Perennial Classics, 2005

The Ice, Stephen J. Pyne, Weidenfeld & Nicolson, 2003

The Order of Time, Carlo Rovelli, Riverhead Books, 2018

Madhouse at the End of the Earth, Julian Sancton, W.H. Allen, 2021

In the Heart of the Antarctic, Ernest Shackleton, Gardners Books, 2001

South, Ernest Shackleton, Robinson Publishing, 1998

Frankenstein, Mary Shelley, 1818

I May be Some Time: Ice and the English Imagination, Francis Spufford, Faber & Faber, 1996

Terra Incognita, Sara Wheeler, Jonathan Cape, 1996

Inventing Wonderland: The Lives and Fantasies of Lewis Carroll, Edward Lear, J.M. Barrie, Kenneth Grahame and A.A. Milne, Jackie Wullschlager, Free Press, 1996

The Diary of Thomas Orde-Lees
The Diary of Frank Wild
The Diary of Frank Hurley
The Diary of Chippy McNish

Articles and short stories used
'On the slipperiness and utility of defining nature writing', Kamil Ahsan, *The Millions,* 15 August 2018
'Scientists reveal what may be the largest flying bird ever', Riley Black, *Smithsonian* magazine, 26 October 2020
'Nature writing is booming but must a walk in the woods always be meaningful?', Zoe Gilbert, *The Guardian,* 2019
'Sur', Ursula K. Le Guin, *The New Yorker,* 24 January 1982
'The Antarctic Paradox', Alejandra Mancilla and Peder Roberts, *Aeon* magazine, 2022
'A Brooklyn church built a "votive ship" as a symbol of hope amid COVID-19 just before the discovery of its inspiration, the long-lost *Endurance*', Egan Millard, Episcopal News Service, 18 April 2022
'The role of emotion in global warming policy support and opposition', N. Smith and A. Leiserowitz, *Risk Analysis,* May 2014
'Frozen Alive', Peter Stark, *Outside* magazine, 1997
'Young People's Voices on Climate Anxiety, Government Betrayal and Moral Injury: A Global Phenomenon', Elizabeth Marks, Caroline Hickman, Panu Pihkala, Susan Clayton, Eric R. Lewandowski, Elouise E. Mayal, Britt Wray, Catriona Mellor and Lise van Susteren, *Preprints with The Lancet,* 7 September 2021

'A Brief History of People Losing Their Minds in Antarctica', Julian Sancton, *GQ*, 3 May 2021

'The Strange and Twisted Life of "Frankenstein"', Jill Lepore, *The New Yorker*, 5 February 2018

'Conversations about Dante', by Osip Mandelstam, translated by Clarence Brown, appendix to *The Selected Poems of Osip Mandelstam*, translated by Clarence Brown and W.S. Merwin, New York Review Books, 2004

CHAPTER NOTES

Chapter sources

The events of the ice are drawn principally from Alfred Lansing's *Endurance*, Roland Huntford's *Shackleton*, Caroline Alexander's *Endurance* and Ernest Shackleton's *South*, as well as the diaries of the participants in the adventure, most especially Thomas Orde-Lees, Frank Wild, Frank Hurley and Chippy McNish. There are interpolations and interpretations and imaginings of my own, but I couldn't have written this book without their pole stars guiding me. Any errors and inaccuracies are, we may safely assume, my own.

Among the historians of the Antarctic explorers, broadly speaking there are – just as there were during the Heroic Age itself – two camps: Team Scott and Team Shackleton. I am happy to admit that I am Team Shackleton, under the persuasive interpretive sway of Roland Huntford in his biographies *Scott and Amundsen* and *Shackleton*. Sometimes, perhaps to be expected from someone seeking to overturn decades of orthodoxy, Huntford makes his case against Scott a little too immoderately and gratuitously, but in the main I'm persuaded by his arguments, and am immeasurably grateful to his magisterial biography of Shackleton. Perhaps the most forceful modern champion of Team Scott is Sir Ranulph Fiennes, who takes the time in his 2004 book *Race to the Pole* to frown at Huntford for being, not merely not a polar explorer himself, but not even English: he was born in Cape Town, the son of a Lithuanian émigré to South

Africa named Sam Horwitz. I discovered this only recently, and am delighted to have done so.

Prologue

an idle king by a quiet hearth is an adaptation of a line from Tennyson's 'Ulysses', which I consider to be the secret text underpinning this book, and which will return in echoes and resonances throughout.

White Warfare

unable to suppress laughter, especially in serious matters is a paraphrase of Roland Huntford's description of Shackleton.

The Osip Mandelstam observation is contained in 'Conversations about Dante', appendix to *The Selected Poems of Osip Mandelstam*, translated by Clarence Brown and W.S. Merwin (New York Review Books, 2004).

grey mist on the sea's face is an adaptation of a line from John Masefield's 'Sea Fever'.

Angles of Light

The Mary Shelley epigraph is from Robert Walton's Letter 1 in *Frankenstein*.

Sara Wheeler describes Antarctica as a brain and as white pancake batter in her excellent and inspiring *Terra Incognita*.

Admiral Byrd describes Antarctica very beautifully and hauntingly in his classic account *Alone*.

Edgar Allan Poe's 'stupendous ramparts of ice, towering away into the desolate sky, looking like the walls of the universe' is a description from 'MS. Found in a Bottle' (1833).

Small Hands II

The final lines in the second-last paragraph about small hands are an echo of 'Gitanjali' by Rabindranath Tagore:

Thy infinite gifts come to me only on these very small hands of mine.
Ages pass, and still thou pourest, and still there is room to fill

Angles of Light II

pern in a gyre is a reference to a line from W.B. Yeats' 'The Second Coming'.

Small Hands III

I was alerted to the story of Guglielmo Marconi by an episode of the excellent and evocative podcast 'The Memory Palace', written and presented by Nate di Meo, whose beautiful cadences and rhythms probably underpin my retelling of it.

Polar Night

The Herzog epigraph is from an interview with Paul Cronin, published in the book *Herzog on Herzog*.

Poe's stories: I am thinking particularly of 'MS. found in a Bottle' (1833) and 'A Descent into the Maelstrom' and *The Narrative of Arthur Gordon Pym of Nantucket*.

I am deeply indebted for the material about *Belgica* – and about other cases of insanity in the Antarctic – to Julian Sancton's gripping account, *The Madhouse at the End of the World*, and his *GQ* article 'A Brief History of People Losing Their Minds in Antarctica'.

Mary Shelley's comment about the programme for the theatrical production of *Frankenstein* is from Jill Lepore's 2018 *New Yorker* article, 'The Strange and Twisted Life of "Frankenstein"'.

I am grateful for some of the insights into bear-baiting in Toby Ferris' excellent and genre-bending *Short Life in a Strange World: Birth to Death in 42 Panels*.

Aunty Molly

The Graham Greene story referred to (in which the falling pig kills the narrator's father) is 'A Shocking Accident'.

A brief digression about heat

The Calvino epigraph is from his collection of lectures, *Six Memos for the New Millennium*, which he made just before his death, published posthumously.

I am greatly indebted to Carlo Rovelli's *The Order of Time*, as well as various speeches, talks and interviews, and I would like to apologise to him for any fumblings and inaccuracies in my partial account of his account of heat and time. I am sure – and so is every physics teacher I had in school – that any accuracy of my understanding is entirely fortuitous.

Ocean Camp

The epigram by Antoine de Saint-Exupéry is from *Wind, Sand and Stars*.

'Lying in a damp ditch' is the phrase Beryl Bainbridge uses in *The Birthday Boys*, and I think she derives it from Apsley Cherry-Garrard's *The Worst Journey in the World*.

The quote from Sara Wheeler about her happiness in the Antarctic is taken from the final chapter of *Terra Incognita*.

Caroline Alexander's observation is from *Endurance*.

'Ears on both sides' is an expression Orde-Lees used in his journal to describe the thinness of the fabric of the tents.

The Zoe Gilbert quote is from 'Nature writing is booming but must a walk in the woods always be meaningful?', *The Guardian*, 2019.

'Day after day, day after day they were stuck, without breath, without motion, as idle as a painted ship, upon a painted ocean' is obviously a paraphrase from a verse in Coleridge's *The Rime of the Ancient Mariner*.

Mutiny

The epigraph is from *Frankenstein* by Mary Shelley.

What is Large

'... the end of all his exploring was not to arrive where he started and to know the place for the first time, but to arrive home and set out again ...' This is a paraphrase of the lines from T.S. Eliot's 'Little Gidding', *Four Quartets*, 1943:

We shall not cease from exploration
And the end of all our exploring
Will be to arrive where we started
And know the place for the first time.

The Pessimist

The epigraph is from Thomas Pynchon's *V.*

'flames out like shining from shook foil' is from Gerard Manley Hopkins' 'God's Grandeur'.

The End of the World

The connection between Scott and Barrie was first brought to my attention by Jacky Wullschlager in her book about the boyhood fantasies of Edwardian fiction, and is well elaborated by Francis Spufford.

The 2021 survey is the 2021 Ipsos/Futerra global poll, an online survey of connected citizens weighted to the national profile of each country: 19,520 adults aged 16–74 in 27 participating countries, 18 January 2021–5 February 2021.

The calculation about the tent drifting out to sea is quoted by Francis Spufford.

Patience Camp

The Shelley epigraph is from the end of 'Prometheus'.

The quotation from Bewick – and that Jane Eyre was reading it – was brought to my attention by Francis Spufford's *I May be Some Time*.

Captain Bengu

I am extremely grateful to Captain Bengu for his time and patience in talking to me, answering my questions, explaining the ice and his life, and for guiding me around the ship and for not keel-hauling me when I broke the handle on the storage-room door. Any errors of understanding are all mine.

What is Large

At least one historian has made the claim that she might have slept with the Norwegian explorer Fridtjof Nansen while Scott was on the ice. Another claims that she had a red-hot summer of passion with the Australian explorer Douglas Mawson in London in 1916. The two historians are respectively Roland Huntford, in his biography of Shackleton, and David Day in his biography of Douglas Mawson.

It wouldn't have taken her long to notice the patterns: that the end of all his exploring was not to arrive where he started and to know the place for the first time, but to arrive home and set straight out again. This is paraphrased from the lines from 'Little Gidding' in *Four Quartets* (1943).

In the Boats

A great many tears are shed over answered prayers is a reference to the epigraph to Truman Capote's unpublished novel, 'Answered Prayers': 'More tears are shed over answered prayers than unanswered ones.' Capote attributes the quote to Saint Teresa of Avila, but he probably made it up.

Mom

The story that Richard Cabell inspired *The Hound of the Baskervilles* is speculative, but firmly argued by local historians. Conan Doyle wrote in a 1907 letter to Cecil Turner: 'My story was really based on nothing save a remark of my friend Fletcher Robinson's that there was a legend about a dog on the moor connected with some old family.' Fletcher Robinson did indeed visit Buckfastleigh, and did see Richard Cabell's grave, facing my Bovey ancestor's, and that is more than enough for me.

In the Boats II

For the details and timeline about hypothermia and how you freeze to death, I am extremely grateful to 'Frozen Alive', Peter Stark's indispensable and classic article in *Outside* magazine, first published in 1997, and collected and reprinted many times since then, including in his book *Last Breath*, published by Random House in 2001.

The Infinite Game

The epigram is from Simon Sinek's *The Infinite Game*, published in 2019, but the definition and identification of finite and infinite games is from James Carse's *Finite and Infinite Games*.

The Hero with a Thousand Faces

The title of the chapter is a reference to the title of the work of comparative mythology by Joseph Campbell, which popularised the notion (and the structural analysis, especially in screenwriting) of the 'hero's journey'.

The Aivazosky painting is 'The Ninth Wave', which I saw with great admiration in the Russian State Museum in the Hermitage in St Petersburg in 2004. I hope to see it again one day.

They turned and looked at each other, like stout Cortez and his men, silent on a peak in Darien is a reference to the poem 'On first looking into Chapman's Homer' by John Keats.

Harold Nicolson's comment about ptarmigan is quoted in J.B. Priestley's *The Edwardians*.

Elephant Island

We sometimes fret today that we lack our former mettle and temper, that we have not now that strength that in old times moved heaven and earth is a reference to the lines from Tennyson's 'Ulysses'.

Aftermath

My purpose holds, he said, to sail beyond the sunset, and the baths of all the stars, until I die. This is a reference to a line from Tennyson's 'Ulysses'.

When Ernest Shackleton's ship *Endurance* was discovered below the Antarctic ice in March 2022, 106 years after it sank, the world thrilled anew to one of the greatest survival stories of all time.

Acclaimed South African writer Darrel Bristow-Bovey has a deeply personal relationship with the story of *Endurance*, and in this lyrical, loving journey into past and present, into humanity and the natural world, he revisits the famous story, wondering why it seems to mean so much more today than ever before.

Drawing on literature, natural history, personal memoir and the stirring epics of polar adventure, this is a celebration of hope and generosity and a special kind of optimism. In the face of self-inflicted natural disaster, miracles can still happen: human miracles, performed by flawed people in helpless situations.

Not all is lost, and some of what is taken may yet be given back.